Islamic Feminisms

AF849175

"This book is an important contribution to the study of Iranian women's struggle for legal equality since the early twentieth century. With a fascinating personal account of the aftermath of the 1979 revolution that brought clerics to power, Fazaeli chronicles the coming of age of an indigenous feminism that has challenged the official interpretation of 'Shari'a'."

–Ziba Mir-Hosseini, SOAS University of London

"A child of revolution and a martyr's daughter, Fazaeli situates herself in the ongoing resilient political activism of Iranian women in their pursuit of legal and political equality – despite the relentless state obstruction and harassment. She has written a highly engaging, intelligent and readable book. I recommend this book enthusiastically."

–Shahla Haeri, Associate Professor, Boston University

This book explores the contentious topic of women's rights in Muslim-majority countries, with a specific focus on Iran and the Iranian women's movement from 1906 to the present. The work contextualizes the authorial self through the use of personal narrative and interviews. A new critique of Islamic law is produced through an in-depth study of the Iranian Constitution, civil and criminal codes. The work presents a novel reconceptualization of the term "Islamic feminism" by revisiting the arguments of various scholars and through analysis of interviews with Iranian women's rights activists. It is contended that the feminist movements can play a critical role in Islamic law reform and consequently the eventual implementation of international human rights law in Muslim-majority countries. What emerges from this study is not only a feminist critique of two major regimes of law, but also the identification of possibilities for reform in the future. The study transitions from the Iranian national context to the international by way of a comparative legal study of international human rights laws and Islamic laws. The book will appeal both to academics and human rights practitioners.

Dr Roja Fazaeli is Lecturer in Islamic Civilizations, Department of Near and Middle Eastern Studies, Trinity College, Dublin, Ireland. She has published widely on the topics of Islam and gender, Islamic feminism and human rights.

Gender in Law, Culture, and Society
Series Editor
Martha Albertson Fineman
Emory University School of Law, Atlanta, Georgia, USA

For a full list of titles in this series, please visit www.routledge.com

Gender in Law, Culture, and Society addresses key issues and theoretical debates related to gender, culture, and the law. Its titles seek to advance understanding of the ways in which a society's cultural and legal approaches to gender intersect, clash, and are reconciled or remain in tension. The series further examines connections between gender and economic and political systems, as well as various other cultural and societal influences on gender construction and presentation, including social and legal consequences that men and women uniquely or differently encounter. Intended for a scholarly readership as well as for courses, its titles are a mix of single-authored volumes and collections of original essays that are both pragmatic and theoretical. It draws from the perspectives of critical and feminist legal theory, as well as other schools of jurisprudence. Interdisciplinary, and international in scope, the series offers a range of voices speaking to significant questions arising from the study of law in relation to gender, including the very nature of law itself.

Other titles in the series

In Search of Common Ground on Abortion
From Culture War to Reproductive Justice
Robin West, Justin Murray and Meredith Esser
ISBN 978-1-4724-2045-9

Sister Wives, Surrogates and Sex Workers
Outlaws by Choice?
Angela Campbell
ISBN 978-1-4094-3521-1

Vulnerability
Reflections on a New Ethical Foundation for Law and Politics
Edited by Martha Albertson Fineman and Anna Grear
ISBN 978-1-4724-2162-3

Islamic Feminisms

Rights and interpretations across generations in Iran

Roja Fazaeli

Routledge
Taylor & Francis Group
LONDON AND NEW YORK

First published 2017 by Routledge

2 Park Square, Milton Park, Abingdon, Oxfordshire OX14 4RN
711 Third Avenue, New York, NY 10017

Routledge is an imprint of the Taylor & Francis Group, an informa business

First issued in paperback 2018

British Library Cataloguing in Publication Data
A catalogue record for this book is available from the British Library

Library of Congress Cataloging in Publication Data
Names: Fazaeli, Roja, author.
Title: Islamic feminisms : rights and interpretations across generations in Iran / Roja Fazaeli.
Description: New York, NY : Routledge, 2016. | Series: Gender in law, culture and society | Includes index.
Identifiers: LCCN 2016022555 | ISBN 9781472489159 (hardback) | ISBN 9781315411446 (web pdf) | ISBN 9781315411439 (epub) | ISBN 9781315411422 (mobipocket)
Subjects: LCSH: Women—Legal status, laws, etc.—Iran. | Women (Islamic law) | Women's rights—Iran. | Feminism—Iran. | Equality before the law—Iran.
Classification: LCC KMH517.5 .F39 2016 | DDC 342.5508/78—dc23
LC record available at https://lccn.loc.gov/2016022555

ISBN: 978-1-4724-8915-9 (hbk)
ISBN: 978-1-138-36358-8 (pbk)

Typeset in Galliard
by Apex CoVantage, LLC

For my mother, Dr Nasrin Nakhshab

Contents

Acknowledgements

As I conclude this journey of writing, my foremost gratitude goes to Professor Martha Fineman, without whom this book might not ever have been realized. Martha's support began during my Ph.D. work and has been ever constant. Through Martha I benefitted from time with Emory Law's Feminism and Legal Theory Project, as well as Emory University's Vulnerability and the Human Condition Initiative. Both spaces are imbued with Martha's critical spirit and advance her determined work for gender justice. If a similar spirit and ethic has not been translated into these pages the fault is my own, as I could have had no better mentor.

I am continually thankful as well for the supervision and encouragement I received from Professor William Schabas during his tenure at the Irish Centre for Human Rights, NUI Galway. Bill first helped me to engage the freedom and responsibility that comes with research, and his work continues to be a north star for my own writing. I hope that this work edges closer to his high standards of precise and exhaustive research.

Professor Abdullahi An-Na'im was an early inspiration for my work on Islam and human rights. I am grateful for all the ways that his challenging ideas have influenced and shaped this work. My thanks also go to Professor Joshua Castellino, who first welcomed me to the bustling community at the Irish Centre for Human Rights, as well as Dr Kathleen Cavanaugh, who continues to be a resolute and inspirational colleague. I also extend my gratitude to Professor Lila Abu-Lughod, who kindly supported me during a sojourn at Columbia University.

This book has been largely written at Trinity College, Dublin. I'm especially grateful for the platform and context that the Near and Middle Eastern Studies Department has afforded me during the process of writing. My thanks, in particular, go to Dr Anne Fitzpatrick for her support from the beginning. The earliest stages of this research were made possible by a doctoral grant from the Irish Research Council (IRC). I remain cognizant and quite appreciative of the fact that proper funding can make or break a project, and am thankful to the IRC for helping me start on the right foot.

Very special thanks go to my friend and colleague Maryam Hosseinkhah. Maryam was an extraordinary help and resource to me in this project. From her coordination of many of the interviews to her first-hand knowledge of the Iranian women's movement, Maryam's fingerprints are all over these pages. I'm thankful as well to Afrooz Maghzi and Saghar Qiasvand, who both graciously and generously offered their expert thoughts on the Iranian women's movement at various points throughout the writing process.

My support in Dublin has been augmented tremendously by the presence of Professor Maria Baghramian. Maria's academic advice and friendship have helped this book come together. I am profoundly grateful for her many thoughtful acts of encouragement. Her presence in my corner made writing about the Iranian women's movement all the more meaningful. My thanks as well go to Meline Papazian, whose friendship along the way was constant.

I'm grateful to have several friends and colleagues who generously gave their time to read this work in various drafts and incarnations. Special thanks in this regard go to Dr Anthony Cullen and Ruby Carmen, as well as Lucy and Ruaidhrí Power. I also thank Dr Seyed Noori for his help in strengthening sections relating to religion and theology, as well as his thoughtful and irenic approach to scholarly collaboration.

My sincerest thanks also go to Claire Dowling, Sana Sanai and Shabnam Azad, stellar students and superior research assistants and proofreaders. I look forward to their books and work in the years to come.

My penultimate thanks are reserved for my family. My mother, Dr. Nasrin Nakhshab, and sister, Leila Fazaeli, appear in these pages and are daily companions. The story of rights I am attempting to advance here is our story, and I humbly acknowledge that. I am thankful for the journey we've taken together from Iran to Ireland and all the ways it has led to this book. I'm thankful as well to my brother-in-law, Seán Sweeney, and nephew, Micheál Sweeney, and all of their kindnesses throughout the writing process. My husband, Joel Hanisek, is my best editor; I am thankful for all the ways, big and small, he has midwifed this book into being. And I am thankful for our daughter, Maneli, who makes me laugh and calls me to life beyond the page.

Finally, I acknowledge all the Iranian women's rights activists, past and present. I give thanks for their work and I offer this book to them, with the hope that it will serve.

Introduction
Situating the self

This study, apart from being an academic project, has also been a personal journey. I am a child of the Iranian Islamic Revolution. I make this claim to distinguish myself from other Iranian feminist writers such as Mehrangiz Kar, Azadeh Kian, Shirin Ebadi, Ziba Mir-Hosseini and Nayereh Tohidi.[1] These are writers whose brilliant feminist consciousness seems intrinsically linked to a time before the Iranian Islamic Revolution, while I grew up in the Islamic Republic of Iran during the Iran-Iraq War. At the age of three I lost my father to that war and became a martyr's daughter.[2] As a result I grew up in an all-female family, consisting of my mother, my sister and me. I grew accustomed to my mother's fights for rights. She fought her family for an independent life. She fought my paternal grandfather for our guardianship. She fought male colleagues for rights at the work place. She fought her status as a war widow. She was one of the only female lecturers in the field of horticulture (1989–1992) at a time when horticulture was still an exclusively male subject.[3] My mother, like so many women in the Islamic Republic, was a paradox. Veiled in a dark *maghnae*[4] and wearing a long dark *manteau*,[5] she taught

1 Mehrangiz Kar, *Raf-e Tabeez Az Zanan, Moghayesey-e Convension-e Raf-e Tabeez Az Zanan ba Qavaneen-e Dakheliy-e Iran* (*End Discrimination against Women: A Comparison between the Convention on the Elimination of All Forms of Discrimination against Women and Iranian Laws*) (Tehran: Nashr-e Qatr-e Publications, 2000). Azadeh Kian, "Women and Politics in Post-Islamist Iran: The Gender Conscious Drive to Change," *British Journal of Middle Eastern Studies* 24, no. 1 (1997), 75.

2 In Chapter 4 I write more about the category of martyr in this context, and in particular the way in which it can become a status that binds women to certain social norms without their consent, input or willing participation.

3 As education became segregated, women were prohibited from certain subjects, such as horticulture and legal studies to become a judge. Some of these were reformed in the second decade after the revolution.

4 A scarf-like veil that resembles a wimple.

5 Word borrowed from French meaning a coat. In Iran, manteaux usually fall below the knee. They come in different styles and colours; however, at the workplace and schools darker shades of black, navy, brown and grey are preferred. In some workplaces and universities women are required to wear a black *chador* (literally translated as tent), which is a body-enveloping cloth that covers the whole body apart from the face and the hands.

all-male classes. In one instance she had to compel a student's armed bodyguard to leave the class. The head of the faculty later called her to let her know that she had literally disarmed one of the heads of Gilan province's[6] *Sepah-E Pasdaran.*[7] She was so powerful, and yet powerless all at the same time. I was always fascinated with the outfits I saw my mother wearing in photos from before the revolution, particularly in contrast to her attire after the revolution. Before, she wore seventies-style corduroys, and even short skirts; after, she wore the veil. Throughout the seismic changes in the country she fought for a scholarship to Ireland, only to have the Iranian government discontinue her funding six months after our arrival. The law, it turned out, did not allow a single woman (whether widowed, unmarried or divorced) to study abroad with governmental support.[8] I always saw my mother as a powerful woman, but I also became aware, from an early age, of the power dynamics inherent in every public institution, particularly those that sapped her strength and subjected her to multiple dependencies.

Memories

One of my earliest memories is of standing on a mound of mud. I am wearing a navy tracksuit with a red stripe down each leg. Women clad in black *chadors* huddle around a large opening in the ground. They wail and scream, conveying an incredible pain, hitting their chests with their clenched fists. Now and then one of the women attempts to throw herself in the opening while others hold her back. This is how I remember my father's funeral at the martyrs' cemetery in Noor in 1983. I watched from the mound of mud beside the newly dug grave.

We left Noor to live in Tonekabon (formerly known as Shahsavar) with my mother's family shortly after the funeral. My uncle picked us up in my grandfather's white van. I sat pressing myself to my mother's chest while my sister did the same on her other side. The car was filled with the scents of the funeral: rosewater, tears and sweat. In Tonekabon my mother explained to me and my sister that our father was gone and that he was not coming back.

6 A northern province of Iran situated on the coast of the Caspian Sea.

7 The Revolutionary Guards.

8 A 1988 excerpt from *Ettellaat* reads as follows "Sisters applying for scholarships to go abroad must be accompanied by their husbands at the time of being sent and during education abroad." See *Ettellaat,* 13 July 1988. In 2000 a bill was passed by the *Majlis'* Committee on Education and Research to allow single women to apply for the Ministry of Higher Education scholarship to study abroad. However, the bill was harshly criticized by some Ayatollahs, such as Makarem Shirazi, who consequently condemned the decision. Ultimately, in 2001 the bill was rejected by the Guardian Council. See Hammed Shahidian, *Women in Iran: Gender Politics in the Islamic Republic* (Westport: Greenwood Publishing Group, 2002), 233. Also refer to *Hayat-e No*, 24, August 2000.

My mother tells me the story that when I heard the news of my father's death I was adamant we should buy a new father from our local market, one identical to the one who died: handsome with a mighty moustache of the 1970s Iranian left. My mother was widowed at the age of thirty.

Soon after moving to Tonekabon my mother found a job as a horticulturist in a research centre. She traveled back and forth to Tehran to finish her master's degree, which she had started before the Cultural Revolution. I remember time and time again sitting on the windowsill of my grandmother's kitchen, peering through the window and waiting for a car to stop with my mother in it. I lived in fear of losing her. The roads from Tonekabon to Tehran were treacherous and Tehran was regularly bombarded.

During the nights when my mother was away in Tehran, I used to sneak into my grandparents' room and squeeze myself in between the two of them. Both my grandfather (*babajoon*) and grandmother (*madarjoon*) were religious, but they bickered as soon as my grandmother's night prayers began. Grandfather often ended up telling her that God would award her more in the hereafter if she would stop her night vigils and let her husband sleep. My grandmother took me to *jalasah*,[9] *rowzeh*,[10] *sofreh*[11] and sometimes to martyrs' funerals.[12] I remember well the funeral of my mother's young cousin in the village of Mazarak, the place where my mother's family came from and where their orange groves remain to this day. I clenched my mother's arm and my grandmother walked ahead of us as we entered the yard. I heard the

9 Religious gatherings where women come together, read and interpret the Qur'an. *Jalasahs* are conducted throughout the year. They are held by women, for women, in private homes on a regular and rotational basis. Usually the *jalasahs* are conceptually dedicated to a member of the family of the Prophet Muhammad, in particular to Fatima (Muhammad's daughter) or Hussein (grandson of Muhammad and son of Fatima and Ali, the Shi'a third Imam). For more, please refer to Aam Torab, "Piety as Gendered Agency: A Study of Jalaseh Ritual Discourse in an Urban Neighbourhood in Iran," *The Journal of the Royal Anthropological Institute* 2, no. 2 (1996), 235–252.

10 *Rowzeh* and *jalaseh* are religious meetings held in private houses or religiously endowed buildings. The terms *rowzeh* and *jalaseh* are often used interchangeably; however, *rowzeh* meetings are mainly for the months of *Ramezan* and *Muharram*. Also see Zahra Kamalkhani, *Women's Islam: Religious Practice among Women in Today's Iran* (London: Kegan Paul International, 1998), 12–31.

11 The word *sofreh* translates to a spread (tablecloth) which is extended on the floor and food is placed on it. People sit around the *sofreh* to eat. However, in this context I am referring to "*sofreh-e Nazri*" which is "the *sofreh* used for a ceremonial votive meal (*ghaza-e Nazri*) given to honor a saint or pray for a certain outcome". Faegheh Shirazi, "The Sofreh: Comfort and Community among Women in Iran," *Iranian Studies* 38, no. 2 (2005), 293.

12 The first three are all female religious gatherings organized by women for women in private homes. Self-professed pious women gather to read and interpret the Qur'an. The meetings are usually led by female preachers. Although an in-depth study of such meetings is out of the scope of this study, I find them important as "sites for interpreting cultural notions regarding gender". These notions in turn have formed parts of my own understandings of gender, Islam and piety, which are reflected in this study.

laments, the wailings and I wanted to run back. We walked to where the women were sitting. Everyone was wearing black. I hated going to funerals of *shahids* (martyrs) because, if anyone recognized me as a daughter of *shahid* Fazaeli, they would begin wailing even louder. I would then be made to sit on the women's laps for a few moments while they would kiss my face and cover me with the smell of rosewater, tears and sweat. I despised being branded a martyr's daughter and all the sorrowful attention it brought. I therefore made a decision that I would no longer be a martyr's daughter and that if any one asked about my father I would tell them that he was alive and lived far away.

I began first grade in 1985 at the age of five. The months leading up to the first day of school were filled with excitement. I loved my new books and pencils and the uniform. We wore little *manteau*, which came in three colors of navy, brown and black with matching trousers and a similar color (or white) *maghnae*. At school it was the norm to ask about someone's father and mother and their occupations before making friends. When asked by potential friends about my parents' professions, I told them gladly about my mother and continued my narrative by telling them that my father was a medical doctor who worked in Sardasht, on the border with Iraq, near the front. This was, in fact, where he had worked before his death. Two years passed and I kept my secret. Then a nurse visited our school to talk to us about her work at the war front. At the end of her talk she asked if anyone's father or mother was a medical doctor who might volunteer for war efforts. Being short I was, as always, at the very front of the classroom and in clear view of the teacher. I felt my body sinking into my chair while the nurse spoke. My eyes welled up with tears when I heard one of my classmates shout, "Miss! Roja's father is a medical doctor." The nurse immediately turned to me. I began sobbing because my lie was being uncovered in front of the whole class. I told her yes, indeed he was a medical doctor, but that he worked in Sardasht. The same day my mother received a phone call from my school telling her that I might be in denial about my father's death. My mother, however, understood that it was not denial, but a mode of self-preservation. She then bravely proceeded to throw us a huge birthday party, although it was neither my birthday nor my sister Leila's. Then, less than a year after my father's death, my mother banned us from wearing any dark colours. She herself wore black.

Our school was run in shifts. One week the classes began at 7.30 a.m. and ended by 1.00 p.m. The next week we switched to afternoons, 1.30 p.m. to 5.00 p.m. The shift system was set in place to accommodate the growing number of students resulting from a rise in population after the 1979 Iranian Revolution. It also provided for gender-segregated schooling. The weeks were shared between girls and boys. When we had the mornings, they had the afternoons and vice versa.

Eight years of war with Iraq (1980–1988) took its toll. Iran lost approximately one million young men. The economic impact on the oil-rich country was undeniably harsh. The northern provinces Gilan and Mazandaran were rarely bombed and, given the rich farming culture of the region, we did not feel the economic sanctions and the hardship as much as other regions. However, even the north was not shielded from long queues at the bakery every morning, or the search for coupons required to get cooking oil and other household necessities. We often studied under oil lamps, scrunched over on the ground, writing our homework and hoping the electricity would soon be back. When it did return, we might have watched television, reruns of the Japanese drama *Oshin*, or one of the post-revolutionary soaps. One of my errands in the summer was to queue to buy bread. My grandmother had given me a white flowery *chador* to wear when I went out. Although I was young enough not to need to wear the *chador*,[13] I saw it as my religious duty to do so. It also gave me a feeling of being grown up. In the mornings I would throw the *chador* over my head and run, rather than "piously" walk, to the bakery. I would wait there in the queue for hours and sometimes, just before it was my turn, the baker would announce that they had run out of supplies for the day. On those days, I would return home empty-handed and teary-eyed. On good days I came back with a freshly baked pile of *lavash* in my little hands, trying not to burn myself.

After my father's death, my mother managed to become our custodian (*hezanat*), but my grandfather legally remained our guardian (*vali*). My mother's relationship with my father's family became more strained because of this but she always insisted that my sister Leila and I should spend time with our father's family. As a result, we would spend a couple of weeks to a month of our summer holidays in Noor with our six aunts, two uncles and thirty-something first cousins. Leila had her group of cousins to play with and I had mine. But my favourite person to spend time with during the holidays was my Uncle Behzad. He was similar in looks to my Dad and I preferred to go to his hardware shop instead of playing with my cousins. He would spoil me by buying me ice cream and taking me on excursions to the forest of Noor (*Park Jangali-e Noor*), where we would sometimes fish in the streams. Other times he would take me to the seaside. At nighttime, we would all sleep in my grandmother's house. Leila and I would ask her to sleep in between the two of us on the bedroll and she would caress our backs and tell us stories about white giants and unlucky thieves.

13 According to most Islamic schools of law (*madhahib*), a girl reaches the age of maturity at nine lunar years. One of the consequences of reaching the age of maturity for girls is that they are required by law to cover their hair in public and to wear one form of *hejab*, depending on where they come from.

The years between 1983 and 1988 were a time of repression in Iran. Almost everything seemed to be regulated. I remember when my Mum took us to Teriatooka, a fancy restaurant not too far from my grandparents' house in Tobekabon. We had (for the first time in public) grilled sturgeon. This fish, once deemed *haram*, became *halal* following a *fatwa* by Ayatollah Khomeini in 1983.[14] I also remember how excited I was when chess was once more deemed permissible. We used to have chess tournaments with my cousins until the early hours of the morning. Other restrictions kept us in a perpetual state of fear of reprisal from authorities. During family gatherings, weddings or birthday parties where there was music or a mixed crowd, Revolutionary Guards would turn up to smell drinks for alcohol or to tell us to stop the music. Even a simple trip out to the shops or for a walk was controlled. When I was eleven and Leila was thirteen we went shopping with my aunts, who all wore the *chador*. On our way back we were stopped by a patrol car full of Revolutionary Guards. The women guards in black *chadors* got out of the car first. They came towards Leila, shouting at her to cover her hair. Before she could do so, they had grabbed her by the hand and were trying to drag her into the car. From one side, she was being pulled by the "sisters"; from the other, we were tugging to keep her with us. We finally reasoned with the guards to let Leila go. I remember one of my aunts told them that Leila was a martyr's daughter. Incidents such as this were not infrequent. My mother was once arrested for indecent clothing. She had dressed hastily because she was going to the pharmacy to find eye medication for me. The war and the sanctions made it difficult to access the most basic medications, no matter the amount of money you offered. Shocked at her arrest and the insults the Revolutionary Guards had shouted at her, she sat waiting for her turn to be interrogated at the police station. It was there that a passing young Revolutionary Guard asked her to button up her *manteau*. Only then did she realize that in the midst of all the pushing and pulling in the pharmacy she had lost a button. She was released shortly afterwards, because her supervisor at the research centre vouched for her upright character.

After seven years of living in Tonekabon, my mother was offered a lectureship in the Faculty of Horticulture at Rasht University. In Rasht we moved into a two-bedroom apartment where Leila and I shared a bedroom. I became more religious, at least as religious as a ten-year-old can be. I had come to terms with my identity as a daughter of a martyr, so much so that I even took part in competitions for martyrs' children. I became the "good" girl of our class, the one who studied, wore her *maghnae* framed tightly around her thin face, and took part in Maths Olympiads. As Leila was slowly

14 See "Khaviar Halal Shod (Khaviar became Halal)", *Ettelaat*, 6 September 1983, republished in *Mardomsalari*, online www.mardomsalari.com/template1/News.aspx?NID=149176, (accessed 4 January 2016).

becoming a rebellious teenager, I was becoming an introvert obsessed with getting As. I liked Rasht in many ways. Occasionally the vice principal of the school would come looking for me and say that my Mum was waiting to take me to the doctor. Knowing that I was not sick, I would step out of the class and see my mother there with a mischievous gleam in her eyes. She would take my hand, and once outside the front gate of the school, she would ask which movie I wanted to go and watch. After two years of living in Rasht, my mother secured a scholarship to study for her Ph.D. in Ireland. We moved to Dublin in October 1992.

When we first moved to Ireland, I was homesick and wanted to go back. Leila and I did not speak a word of English. The school we attended did not have many non-Irish students. We were bullied by a couple of students, and the teachers were not quite sure how to deal with us. On the one hand, we were scoring 100 per cent on our algebra exams; on the other, we were failing English. Because my mother's scholarship was from the Ministry of Horticulture in Iran, we had to abide by the laws of the Islamic Republic and keep our scarves on at all times in public. The principal of the school we registered with did not allow us to wear our scarves on the school premises. Therefore, we took them off on entering the school and put them back on once we approached the exit. When after six months my mother's scholarship was cut by the Iranian government, we were left with little money and were unable to buy tickets to go back to Iran. Leila and I had to learn English at a much quicker pace than either of us had anticipated.

After eleven years in Ireland I went back to Iran. It was the summer of 2003 and I was researching my master's thesis on "family honour and women's rights in Iran".[15] The country had changed considerably. I was most impressed with the women I interviewed. Women's participation in the public sphere after the revolution had increased. Gripped by the reform dynamics, I returned to Iran again in the spring of 2004 to work on a co-authored book project about civil society in Iran. During that time, I also worked for a former parliamentarian, Azam Talleghani, and participated in a youth-studies organization. I became friends with young reformists and attended talks at the reformist political party *Jebheye Mosharekat* (Front for Consolidation). In the first two months of that spring I interviewed a wide array of civil society members from various parts of Iran. But in the third month of my stay the book project fell through, and soon thereafter[16] I found myself under house

15 Roja Fazaeli, *Family Honour and Women's Rights in Iran*, Trinity College, Dublin, 2003 (Master's Thesis).

16 This was after coming back from Japan, where I attended the United Nations Asia-Pacific Youth Leadership Summit as one of the two Iranian delegates. See Pan-Asian Youth Leadership Summit, Hiroshima, Japan, September 19–21, 2004. See also, online www.shumei-international.org/youth/hiroshima.html, (accessed 6 January 2016).

arrest and subject to intense daily interrogations. During these interrogations, I was often referred to as an "immoral Western feminist". Yet at times I was also granted the elevated status of a martyr's daughter. I thought of myself as a women's rights activist but, quite unwillingly, I had also become a political dissident. I realized then that, in fact, I embodied multiple identities. This realization over time led me to engage with questions of Iranian feminist identity across generations. This book is an attempt to engage with these questions as a child of the revolution, a martyr's daughter, an Iranian-Irish woman, an activist and an academic.[17]

17 The term "fifth-generation Iranian feminist" was first cited in Noushin Ahmadi Khorasani, "The 'One Million Signature Campaign': Face-to-Face, Street-to-Street," trans. Sholeh Irani, *Change for Equality*, 29 March, 2007.

1 Iranian women's movement

Narratives of dissent

Overview

An overview of the Iranian women's movement from the later 1800s to the present is necessary to contextualize the current state of the movement. This chapter examines patterns in the Iranian women's movement from its origins to the present time, including its struggles with institutions of power, its relationship to religion and religious authority, and its dependencies on national and international institutions, as well as its innovations in the face of setbacks. The past three decades have witnessed a revival in historical studies of the early Iranian women's movement. Scholars such as Parvin Paidar, Afsaneh Najmabadi, Ali Akbar Mahdi, Eliz Sanasarian, Hammed Shahidian, Homa Hoodfar, Nikki Keddie, Mehrangiz Kar and Shirin Ebadi,[1] to name a few, have all written on aspects of the Iranian women's movement from historical, sociological and politico-legal perspectives covering the movement's

1 Parvin Paidar, *Women and the Political Process in Twentieth-Century Iran* (Cambridge: Cambridge University Press, 1995); Afsaneh Najmabadi, *Women with Mustaches and Men without Beards: Gender and Sexual Anxieties of Iranian Modernity* (Berkeley: University of California Press, 2005); Ali Akbar Mahdi, "The Iranian Women's Movement: A Century Long Struggle," *The Muslim World* 94 (2004), 427–448; E. Sanasarian, *The Women's Rights Movement in Iran: Mutiny, Appeasement, and Repression from 1900 to Khomeini* (New York: Praeger, 1982); Hammed Shahidian, *Women in Iran: Gender Politics in the Islamic Republic* (Westport: Greenwood Publishing Group, 2002); Homa Hoodfar, "Against All Odds: The Building of a Women's Movement in the Islamic Republic of Iran," in from Changing Their World 1st Edition, ed. Srilatha Batliwala, *The Association for Women's Rights in Development (AWID)*, (2008), 1–16, accessed online www.awid.org/sites/default/files/atoms/files/changing_their_world_-_building_of_a_womens_movement_in_the_islamic_republic_of_iran.pdf, (accessed 27 July 2016); Nikki R. Keddie; with a section by Yann Richard, *Modern Iran: Roots and Results of Revolution* (New Haven: Yale University Press, 2003); Mehrangiz Kar, *Raf-e Tabeez Az Zanan, Moghayesey-e Convension-e Raf-e Tabeez Az Zanan ba Qavaneen-e Dakheliy-e Iran (End Discrimination against Women: A Comparison between the Convention of All Forms of Discrimination against Women and Iranian Laws)* (Tehran: Nashr-e Qatr-e Publications, 2000); Shirin Ebadi, *Huqu-e Zan Dar Ghavanin-e Jomhoriye Islamiy-e Iran (Women's Rights, in the Laws of the Islamic Republic of Iran)* (Tehran: Ganje Danesh Publication, 2002).

beginnings until the time after the 1979 Iranian Revolution. As Janet Afary observes, following the 1979 Iranian Revolution academics and female activists "began to search in the dustbin of history for the origins of feminism in literature and politics".[2] This search is particularly noteable in books such as *Senator: the Works of Senator Mehrangiz Manouchehrian for Legal Rights for Women* by Noushin Ahamadi Khorasani and Parvin Ardalan. By way of Manouchehrian's story, this work explores the history of the women's movement in Iran from the post-constitutional era to the Pahlavi dynasty. It also includes the early period following the 1979 Islamic Revolution.[3] More recently, Ahmadi Khorasani's book *Bahar Jonbesh Zanan* (The Spring of Iranian Women's Movement), published in 2012, gives an intimate account of the movement.

Following 1979 an important part of the history of the women's movement in Iran has been the transition of women's publications from print to online media. This transition has facilitated a broader range of activism, both nationally and internationally, and has blurred public and private divides, for example, between the home and the prison. The media transition has also had implications for censorship and must be understood alongside the closure of many reform print media outlets[4] as well as in light of changes in the political discourse, particularly those leading to the harassment and arrest of journalists, human rights activists (in particular, women's rights activists) and bloggers.

One forum where women's rights activists and reform-minded intellectuals traditionally voiced their concerns regarding discrimination, and where debates and discussions of a religious and secular nature took place, was that of women's reformist media. The role of women's reformist media has been the topic of many articles and books.[5] Women's magazines such as *Zanan*, *Farzaneh* and *payam-e Hajar* have been thoroughly studied as platforms

2 Janet Afary, *The Iranian Constitutional Revolution, 1906–1911: Grassroot Democracy, Social Democracy, & the Origins of Feminism* (New York: Columbia University Press, 1996), 176.

3 Noushin Ahmadi Khorasani and Parvin Ardalan, *Senator: Faliyathaye Mehrangiz Manouchehrian ba Bastar Mobarezat Hughughi Zanan dar Iran (Senator: The Works of Senator Mehrangiz Manouchehrian for Legal Rights for Women)* (Tehran: Nashr Tose-e, 1382/2003).

4 Kian, Shargh, Yas-e Nou, Etemaad Meli, Vaghaye, Etefaghiye, Jame-e, Neshat, Sobh-e Emrooz, Asr-e Azadegan, Aftaab Emrooz, Payam-e Emrooz, Payam-e Hajar, Zanan, Salaam, Etemaad Meli, Iran Dokht, Shahrvand, Ham Vatan, Zan, Bahar, Bayan and many more.

5 Roza Eftekhari, "Zanan: Trials and Successes of a Feminist Magazine in Iran" in *Middle Eastern Women on the Move: Openings for and the Constraints on Women's Political Participation in the Middle East*, (Washington, DC: Woodrow Wilson International Centre for Scholars 2003), 15–22, online www.wilsoncenter.org/sites/default/files/MEP_women.pdf, (accessed 27 July 2016). See also, Ziba Mir-Hosseini, "Stretching the Limits: A Feminist Reading of the Shari'a in Post-Khomeini Iran" in *Feminism and Islam, Legal and Literary Perspectives*, ed. Mai Yamani (United Kingdom: Ithaca Press, 1996), 285–321. See also, Valentine M. Moghadam, "Islamic Feminism and Its Discontents: Towards a Resolution of the Debate," *Signs: Journal of Women in Culture and Society* 27, no. 4 (2002), 1136–1167.

where women's issues were discussed and religious texts were reinterpreted.[6] These previous studies form the basis for understanding the present women's movement. However, there is a clear paucity of academic study when it comes to Iranian online publications and blogs. These sites have become an integral part of the women's movement and are places where collective and individual narratives join together in innovation in the fight for equality.

The final section of this chapter examines a new medium for women's public voices: prison narratives from women rights activists that are published online. These narratives afford women prisoners a voice and raise questions about the nature of private and state-owned prisons. By giving these testimonies, the women defy the state, which has otherwise imprisoned them, and also create a new space for their activism. These narratives from the ***band nasvan*** (women's ward) are important as they not only give a human face to women who are otherwise dismissed as criminals, but also because they critically analyse the reasons for which these women have broken laws.

The Iranian women's movement: a brief historical account (1872–2012)

The beginning of the Iranian women's movement can be traced back to the late nineteenth century. It is intrinsically linked to Iran's relationship with Western powers, in particular Russia and Britain, and consequently to the Iranian nationalist movement and the so-called Constitutional Revolution (1905–1911).[7] Women became part of the active nationalist opposition to territorial and commercial concessions gained by both Russia and Britain. They actively opposed the Reuter concession of 1872, "which sold almost all of Iran's resources at a very low price", and they joined the Tobacco Protest (1891–1892).[8]

6 Haleh Afshar, *Islam and Feminism: An Iranian Case Study* (London: MacMillan, 1998). Haideh Moghissi, *Feminism and Islamic Fundamentalism: The Limits of Postmodern Analysis* (London: Zed Books, 1999). Valentine M. Moghadam, *Modernizing Women: Gender and Social Change in the Middle East*, 2nd ed. (Boulder, CO: Lynne Reinner Publishers, 2003). Ziba Mir-Hosseini, *Islam and Gender: The Religious Debate in Contemporary Islam* (New Jersey: Princeton University Press, 1999). Janet Afary, "Seeking a Feminist Politics for the Middle East after September 11," *Frontier Journal of Women's Studies* 25, no. 1 (2004), 128–137. Azadeh Kian, "Women and Politics in Post-Islamist Iran: The Gender Conscious Drive to Change," *British Journal of Middle Eastern Studies* 24, no. 1 (1997), 75–96. Mehrangiz Kar, *Raf-e Tabeez Az Zanan, Moghayesey-e Convension-e Raf-e Tabeez Az Zanan ba Qavaneen-e Dakheliy-e Iran (End Discrimination against Women: A Comparison between the Convention on the of All forms of Discrimination against Women and Iranian Laws)* (Tehran: Nashr-e Qatr-e Publications, 2000).

7 Although not a part of a widespread women's movement, one should not forget the activism of Qurrat al-Ain (1814–1852), a Babi disciple who championed the cause of women's emancipation (though not to much avail) in the 1800s.

8 Nikkie Keddie, *Iran: Religion, Politics and Society: Collected Essays* (London: Taylor and Francis, 1983), 54.

The Tobacco Movement, sparked by a *fatwa* issued in December 1881 by a leading Shi'a cleric, Haji Hassan Shirazi, resulted in a nationwide boycott of tobacco. This occurred against the background of near-constant public criticism of Naser al-Din Shah's concession to a British company that cured and sold tobacco.[9] Women played an effective part in the protests. During the public protests, women attacked shops, forced them to close down and shouted insults at the Shah. Among other things they called him "the female with the moustache", "the scarf wearer" and "unbeliever".[10] His submissiveness to the West had feminized him in the eyes of the public and brought his masculinity into question. The Shah's wives also took part in the protests by refusing to smoke tobacco. The Shah's wife Anis al-Dawlah took a lead in boycotting tobacco in the *andarun* and a boycott of tobacco in the *harem* was announced in the following way: "Tobacco has been boycotted by those who have married us to you."[11] This statement highlights the power the clergy possessed during that period and how closely it was linked to women's activism. Having succumbed to the pressure of the mass protests, in 1892 Naser al-din Shah cancelled the concession.[12] According to Ali Akbar Mahdi this "was the first of a series of collective protests" staged in the hope of establishing a constitution and bringing about "parliamentary rule and democracy" by limiting the relative power of the monarch.[13]

The movement culminated in the aforementioned Constitutional Revolution and was centered on the debate over the relevance of "Western" modernity to Iranian society. It was a movement intimately concerned with Qajar vulnerability to Western intrusion. Opposition to the state was articulated in strong nationalist terms. Alliances between the groups that constituted this opposition movement included "the *Shi'a* clergy, the business community and the secular intelligentsia".[14] Both men and women supported these movements, with class and education remaining a significant predictor of support. The educated upper classes were more inclined to be supportive. This was especially true for the women who took part. The Shi'a clergy were also supportive and supported, both because of their institutional base within the Iranian community and their autonomy. Paidar summarizes the

9 Parvin Paidar, *Women and the Political Process in Twentieth-Century Iran* (Cambridge: Cambridge University Press, 1995), 50.

10 Ibid., 51.

11 Ibid.

12 Ibid.

13 Ali Akbar Mahdi, "The Iranian Women's Movement: A Century Long Struggle," *Muslim World* 94, no. 4 (October 2004), 427–428. See also, Nahid Yeganeh, "Women, Nationalisms and Islam in Contemporary Political Discourse in Iran," *Feminist Review*, no. 44, Nationalisms and National Identities (Summer 1993), 4.

14 Ibid.

power of the clergy before and after the Constitutional Revolution. She states:

> Under the Qajars, power and authority were invested in both the king and the *mojtahed*, and the state and the religious establishment maintained a relationship of mutual interdependence. During the Constitutional Revolution the clergy's influence in political affairs increased. With the establishment of parliamentary democracy, the clergy consolidated its role in politics by taking up seats in the Majles as people's representative. The Shii establishment had throughout the post-constitutional period exerted tremendous power and influence in the affairs of state, nation and individual. It had, on the other hand, lost control over education after the establishment of a national education system in 1918.[15]

The events leading up to and following the Constitutional Revolution marked the beginning of the women's movement and activism in Iran.[16] The movement was formed against the backdrop of a new nationalism and supported by a number of the Constitutionalists. Women also supported the Constitutional movement through protests, strikes and other financial means. According to Afary, "In 1905 women reportedly created human barriers and protected the 'ulama' who had taken sanctuary at the Shah 'Abd al-'Azim Shrine from the armed government forces."[17] The signing of the August 1906 royal proclamation was followed by women's involvement in a "plan to form a national bank" and support "the boycott of foreign goods".[18] Women's patriotism was demonstrated by their efforts to collect and donate funds to the national bank, with some of them giving their inheritance share and others selling their jewelry and household items.[19] Either in spite of, or because of, the history and extent of women's dependencies during the Qajar dynasty, women recognized the importance of autonomy for national aspirations and attempted to boycott European imported textiles by wearing "native fabrics".[20] "It was believed that the boycott of European textiles in Iran would free the

15 Parvin Paidar, *Women and the Political Process in Twentieth-Century Iran* (Cambridge: Cambridge University Press, 1995), 83.

16 For more on the link between nationalism and the women's movement see Firozeh Kashani-Sabet, "Patriotic Womanhood: The Culture of Feminism in Modern Iran, 1900–1941," *British Journal of Middle Eastern Studies* 32, no. 1 (2005), 30.

17 Janet Afary, *The Iranian Constitutional Revolution, 1906–1911: Grassroot Democracy, Social Democracy, & the Origins of Feminism* (New York: Columbia University Press, 1996), 178.

18 Ibid.

19 Ibid., 179.

20 As Afary writes "This movement had close similarities to the Swadeshi boycott (1904–1911) by Indian women of British good in the same period." Ibid.

nation from its dependence on European merchants and manufacturers."[21] In one instance, driven by fear of the newly formed *Majlis-e Shoraye Eslami*[22] (Islamic Consultative Assembly) delegating unlimited power to the Russians, the following plan was executed:

> Women whose husbands and male relatives made up the *majlis*, met secretly in one another's homes and planned a dramatic protest. Three hundred strong, they marched to the *majlis* building; there the women, heavily veiled and in *chadors*, demanded to see the President. When he appeared the women brandished their revolvers and declared that they would kill all their men folks if the deputies did not uphold the integrity of the Constitution. The women won their point. Similarly, when the Ministry of Finance delayed paying their employees, women relatives stormed the Ministry offices and demanded payment.[23]

Women participated in the national struggle by "circulating information, spreading news, acting as informers and messengers, participating in demonstrations, and taking up arms in protest".[24] Traditional gatherings such as *rowzehs* also turned into political meetings. Mosques were used as spaces for political knowledge sharing. Consequently, a number of secret or semi-secret women's societies were formed. Women's participation in the national movement led to the establishment of *anjumans* (societies) and schools by women for women. Two noteworthy societies were *Anjuman Azadi-yi Zanan* (the Society for Freedom of Women) and *Anjuman Mukhadarat-i Vatan* (the National Ladies Society). Each of these societies had up to sixty members. It is for this reason that Morgan Shuster writes in his book *The Strangling of Persia*, that:

> . . . the Persian women performed the crowning act of the noble and patriotic part which thousands of their sex had been playing since Persia's *risorgimento* began. The Persian women since 1907 had become almost at a bound as the most progressive, not to say radical in the world. That this statement upsets the ideas of centuries makes no difference. It is the fact.[25]

21 Janet Afary, *The Iranian Constitutional Revolution, 1906–1911: Grassroot Democracy, Social Democracy, & the Origins of Feminism* (New York: Columbia University Press, 1996), 179.

22 Hereafter *Majlis.*

23 Reza Arasteh, "The Struggle for Equality in Iran," *Middle East Journal* 18, no. 2 (Spring 1964), 192.

24 Parvin Paidar, *Women and the Political Process in Twentieth-Century Iran* (Cambridge: Cambridge University Press, 1995), 52.

25 Morgan W. Shuster, *The Strangling of Persia* (New York: The Century Co., 1912), 191.

As Ahmadi Khorasani and Ardalan note, two main strands of female activism stemmed from the period following the establishment of Iran's first Constitution and the subsequent first parliament. The first strand of activism was concerned with the right of women to vote. Women realized that, regardless of their activism during the Constitutional Revolution, they were still rendered powerless in the political arena. The Constitution itself did not mention women. Article 10 of the Electoral Law of 1908 explicitly names eight categories of people, including women, who were banned from voting:

> 1) Women; 2) those who are mentally disabled (have not reached a mental maturity) and who are under legal guardianship;[26] 3) Foreign nationals; 4) Those who have exited from religion of Islam in the presence of a Islamic jurist (*hokam Shar' Jame al'Sharayet*) 5) Those under the age of twenty; 5) Those bankrupt due to a false (criminal) action on their part; 6) Beggars and people who earn their living immorally; 7) Murderers, thieves and other criminals who have been convicted under Islamic law; 8) Political offenders who have revolted against the bases of the nationalist government and the independence of the nation.

Similarly, Article 13 of the same law specifies six categories of people not allowed to be elected to parliament:

> Princes in the line of succession (sons, brothers, uncles of the king); 2) Women; 3) Foreign nationals; 4) Those serving in the security forces (police forces), those in the army and the navy, apart from those who hold honorific titles; 5) Governor generals, provincial governors and their deputies in the (geographical) contexts they are serving; 6) Financial officers in the (geographical) contexts they are serving in.[27]

Not only were women not permitted to vote or be elected, but also they were lumped in the same category with a number of very diverse groups: thieves, criminals, the mentally disabled and children. The Secret Union of Women (*Ittihadiyahy-e Ghaibiy-e Nasvan*) was one of the organizations that promoted women's civil and political rights in this context. According to Afary, it had strong revolutionary tendencies.[28] However, some male Constitutionalists

26 Note that this category is often referred to in the literature as mentally ill or mad.

27 Noushin Ahmadi Khorasan and Parvin Ardalan, *Senator: Fa'aliatha-ye Mehrangiz Manucheh-rian bar bastar-e mobarezat-e hoququi-e zanan dar iran (Senator: The Work of Senator Mehrangiz Manouchehrian in the Struggle for Legal Rights for Women)* (Tehran: Tose'eh, 2003), 180–181.

28 Janet Afary, *The Iranian Constitutional Revolution, 1906–1911: Grassroot Democracy, Social Democracy, & the Origin of Feminism* (New York: Columbia University Press, 1996), 184.

were not content with the women's rights–based critique of the Constitution. They believed any critique of the newly formed Constitution was an attack on Iranian independence. Thus, the Iranian women's suffrage movement began its half-century–long struggle.

The other strand of women's activism was concerned with promoting female education. This strand was, by and large, supported by the Constitutionalists. Women's societies were organized to carry out charity work, as well as literacy classes and training workshops in skills such as sewing. However, these organizations also showed political awareness and some eventually became politically active. The *anjumans* associated with raising funds for schools, orphanages and hospitals included, among many others, the Association for the Welfare of Women of Iran (*Shirkat-i Khavatin-i Irani*) and the Society of Ladies of Iran (*Anjuman-i Khvatin-i Iran*).[29]

Although the first girls' schools were opened by American missionaries in Urummiayh, Province of Western Azerbaijan, in March 1838, Afary argues, "it was only with the Constitutional Revolution that a grassroots campaign for women's education began. By April 1910 fifty girls' schools had opened in Tehran and a women's congress on education took place in the capital."[30] By 1913 the journal *Shokofeh* was able to publish a list of sixty-three girls' schools in Tehran alone. The success of these schools was owing to the activism of women pursued mainly through the *anjumans*. However, as Guity Neshat notes, "the first public school for girls did not open until 1918".[31] Neshat also highlights the opposition of some clerics to the opening of the early girls' schools and the subsequent harassment of founders and teachers. She writes, "(t)hese schools were regarded as the means of 'luring Muslim girls and leading their minds astray and turning them into unbelievers and wantons by pretending to give them lessons.' "[32] The fact that these women were also at times "harassed by the members of their own families"[33] highlights feminist dependency on family in the early years of the Iranian women's movement. One important example is that of Bibi Khanoom Astarabadi,[34] who founded *Dabestan Dooshizegan* (School for Young Ladies) in Tehran in 1907. This was one of the first all-female

29 Ibid.

30 Ibid., 182.

31 Guity Neshat, "Introduction," in *Women in Iran from 1800 to the Islamic Republic*, ed. Lois Beck and Guity Neshat (Champaign, IL: University of Illinois Press, 2004), 21.

32 Ibid., 24.

33 Ibid.

34 Bib Khanoom Astarabadi (b. 1858) was an educated woman (educated by her mother) and one of the first vocal Iranian feminists who lobbied for education for girls as well as equal gender rights. She is also known for her feminist treatise "Ma'ayeb al-rijal (the Vices of Men)" written in 1894.

schools to be opened by Iranians.[35] The school was forcibly closed down following the publication of a newspaper article that accused the school of having been "established by foreigners to promote decadence".[36] The article was also accompanied by clerical opposition to the school, with one cleric proclaiming in a sermon delivered at Haram Hazrat Abdul Azim that "one should weep for a nation where a school has been opened for young ladies".[37] A second example of this type of dependency is afforded by Fakhr Afaq Parsa (b.1898), one of the first Iranian female journalists of the Constitutional era. Parsa established a magazine (*Jahan-e Zanan* [Women's World]) with the support of her husband Fakhr al-Din Parsa, which published articles on housekeeping, child minding, and the education of women and girls, as well as children's hygiene. Parsa's articulation of women's rights was predicated on a discourse that had the explicit support of men in power. She did not advocate for women's direct political participation. Hers was a mediated feminism that assumed interdependence rather than independence. *Jahan-e Zanan* was suspended after "publishing a letter to the editor that criticized sermons and popular Shi'i mourning rituals".[38] This subsequently led to Parsa's temporary exile in Arak. She rejoined her family in Qom two years later.

Both before and during the Constitutional Revolution, while women's roles were being reinvented, the masculinity of the nation's men was also brought under scrutiny. This was often done in the name of "the collective sense of honor (*namus*) and zeal (*ghairat*)".[39] In other words, it was asserted that the men had failed in their duty to protect the weak and the vulnerable, the women and the children, against the forces of oppression both internally and externally. Women's honor in this way was joined with the honor of the nation and its men.

The women's movement, which had hitherto been "an integrated part of the constitutional movement",[40] enjoyed relative independence from political parties in the post-revolutionary period (1911–25). According to some

35 The first all-female school established by an Iranian is credited to Tubi Rushdieh, whose school named "Parvaresh" (est. 1903) remained open for four days before it was forced shut by opposition to female education.

36 Roznameh Matboeh dar Astaneyeh Hazrat Abdul Azim, 29 July 1907. It is important to note that school did re-open after lobbying by education activists.

37 Cited in Mandan Kazazi, Zeyban Akbari and Mina Jamaat, "Naghsh Zanan dar Shekl Giri Amoozesh va Parvaresh Jadid Dokhtaran Iran (Women's Role in shaping modern education for Iranian girls)," *Pajuhesh dar Tarikh* no. 10, Year 3 1392 (2013), 97.

38 Farzin Vejdani, *Making History in Iran: Education, Nationalism, and Print Culture* (Stanford, CA: Stanford University Press, 2015), 104.

39 Ibid.

40 Parvin Paidar, *Women and the Political Process in Twentieth-Century Iran* (Cambridge: Cambridge University Press, 1995), 91.

scholars, such as Paidar, although the seeds of the women's movement were sown before the Constitutional Revolution, the actual movement was formed in this post-Constitutional period.[41] The movement, although not politically homogenous in its membership, created a united front in terms of demands, which included the right to vote and the right to education. It also raised questions about law reform and regulations on veiling, segregation, child marriage and polygamy.[42]

At the demise of the Qajar dynasty, a nationalist state was formed by Reza Shah (r. 1925–1941) and the Pahlavi dynasty subsequently was established. The new dynasty enjoyed a relative independence from foreign forces. Although Britain and Germany exerted some influence on the new dynasty, "this was not comparable to that enjoyed by foreigners before 1920".[43] The Pahlavi attempts at centralization, modernization and state formation influenced the direction of the women's movement from independence to state dependence. Women's emancipation became an integral part of Reza Shah's policy of state building, modernization and national progress. As Paidar writes, "(t)he era of state building consolidated the link hitherto made between gender equality and national progress and transformed some of the gender demands of the constitutional movement into state policy."[44] The control of women's activism by the state apparatus was combined with pressure on independent women's organizations and *anjumans*. This culminated in the inception of "Reza Shah's state feminism project called the Women's Awakening (*Nehzat-e Banovan*) in 1936".[45] Censorship was a main tool for control of the press, which eventually led to a dramatic decrease in the number of newspapers (including women's presses) from 150 in 1925 to 50 in 1941.[46]

Eventually, and perhaps linked to Reza Shah's trip to Turkey, *Kanun Banovan* (Society for Women), a state-sponsored women's center, was established in May 1935 under the directorship of the Shah's daughter Princess Shams Pahlavi (1917–1966) and the patronage of the Ministry of Education.[47] Among its objectives, which included the physical and spiritual training of

41 Ibid.
42 Ibid.
43 Nikki R. Keddie, "Iranian Power Structure and Social Change 1800–1969: An Overview," *International Journal of Middle East Studies* 2, no. 1 (January 1971), 11.
44 Parvin Paidar, *Women and the Political Process in the Twentieth-Century Iran* (Cambridge: Cambridge University Press, 1995), 103.
45 Camron Michael Amin, *The Making of the Modern Iranian Woman: Gender, State Policy, and Popular Culture, 1865–1946* (Gainesville: University Press of Florida), 4.
46 Naser Rahim Khani, "Negahi be Majaleye Peyk Sadat Nasvan (A Look at the Magazine 'Courier of Women's Happiness')," online www.akhbar-rooz.com/article.jsp?essayId=44191, (accessed 8 January 2016).
47 Parvin Paidar, *Women and the Political Process in the Twentieth-Century Iran* (Cambridge: Cambridge University Press, 1995), 104.

women implemented through "the spread of the Girls' Scouts (*pish ahangi*)", was de-veiling (*kashf hejab*).[48] Eventually, on 7 January 1936, the Shah's most controversial reform was instituted through the promulgation of the unveiling decree, which forbade the public wearing of *chador* and scarf and was immediately opposed by a large sector of women and the clergy.[49] In general, the clergy saw their power wane during this time, in particular, in the areas of education and legislation. However, they did demonstrate their popularity with, and influence on, the Iranian people during the veil ban.

Reza Shah's other reforms included "provision of free education, and the opening up of employment opportunities for women".[50] These reforms, however, furthered gendered roles. Yeganeh writes, "(t)he ambition of the state, however, in instituting these changes was to achieve national progress through the legal construction of women as social participants, educated mothers and subservient wives. The latter was regarded to be a matter of national honor and duplicated the sentiment which had insisted on a women's movement subservient to the state."[51] Furthermore, as discussed in Chapter 3, the legal reforms of Reza Shah's reign did not include many legal rights for women. The family law, enacted as part of the Iranian Civil Code in 1931, discriminated against women in laws pertaining to marriage, divorce, custody and guardianship. The 1937 supplements did not improve women's *de jure* status significantly.[52] Women were also not granted the right to vote or to be elected. Furthermore, Reza Shah's reforms, particularly his unveiling decree, "were not in step with the needs and realities of Iranian society at that time. The absence of social and economic conditions that could support those policies ensured that once force was removed they would be abandoned."[53]

48 Ibid, 105 and Firoozeh Kashani-Sabet, "Patriotic Womanhood: The Culture of Feminism in Modern Iran, 1900–1941," *British Journal of Middle Eastern Studies* 32, no. 1 (May 2005), 41.

49 Firoozeh Kashani-Sabet, "Patriotic Womanhood: The Culture of Feminism in Modern Iran, 1900–1941," *British Journal of Middle Eastern Studies* 32, no. 1 (May 2005), 42–43. And Parvin Paidar, *Women and the Political Process in Twentieth-Century Iran* (Cambridge: Cambridge University Press, 1995), 107.

50 Nahid Yeganeh, "Women, Nationalism and Islam in Contemporary Political Discourses in Iran," *Feminist Review*, no. 44, Nationalisms and National Identities (Summer 1993), 5.

51 Ibid.

52 Although, it is important to note that these reforms did entail a rise in the age of marriage for girls to fifteen and for boys to eighteen years of age, as well as a requirement for all marriages to be registered by the state. See Guity Neshat, "Women in Pre-Revolutionary Iran: A Historical Overview" in *Women and Revolution in Iran*, ed. Lois Beck and Guity Neshat (Boulder: Westview Replica Edition, 1983), 26 ff.

53 Guity Neshat, "Women in Pre-Revolutionary Iran: A Historical Overview" in *Women and Revolution in Iran*, ed. Lois Beck and Guity Neshat (Boulder: Westview Replica Edition, 1983), 28.

After the forced abdication of Reza Shah by the Allies and the coming to power of his son Muhammad Reza Shah on 16 September 1941, the Iranian women's movement once again gained a relative independence. The women's suffrage movement gained a new momentum. In 1942 the Tudeh Party put the political rights of Iranian women on the agenda of a congress organized in Tehran. In general, the Tudeh Party was successful in gathering support for its campaigns to advocate for women's rights and attracted, among others, some of the early women's rights activists.[54] Also, in the same year, the Iranian Women's Party (*Hizb-e Zanan-e Iran*) established by Fatemeh Siyah and Safiyeh Firooz began a widespread campaign to gain the vote for women. One lobbying strategy used by the members of the Women's Party in their fight for the vote was to target the support of male parliamentarians. The dependence of these early feminists on men in the state apparatus is comparable to that of the state feminists mentioned in Chapter 2.[55]

In 1949 the Society of Democratic Women (*Jamey-e Democrat-e Zanan*) was established and linked to the Tudeh Party. The Society campaigned for women's political rights, especially for women's right to vote and for equal remuneration for equal work. They also campaigned for the right of women to education. One strategy that the Society undertook in 1952, that of signature collection, is comparable to a strategy used by the later One Million Signatures Campaign, which is discussed later in this chapter. As Neshat observes, the Society of Democratic Women "demanded the extension of suffrage to women in 1952 on the 45th anniversary of the Constitutional Revolution. The party was able to collect 100,000 signatures for the extension of the vote to women. The Constitutional Amendments were discussed in the Parliament, but the prime minister, Dr. Muhammad Musaddiq [sic], had to withdraw the bill under pressure from religious authorities."[56] The clergy, who had lost considerable power during Reza Shah's time, began gaining support during the reign of Muhammad Reza Shah. One way they managed to do so was by restoration of the veil. Some clergy also continued their opposition to women's education.[57]

The overthrow of the nationalist prime minister (1951–1953), Muhammad Mossadegh, in 1953 led to the authoritarian rulership of Muhammad Reza Shah and put an end to opposition parties such as Tudeh. While the late '40s and early '50s saw a surge in the *ulama's* power, the period after the 1953 coup witnessed a decade of relative quietism. For some women

54 Ibid., 29.

55 The interview with Fatemeh Haghighatjoo in this section, in particular, is a testament to a legacy of ongoing dependencies in the twenty-first century where women members of the parliament in the sixth *majlis* depended on the support of male parliamentarians (often clergy members) to advance their work for equal rights.

56 Ibid.

57 Ibid., 28.

activists the decrease in clerical influence during this time ensured a "more favourable climate in which individuals and small groups of women could step up their efforts to improve women's rights".[58] Women's rights rhetoric became common in organizations such as *Hezb-e Zanan* (the Women's Party) and the Women's League (which later was renamed the Women's League of Supporters of Human Rights).[59] The lobbying of these organizations and the activism of many more women's rights advocates led to the success of the women's suffrage movement being included as one the six points of Muhammad Reza Shah's White Revolution. In the 1960s and 1970s women made some headway towards attaining equal rights. This may have been related to the rapid socio-economic development of these decades and growing Iranian oil revenue. The 1967 Family Protection Act (FPA),[60] as mentioned in Chapter 3, restricted polygamy, raised the age of marriage for girls and allowed women the right to divorce. Women also gained an equal right to employment in most public sectors, including in the judiciary as judges. They were allowed to enroll in the majority of third-level courses, including law. They were free to interact with their male counterparts in public sectors, whether veiled or unveiled. However, more religious families would still restrict women's movement in public. Despite these relative freedoms, the Shah's regime faced much opposition, particularly to its corruption. In addition, the Pahlavi modernization process was often regarded as overly dependent on Western influence.[61] The regime was criticized on the grounds that it "followed an autocratic and Western-oriented modernisation approach, which was heavily supported by the United States and other Western countries."[62] Iran was, after all, a Muslim country, with the clergy having strong support from the Iranian public.[63] The more the Shah increased his power over the state apparatus, the more defiant the clergy and their followers became. This

58 Ibid., 29.

59 Ibid., 29–30.

60 See Doreen Hinchcliff, "The Iranian Family Protection Act," *The International and Comparative Law Quarterly* 17, no. 2 (1968), 516–521. The 1967 FPA gave women more rights in the areas of law concerned with custody, polygamy and divorce among others. Former (pre-1979) Iranian Civil Code Articles 1133, 1121, 1092, 1123, 1101, 1122, 1129.

61 See Parvin Paidar, "Gender and Democracy: The Encounter between Feminism and Reformism in Contemporary Iran," *Democracy, Governance and Human Rights*, Programme, no. 6 (United Nations Research Institute for Social Development, October 2001), 2–3. Refer also to Azar Tabari, "The Women's Movement in Iran: A Hopeful Prognosis," *Feminist Studies* 12, no. 2 (1986), 343–360.

62 Parvin Paidar, "Gender and Democracy: The Encounter between Feminism and Reformism in Contemporary Iran," *Democracy, Governance and Human Rights*, Programme, no. 6 (United Nations Research Institute for Social Development, October 2001), 2.

63 The Shah, for example, banned abortion in 1978 as a compromise with religious leaders. See Azar Tabari, "The Women's Movement in Iran: A Hopeful Prognosis," *Feminist Studies* 12, no. 2 (1986), 353.

opposition intensified throughout the 1970s, culminating in the overthrow of the Shah and the start of the Islamic Revolution.

The 1979 Islamic revolution

There was mass participation of Iranian women in the 1979 Islamic Revolution. Women were encouraged to take part in mass demonstrations, became involved in the militia and partisan armed groups and fought in clashes. Women were also killed in clashes during the demonstrations. The Cinema Rex incident and Black Friday are two examples of occasions on which many women lost their lives.[64] Women also assumed the task of spreading news through opposition literature, tapes and revolutionary slogans, doing so once again through networks of *rowzeh* and *sofreh*. It was not only the elite or the educated women who took an active part in the revolutionary movement, but also women from all levels of society.[65] Women still played the gendered role of nurturer as well as being organizers within the revolutionary movement. They supported their families, relatives, friends and neighbours.

However, with its inauguration, the Islamic Republic imposed a series of misogynistic laws and decrees limiting the access of women to much of the public domain. Strict Islamic gender relations were used to the advantage of the hardline regime, and women's appearance and behaviour was regulated. In Khomeini's scheme of thought, as Paidar indicates, "women were regarded as signifiers of national identity, their appearance, behaviour and position first had to be Islamized".[66] The rise of political Islam had transformed Iranian women. In the process they were projected as a single entity, and their *hejab* became a symbol of the Islamic Republic. According to Haleh Afshar, "[as] the symbol of reasserting Islamic identity and purification of society from Western culture, *hejab* is the focal point of the state propaganda and gender politics."[67] As the symbol of the veil became the public face of the revolution, Muslim women were ironically required to resume their maternal and domestic duties and retreat to the privacy of the home.

Whereas before the revolution the practice of religion was largely a private affair and not forced upon people, after the revolution the private domain of religion was displaced. Women were moved behind the veil and sent back to their homes as a public form of religion largely regulated by men began to rule the streets. Before the revolution, the state did not punish so-called unbelievers. After the revolution, a different understanding of Islam, arguably

64 "Iran's Constitutional Revolution (Chronicle of the Constitutional Revolution)," online www.iranianstudies.ca/Const_Revolution/chronicle.html, (accessed 15 May 2008).

65 Haleh Afshar, *Islam and Feminism: An Iranian Case-Study* (Great Britain: MacMillan Press Ltd., 1998).

66 Ibid., 3.

67 Ibid., 197.

derived from male-centric interpretations of Islamic law via the Shi'a tradition, was incorporated into the state apparatus. As Mir-Hosseini narrates, "it was no longer enough to believe; one had to wear one's beliefs in the form of *hejab*."[68] The state took it upon itself to enforce the religious mandates that had previously been the concern of the family. The establishment of the theocratic government following the success of the 1979 Islamic Revolution brought forth the renewal of traditional interpretations of Islamic law. After the revolution the legitimacy of clerics increased even more and became codified in the Iranian Constitution.

This direct rule of the cleric is one of the most startling phenomena of the past few decades. Significant political offices in Iran are filled by Shi'a clergy. The utmost authority is given to the *Vilayat-e al-Faqih*. This title of Supreme Jurist was held by Ruhollah Khomeini from 1979 to 1988. Since Khomeini's death it has been held by Ali Khamenei.[69] According to Ashk Dahlén:

> . . . the new theocratic order confronts a political reality that is not addressed by definite formulations in the traditional *fiqh* corpus. Since there is no clear or hard position under *Shari'at* in many areas of law, such as substantive laws, the Shi'i *fuqaha* (jurists) are divided among themselves as to the best legal solutions to many problems facing contemporary society.[70]

The idea that Islamic states take precedence over all others is evident. Khomeini asserted, "[the Islamic state] is a branch of the absolute trusteeship of the Prophet . . . and constitutes one of the primary ordinances of Islam which has precedence over all other derived ordinances, such as prayer, fasting and pilgrimage."[71] The role of the *faqih* is also enshrined in the Iranian Constitution. Article 91 states:

> With a view to safeguard the Islamic ordinances and the Constitution, in order to examine the compatibility of the legislation passed by the Islamic Consultative Assembly with Islam, a council to be known as the Guardian Council is to be constituted with the following composition:
>
> 1 Six *faqih-adil* (just clerics), conscious of the present needs and the issues of the day, to be selected by the Leader, and

68 Ziba Mir-Hosseini, "The Quest for Gender Justice Emerging Feminist Voices in Islam," Presented at the conference: Reframing Islam, Irish Centre for Human Rights (National University of Ireland Galway, Ireland 2005), 1.

69 Note that Khamenei was elevated to the status of a *Valiy-e Faqih* in a very short space of time (and even his title as an Ayatollah was given to him rather suddenly). This was a shock to many high-ranking clerics at Qom and brought forth a major political rift.

70 Ashk P. Dahlén, *Islamic Law, Epistemology and Modernity: Legal Philosophy in Contemporary Iran* (New York: Routledge, 2003), 4.

71 Sami Zubaida, *Law and Power in the Islamic World* (London: I.B. Tauris, 2003), 2.

2 Six jurists, specializing in different areas of law, to be elected by the Islamic Consultative Assembly from among the Muslim jurists nominated by the Head of the Judicial Power.

The Guardian Council exercises great power over Iranian legislation, as demonstrated in Chapters 3 and 4. Any laws passed by the *majlis* must be sent for approval to the Council, which then decides whether these laws are in accordance with Islamic tenets or not. Furthermore, as Article 98 of the Constitution states, the Guardian Council is vested with the authority to interpret the Constitution. Acts of interpretation require consent of three-fourths of its members.

In addition to the Guardian Council, the Islamic Consultative Assembly (*Majlis-e Khobregan*) is another clerical body. The Islamic Consultative Assembly is composed of eighty-six members and is vested with the power of electing a new supreme leader after the death, dismissal or resignation of the supreme leader. The *Khobergan* are elected by the people. However, the Guardian Council must first determine who is eligible to run for assembly seats. In addition to the Guardian Council and the Assembly of Experts there is the Expediency Council (*Majma-e Tashkhis-e Maslehat-e Nezam*). The members of this council are mainly clerics chosen by the supreme leader. The Expediency Council has supervisory power over all branches of government and the power to adjudicate disputes over legalization between the Consultative Assembly (*Majlis*) and the Guardian Council.[72]

Such is the general governmental context surrounding the Iranian women's rights movement. To the discontent of many who supported the revolution, women lost many of their rights to the discriminatory laws promulgated after 1979. The 1967 Family Protection Act (FPA)[73] was abrogated. Women were banned from working as judges[74] and the legal age of marriage for girls was lowered to thirteen.[75] Girls were barred from technical and vocational schools and also from higher education fields such as engineering, agriculture and mathematical sciences.[76] Veiling was

72 See Articles 107, 108, 111 and 112 of the Constitution of the Islamic Republic of Iran, 24 October 1979, amended 28 July 1989.

73 See Doreen Hinchcliff, "The Iranian Family Protection Act," *The International and Comparative Law Quarterly* 17, no. 2 (1968), 516–521. The 1967 FPA gave women more rights in the areas of law concerned with custody, polygamy and divorce among others. Former (pre-1979) Iranian Civil Code Articles 1133, 1121, 1092, 1123, 1101, 1122, 1129.

74 The Laws Governing the Appointment of Judges, ratified 1982.

75 In the year 2002, the sixth parliament proposed that the age of marriage for both boys and girls be increased to eighteen; however, this met fierce opposition from the Guardian and Expediency Councils.

76 Haideh Moghissi, *Feminism and Islamic Fundamentalism: The Limits of Postmodern Analysis* (London: Zed Books, 1999), 100.

also gradually enforced, starting with "the public harassment of women lacking *hejab* at the hands of religious revolutionaries."[77] On the eve of International Women's Day, 7 March 1979 Ayatollah Khomeini "referred to unveiled women as 'naked' and demanded that they observe Islamic *hejab* at offices and places of work."[78] Consequently the project of "Islamification of offices" required women to observe the veil or face consequences in the form of violence or loss of their jobs. Both "unveiled" (*bi-hejab*) and "improperly-veiled" (*bad-hejab*) women were condemned by the clerical leaders. The veiled woman became both the emblem of the new Islamic state and one of its legitimizing factors. Veiling became a way of controlling women's bodies and sexuality.[79] The *hejab* law eventually came into force on 9 August 1983 as Article 102 of the Penal Code, which asserts "Women who appear in public without religious *hejab* will be sentenced to whipping up to 74 lashes."[80] Women did not passively accept these discriminatory laws. They came out in the thousands on 8 March 1979 to protest Khomeini's speech. There were also scattered protests about the abrogated Family Protection Act and the enactment of *hudud* and *qesas* laws.

Some of these laws were progressively reformed thanks to the persistence of the women's movement. For example, in December 1992 the *majlis* passed the Amendment to Divorce Law, which outlawed "registration of all divorces without a court document certifying 'impossibility of reconciliation'".[81] This amendment obliged the husband to pay the wife he intended to divorce *mahr* (bride price or bride gift) and *nafaqa* (maintenance) and to financially support her during her *idda* (waiting period). However, it should be noted that if the wife initiates the divorce, then "she forgoes all her dues in return for her release."[82] Other reforms and amendments included "the appointment of women judges as advisers to the main judge," and women being paid wages in kind for their housework (*ujrat al-mithl*).[83]

Significantly, early revolutionary acts and subsequent examples of reform were separated by a major inter-state conflict. During the Iran-Iraq war

77 Justice for Iran, *Thirty-Five Years of Forced Hejab: The Widespread and Systematic Violation of Women's Rights in Iran* (London: Justice for Iran, March 2014), 9.

78 Ayatollah Khomeini's speech at the Refah School cited in ibid.

79 Hamideh Sedghi, *Women and Politics in Iran: Veiling, Unveiling, and Reveiling* (Cambridge: Cambridge University Press, 2007), 201–212.

80 Justice for Iran, *Thirty-Five Years of Forced Hejab.*

81 Ziba Mir-Hosseini, "Stretching the Limits: A Feminist Reading of the Shari'a in Post-Khomeini Iran" in *Feminism and Islam, Legal and Literary Perspectives*, ed. Mai Yamani (Reading: Ithaca Press, 1996), 292.

82 Ibid. Please also note that all the mentioned terms are described in more depth in Chapter 3.

83 Ibid.

(1980–1988) women's struggle for equality was largely overshadowed by "the predominant values of self-denial, devotion and sacrifice, rooted in the *Shi'a* culture and internalized by the young volunteers".[84] The war was used by politicians and the clerical elite to dismiss women's social problems. Yet, during the war, because of the mobilization of all Iranian men, a number of employment opportunities were also created for educated women in health, educational and public administration sectors.[85] As Valentine Moghadam has stated, "these jobs went to ideologically correct women, but their presence suggested both the determination of women and the flexibility of the Islamic Regime."[86] Some women were even recruited as Revolutionary Guards and trained for military action in the war.[87] Tellingly, when the regime needed support, the role of women citizens was expanded accordingly.

During the Iran-Iraq war the regime needed support. The war undermined Iran's economy. Government revenue declined. Unemployment and poverty soared. Iran found itself in grave debt. The collective "West" became an object of Islamic propaganda and a scapegoat. Anything Western was deemed morally corrupt and hence against Islamic values. For example, contraceptives were seen both as a Western means of controlling a growing Muslim population (a growth which the government desired during wartime) and as devices to facilitate moral deviance. Therefore, to quash moral deviance and to ensure an increase in army numbers, certain laws were rewritten. For instance, the age of puberty, and hence of marriage, for girls was decreased to nine years of age.[88] The government maintained that marriage was the duty of every mature Muslim and officially encouraged early marriage to the great detriment of a generation of girls. Yet, in an about-turn typifying the pragmatic flexibility of the regime, the final years of the Iran-Iraq war witnessed a policy debate around the permissibility of contraception in Islam.[89] Faced with an economic crisis and a population of fifty million, the government realized that some form of birth control was necessary. Moderate religious leaders led the way in advancing this argument. Finally, because the war left many orphans and widows in its wake, some women remained outside the

84 Azadeh Kian, "Women and Politics in Post-Islamist Iran: The Gender Conscious Drive to Change," *British Journal of Middle Eastern Studies* 24, no. 1 (1997), 78.

85 Ibid.

86 Valentine M. Moghadam, "Islamic Feminism and Its Discontents: Towards a Resolution of the Debate," *Signs: Journal of Women in Culture and Society* 27, no. 4 (2002), 1139.

87 See also Mehrangiz Kar, "*Hoquqe Siyasie Zan dar Iran z Bahman Panjaohaft ta Emroz* (Women's Political Right in Iran from 1979 until Today)," *Zanan*, October 1994, 18–25.

88 This law was later reformed and age of marriage for girls was raised to thirteen.

89 Homa Hoodfar, "Devices and Desires: Population Policy and Gender Roles in the Islamic Republic," *Middle East Report* 24, no. 190 (1994), 11–17. See also Valentine M. Moghadam, "Islamic Feminism and Its Discontents: Towards a Resolution of the Debate," *Signs: Journal of Women in Culture and Society* 27, no. 4 (2002), 1139.

home and were employed by reconstruction projects in jobs created to support their families.[90]

The sanctioned and necessary presence of women outside the home became another important factor leading to the advancement of women's rights in Iran during the reform period. The end of the Iran-Iraq war, the death of Khomeini in 1989 and the election of Hashemi Rafsanjani to the presidency coincided with the growth of liberal publications and an increase in the number of active non-governmental organizations. According to Zarir Merat, during this time "the Ministry of Culture and Islamic Orientation began making subtle gestures in favor of intellectual journals and reviews".[91] Civil society groups mushroomed after the 1997 elections[92] and with them emerged a new political space. Despite certain misconceptions, women became strong political forces in post-revolutionary Iran. Women's agency and the development of what some call Islamic Feminism is a paradoxical consequence of the rise of political Islam in Iran.[93] Mir-Hosseini even argues that the rise of political Islam "helped create a space, an arena, within which Muslim women can reconcile their faith and identity with their struggle for gender equality".[94] As a result, a growing number of women have come to see no inherent link between patriarchy and Islamic ideals, and no contradiction between Islam and feminism.[95]

From the reform era to Ahmadinejad's reign

The reformist movement (*jonbesh-e eslah-talab*) in Iran came into greater prominence with the presidential election of Muhammad Khatami in May 1997. There was mass participation of women and youth in the elections that year.[96] This movement was regarded as an opposition movement within Iran led by moderate Islamists against powerful Islamist hardliners. In the first four years of Khatami's presidency, separate women's units were established in a

90 Homa Hoodfar, "Devices and Desires: Population Policy and Gender Roles in the Islamic Republic," *Middle East Report* 24, no. 190 (1994), 11–17.

91 Zarir Merat, "Pushing Back the Limits of the Possible: The Press in Iran," *Middle East Report* 212 (Fall 1999), 32.

92 Parvin Paidar, "Gender of Democracy: The Encounter between Feminism and Reformism in Cotemporary Iran," *Democracy, Governance and Human Rights*, Programme Paper No. 6 (United Nations Research Institute for Social Development, October 2001), 6.

93 Ibid.

94 Ziba Mir-Hosseini, "The Quest for Gender Justice Emerging Feminist Voices in Islam," Presented at the conference, Reframing Islam, Irish Centre for Human Rights (National University of Ireland Galway, Ireland 2005), 1.

95 Parvin Paidar, "Gender of Democracy: The Encounter between Feminism and Reformism in Cotemporary Iran," *Democracy, Governance and Human Rights*, Programme Paper No. 6 (United Nations Research Institute for Social Development, October 2001), 1–47.

96 Ibid., 1. Also note that Iranian girls and boys have the right to vote at the age of fifteen.

majority of the government departments and executive agencies.[97] Khatami used the slogan of women's emancipation as one of his primary campaign tools. In one speech he said, "the Islamic system and community should confidently appoint women to sensitive posts. . . . Limitations should not come in the way of broad participation by women in management, politics and society."[98] Even though during Khatami's reign more women became active in politics, they were mainly women who were somehow already linked to the state apparatus. Nonetheless, women parliamentarians in the *majilis-e sheshom* (sixth Islamic Consultative Assembly) were able to make some headway concerning women's rights. Some amendments were made to the existing laws to improve the rights of women,[99] and a campaign was launched for Iran to ratify the United Nations Convention on the Elimination of all Forms of Discrimination against Women (CEDAW).

Yet even during the reform period most of the state power remained concentrated in the hands of the hardliners. During this time many reformist presses were closed down. Journalists were jailed. Lawyers were harassed, and many other reformist supporters both within and outside the government lost their jobs. In September 2004 a right-wing newspaper, *Jomhuri-ye Eslami,* printed an extended article accusing women's non-governmental organizations (NGOs)of being agents of the West. The article's publication was followed by a wave of arrests.[100] Reformist journalists, webloggers and women's rights activists were arrested. Iran's reform movement came to an end in February 2004 when the conservatives took control of the seventh Islamic Consultative Assembly (*majlis-i haftom*). The seventh (2004–2008), eighth (2008–2012) and ninth (2012–2016) Consultative Assemblies showed a high degree of hostility towards civil society and the women's movement in general.

Since the defeat of the reformists in the *majlis-i haftom* and the election of President Mahmoud Ahmadinejad in June 2005, civil society and women's movements have faced new challenges. Only three weeks after the new president took office, the Regional Civil Society Forum on an Information

97 It is important to note that some reforms also re-emerged from the fourth and fifth parliament. Also a women's commission was set up before Khatami by Rafsanjani. However, the commission was extended more noticeably after Khatami's election.

98 Parvin Paidar, "Gender of Democracy: The Encounter between Feminism and Reformism in Cotemporary Iran," *Democracy, Governance and Human Rights*, Programme Paper No. 6 (United Nations Research Institute for Social Development, October 2001), 11.

99 One such amendment is the case for female scholars to study abroad. From the start of the revolution until 2001, women were able to pursue studies abroad on government funding only if they were married (this rule did not apply to men). However, in 2001 an amendment was made to this law to allow single females to study abroad.

100 My own house was raided after the publication of this article.

Society for the Middle East and West Asia, which had been scheduled to take place in Iran on the 23rd of August 2005, was banned unexpectedly by government officials. On the 8th of March 2006 women's rights activists took to the streets to protest discriminatory laws against women and to ask the government to reform these laws. The demonstration led to clashes and many of the demonstrators were arrested. This marked the beginning of a round of widespread arrests and intimidation, which continued through the disputed 2009 presidential elections. As of June 2012 it had increased to the point that many women's rights activists, including Parvin Ardalan, Shirin Ebadi, Mahboubeh Abbasgholizadeh and Mansoureh Shojaee, had been forced into exile. Others, including Nasrin Sotoudeh, Bahareh Hedayat, Jila Baniyaghoub, Narges Mohammadi and Haleh Sahabi, were imprisoned. Those who remain in Iran have had to be innovative in their activism. One aspect of innovation consistently embraced by the women's movement has been the strategic use of new forms of media. A brief survey of publications associated with the Iranian women's movement in political and historical context is essential to understand these dynamics, particularly the print to online transitions made by independent and semi-independent women's media.[101]

Iranian women's movement through offline and online media

From the early years of women's activism in Iran, newspapers and periodicals were used as forums for knowledge sharing, lobbying and advocacy. In the early publications edited and written by women, one can read of the promotion of the right to health and to education, as well as narratives about women's public and political participation in Iranian society. Up until the Constitutional Revolution, publications such as *Ghanun* (1889–1892),[102] *Sur-e Israfil* (1907–1908), *Habl al-Matin* (1907–1909), *Musavat* (1907–1909), *Iran-i Naw* (1909–1911), *Neday-i Vatan, Majlis* (1906–1908), *Anjuman* (1906–1909) and *Mulla Nasredin*[103] were all established and run by men. At times, however, they published articles related to women's issues. There are examples of articles on women's suffrage or, on occasion, articles, letters and petitions written by women. Mirza Malkom Khan wrote in *Ghanun*, "(the rush of women to participate in the movement of humanity is

101 Media that is not entirely free from the state apparatus.

102 *Ghanun* was published in London.

103 A number of publication dates are associated with *Mulla Nasredin*. It was first published in Georgia from 1906 to 1917, then in Tabriz in 1921; the publication continued in Baku, Azerbaijan, from 1922 to 1931. *Mulla Nasredin* was published in Azari Turkish and sometimes in Russian.

surprising. The state of affairs is such that many of our noble women have gone ahead of men [in promoting humanity]. Women have understood the meaning and advantage of humanity better than men or rather non-men."[104] In December 1906 *Habl ol-Matin* published a letter to its editor, in which a woman asked, "Why is it that the Constitution has prevented women from gaining their rights?" Women, she continued, "did not take part in the Revolution to have their rights trampled upon."[105]

The eventual rise in the number of women's publications seventy-five years after the first Iranian newspaper, *Kaghaz Akhabar*,[106] debuted is linked to the expansion of women's schools and to a heightened awareness in women of their status and rights.[107] As one traces the history of Iranian women's publications a pattern emerges: Publications begin as free forums only to be closed down when the content of their articles challenges the status quo and the power of officials and clerics.

Danesh (Knowledge), the first Iranian publication with a specific remit for women, was founded in 1910. Dr. Kahali Jadid al-Islam Hamedani, the first Iranian female ophthalmologist, was its managing editor. This weekly journal was apolitical. In fact, it actively tried to avoid politics.[108] Instead, it emphasized the gendered role played by women as mothers and wives. Nonetheless, it broke taboos at a time when nearly 97 per cent of all Iranian women were illiterate.[109] *Danesh* advocated for the importance of education for women and girls and regarded education as a solution to women's problems.[110] In

104 Parvin Paidar, *Women and the Political Process in Twentieth-Century Iran* (Cambridge: Cambridge University Press, 1995), 54.

105 Ibid., 55.

106 *Kaghaz akhbar* is a literal translation of the English word newspaper. It was established by Mirza Muhammad Saleh Mohandes Shirazi, and the first edition was published 1 May 1837 by the order of Muhammad Shah Qajar.

107 Maryam Hosseinkhah, "Mashrooteh Aghaz baray-e Roozna negari Zanan," *Zanan*, 17 Mordad, 1385 (8 August 2006), online http://zanestan.es/issue9/06,08,08,07,13,22, (accessed 3 March 2016).

108 In the first edition of the weekly, one can read "This is a moral, scientific, housekeeping, child-minding, husband-minding journal, useful to girls, women and in totality does not talk about governmental policies nor politics." See Sadr al-Din Elahi, "Tak negari yek rooznameh: <<Danesh>>, Avalin rooznameh farsi zaban baraye zanan Irani, (Signle authored newspaper: <<Danesh>>, the first Persian language newspaper for Iranian women)," *Majaleye Iranshenasi* 24, no. 2, sixth year, (1994), 322.

109 www.iran-forum.ir/thread-61697.html. See also Maryam Hosseinkhah, "Enghelab Mashrooteh Shoroee Baray-e Roozname Negari Zanan (Constitutional Revolution: the Start of Journalism for Women)," *Etemaad* no. 1465 (13 August 2007), 8, online www.magiran.com/npview.asp?ID=1463097 (accessed 29 July 2016); see also Eliz Sansarian, "Characteristics of Women's Movement in Iran" in *Women and Family in Iran*, ed. Asghar Fathi (Leiden, Netherland: E.J. Brill, 1985), 88.

110 Maryam Hosseinkhah, "Mashrooteh Aghaz baray-e Roozna negari Zanan," *Zanan*, 17 Mordad, 1385 (8 August 2006), online http://zanestan.es/issue9/06,08,08,07,13,22, (accessed 3 March 2016).

the first edition of *Danesh*, Hamedani wrote an editorial in which she asked men to advertize the weekly to illiterate women in the following way: "It is assumed that the gentlemen will read the gazette for them each week so that they are not excluded from the joy of (literacy) and perhaps this will encourage them towards attaining literacy."[111] Another issue raised in *Danesh* was the treatment of women by men. Issue 13 of the journal claimed, "No more, has any man the right to belittle and insult women for women's ability/potential and smartness are no less than men."[112] These editorials were written at a time when, according to Eliz Sanasarian, "(t)here was a general belief, consistently reiterated by the religious leaders, that literacy among women would pose a dangerous threat to society. Many believed that women could not be educated because their brains did not have the capacity to absorb knowledge. Others argued that the education of women was against Islam."[113] Sanasarian further elaborates that although some Qajar families allowed women to learn to read they "were strictly prohibited from writing (Shaykh ol-Islami, 1972: 84)."[114] She continues, "It was believed that if women knew how to write they would send love letters to men and disgrace the family (Shaykh ol-Islami, 1972: 84)."[115] These were the circumstances under which women began the difficult task of publishing magazines and newspapers in Iran.

Shokofeh (Bloom), the second women's magazine in the country, was first published in 1913 in Tehran. It was founded by Mayam Amid Sana'i Mozayen al-Saltaneh, who was the daughter of Seyed Reza Raeen al-Atabaa, Nasir al-Din Shah's physician. *Shokofeh* is remembered as the first Iranian bi-weekly published by women for women. Al-Saltaneh was also the founder of the first Iranian women's society and the principal of the "Dar ul-Elm and Sanaye Moznieh" school. *Shokofeh*, at a glance, resembles *Danesh*. Its first editorial states, "It is a literary and moral newspaper, concerning hygiene, children, housekeeping, child-minding, with a direct aim of educating young ladies and women in relations to schools for girls, currently two issues are being published per month. . . ."[116] However, apart from pursuing these goals, the newspaper also published discussions on gender equality, as well as critiques of early marriage. One of the distinguishing features of *Shokofeh* was its publication of socio-political satire. *Shokofeh's* content became more and more politicized once it became the organ of *Anjoman Hemmat Khavatin*

111 *Danesh*, no. 1 (year), 2.
112 *Danesh*, no. 13 (year), 4.
113 Eliz Sansarian, "Characteristics of Women's Movement in Iran" in *Women and Family in Iran*, ed. Asghar Fathi (Leiden: E.J. Brill, 1985), 88.
114 Ibid., 89.
115 Ibid.
116 Masoomeh Khodadad, "Nokhostin Rooznamehaye Zanan Iran (First Newspaper for Women in Iran)," *Majmoeye Maghalat Nashriye Dakheli Hafez* no. 49 (2009), 24.

(the Society for the Efforts of Women). It then began publishing articles explicitly on Iranian nationalist struggles. One of the most striking pieces that appeared in *Shokofeh* was an article that introduced twelve of its own women candidates and asked men to vote for them. This led to the newspaper being banned. However, the ban was later withdrawn.[117]

Iranian journalist, Sadiqheh Dawlatabadi (1882–1961), a pioneer of the Iranian women's movement, founded the first Iranian women's publication registered under a woman's name, *Zaban-e Zanan* (The Voice of Women). This occurred in Isfahan in 1918, three years after the closure of *Shokofeh*. *Zaban-e Zanan* was published bi-weekly, and aimed to combat superstition and ignorance and to spread political awareness among women.[118] The language of rights appears in its very first issue. Dawlatabadi also regularly included political commentary on combating dictatorship.[119] The magazine was subsequently suspended by the order of the government of Isfahan for having broken the 1919 press laws of *Vusugh al-Dawlah* and for having criticized British rule in Iran under the 1919 Anglo-Iranian Treaty.[120] However, when Sedigheh moved to Tehran in 1922 she resumed publication.[121] Much like the contemporary women's movement in its use of online media, which is discussed in subsequent sections, Dawlatabadi "organized women locally and attempted to coordinate their actions through her newspaper."[122]

Numerous other women's weeklies and monthlies were founded and run by women thereafter, although most were short-lived. Some of these publications also addressed issues concerning women's rights and emancipation. One, *Nameh-e Banovan* (Ladies' Letter), was published in Tehran in 1920 under the editorship of the women's rights activist Shahnaz Azad. According to Eliz Sansarian, this publication, which only printed articles written by women, "covered both national and international news, and advocated the unveiling of women".[123] Looking through the archives of *Nameh-e Banovan*,

117 Maryam Hosseinkhah, "Mashrooteh Aghaaz Baray-e Rooznamè Negari Zanan (The Constitutional Era: The Beginning of the Women's Journalism)," *Zanestan*, 17 Mordad 1385 (8 August 2006), online http://zanestan.es/issue9/06,08,08,07,13,22/, (accessed 3 March 2016).

118 Masoomeh Khodadad, "Nokhostin Rooznamehaye Zanan Iran (The First Newspaper for Women in Iran)," *Majmoeye Maghalat Nashriye Dakheli* no. 49 (2009), 24.

119 Ibid.

120 Sadiqah Dawlatababadi, "Women's World in Qajar Iran," online www.qajarwomen.og/archive/collections/12

121 Majmo-e Shakhsi Sedigh-e Dolatabadi, https://socialhistory.org/fa/collections/sédighé-dolatabadi-collection, (accessed 2 August 2016).

122 Eliz Sansarian, "Characteristics of Women's Movement in Iran" in *Women and Family in Iran*, ed. Asghar Fathi (Leiden, Netherland: E.J. Brill, 1985), 92.

123 Ibid.

it is clear that Azad considered female education and emancipation to be closely linked subjects. In fact, a considerable number of the women journal editors and journalists were involved in education as teachers or headmistresses.[124] The inaugural edition of *Nameh-e Banovan* went so far as to claim ". . . the women of Europe are better workers than the Iranian men, it is surprising that Iranians have not yet realized that if women are not educated men will not be what they could be."[125] In the second edition a number of letters from women readers were published that insisted on the importance of education for women in both secular and Islamic terms. They cited examples from Europe and the United States and also examples from Islamic scholars, such as Ayatollah Agha Seyed Sharif Mojtahid from Shiraz, who supported women's education. The second edition also included an article titled, "Wife of Mr Wilson, the President of America." The piece claimed that while President Wilson was sick his wife took over his presidential responsibilities.[126] That she was able to do so, the article contended, was because of her education. The argument held "such women are found in Europe and the U.S. in their millions" but are not found in Iran.[127] The same piece noted that *Nameh-e Banovan* was temporarily seized by the government and reported that Azad had been imprisoned.[128] The third edition of *Nameh-e Banovan* opened with another article in support of female education and included the English proverb, "The hand that rocks the cradle rules the world."[129]

Alam Nasvan (Women's Universe) began initially in 1921 as "a bi-monthly journal of the alumni [sic] of the American School for Girls," and was published in Tehran for thirteen years.[130] The editorial board classified its objectives in non-political terms, explaining that the journal was established to assist "the elevation and progress of women; encouraging them to serve their country and family, and improve their education."[131] The aims of the journal

124 Parvin Ghodsizad, "Jarayed dar Iran (5)," online *Daneshnameh Jahan Eslam* 1, n.d., http://lib.eshia.ir/23019/1/5000, (accessed 29 July 2016).

125 Shanaz Azad, "Nameh-e Banovan," no. 1 (23 January 1920), 2, available online at Women's World in Qajar Iran, Harvard University, online www.qajarwomen.org/en/items/903A1.html, (accessed 27 July 2016).

126 Shanaz Azad, "Nameh-e Banovan," no. 2 (16 August 1920), 8, available online at Women's World in Qajar Iran, Harvard University, online http://iiif.lib.harvard.edu/manifests/view/drs:15395772$16i, (accessed 27 July 2016).

127 Ibid.

128 Reza Arasteh, "The Struggle for Equality in Iran," *Middle East Journal* 18, no. 2 (1964), 193.

129 Shanaz Azad, "Nameh-e Banovan," no. 4 (September 1920), 2, available online at Women's World in Qajar Iran, Harvard University, online http://iiif.lib.harvard.edu/manifests/view/drs:15395772$28i, (accessed 27 July 2016).

130 Parvin Paidar, *Women and the Political Process in Twentieth-Century Iran* (Cambridge: Cambridge University Press, 1995), 94.

131 Ibid.

were divided into six main categories ranging from medical issues, hygiene and housekeeping, nursing, and training children in fashion, literature and poetry."[132] Although the journal declared its aims to be non-political, Paidar notes that during these thirteen years the journal published articles discussing the drawbacks of veiling and seclusion as well the rights of women.[133] On the cover of the third issue of the journal the following verse of poetry was printed: "In a country where the women are belittled (*haghir*), there is no doubt that its men are poor."[134]

One other publication that deserves mention is the monthly *Jamiat/ Anjuman Nesvan Vatankhah Iran* (Journal of the Society of Iranian Patriotic Women).[135] The first issue was produced in 1924 under the editorship of Princess Moluk Eskandari, who described the journal thus:

> First of all, this journal consists of several sections, each of which is important, particularly its literary part. There will also appear, special articles of famous women in the world and their achievements. . . . Besides political and religious news, this journal will try to present material that is essential to the enlightenment of women. Finally, let us beg God to help us achieve these goals.[136]

It is important to note that women such as Sedigheh Dowlatabadi and Fakhr Afagh Parsa, whose own publications were at the time banned, still contributed to the *Nesvan Vatankhah*. The way the journal was divided is also noteworthy. It had a specific section on politics and another on religion, while "the rest of the journal focused on matters 'which were of general use to women' and consisted of articles on social reform, women's rights, girls' education and poetry and literature."[137]

Pahlavi period (1925–1979)

The dictatorial nature of the Pahlavi dynasty eventually brought about the end of independent women's societies; this era also saw the gradual closure of women's

132 Ibid., 95.
133 Ibid.
134 Masoumeh Keyhani, "Negahi be Matbooat Zanan dar Iran (az 1328 Ghamari ta 1371 Shamsi), (A Review of the Press in Iran from (1288 to 1992))," *Kalak* no. 34, (January 1993), 77.
135 Reza Arasteh, "The Struggle for Equality in Iran," *Middle East Journal* 18, no. 2 (Spring 1964), 195.
136 Ibid.
137 Parvin Paidar, *Women and the Political Process in Twentieth-Century Iran* (Cambridge: Cambridge University Press, 1995), 96.

publications that were linked to these societies. The societies and the publications that remained active or began their activities thereafter had to be in line with government policies. The first such of this new line, *Nour Afshan* (The Illuminator), was published in 1926 in Boushehr, a city in the south of Iran.[138] The managing editor, Shokat Salami, was the founder of the first all-girls school in that city. The contributors to this journal included women who were educated in Britain and India. Another journal, *Jamiat Peyk Saadat Nasvan* (The Organisation of the Messenger of Women's Prosperity) was established in Rasht, in the Gilan province of Iran, in 1927 under the directorship of Roshanak Nowdoost, "who was a headmistress in the *Saadat* (Prosperity) school".[139] Nowdoost also edited another journal with the name of *Peyk Saadat Zanan* (The Messenger of Prosperity for Women). *Peyk Saadat* was generally viewed as having leftist tendencies due in part to support from "the pro-Soviet Iranian Cultural Society in Rasht".[140] All told, in Iran by "the mid-1930s, there were 14 women's magazines discussing women's rights, education and veiling".[141] The early 1940s marked the coming to power of Muhammad Reza Shah and the second phase of the Pahlavi dynasty. This was a time during which the tide of women's publications, many of them linked to oppositional political parties, began to turn.

Throughout the 1940s, women's publications included articles on education, as well as discussions on veiling and the rights of women. *Rastakhiz Iran* (Iran's Resurrection) was a weekly magazine that began its publication in 1942. By 1944, it was published as a daily paper under the management of Irandokht Teymortash, who was the daughter of Abdulhossein Teymortash, a minister in the court of Reza Shah. *Rastakhiz Iran* was regarded as a left-leaning political paper and was linked to *Jebheye Azadi* (Freedom Front) and *Hezb-e Mihan* (National Party). *Rastakhiz* was more of a literary journal than a women's publication, and only certain sections of the journal were dedicated wholly to women's issues.[142] Yet, because of its political leanings and its critique of the government, the paper was seized numerous times by authorities.[143]

138 Parvin Taj Mohammadi, "Barresi Harkathaye Siasi-Ejtemai Zanan Bushehr dar Tariskh Moaser," n.d, online www.iranzanan.com/social/cat_14/001546.php?q=print, (accessed 31 March 2016).

139 Parvin Paidar, *Women and the Political Process in Twentieth-Century Iran* (Cambridge: Cambridge University Press, 1995), 97.

140 Ibid.

141 Ali Akbar Mahdi, "The Iranian Women's Movement: A Century Long Struggle," *The Muslim World* 94 (October 2004), 427–428.

142 Masomeh Keyhani, "Negahi be Matbooat Zanan dar Iran (az 1328 Ghamari ta 1371 Shamsi), (A Review of the Press in Iran from (1288 to 1992))," *Kalak* no. 34, (January 1993), 81

143 Parvin Ghodsizad, "Jarayed dar Iran (5)," online *Daneshnameh Jahan Eslam* 1, n.d., http://lib.eshia.ir/23019/1/5000 (accessed 29 July 2016).

The year 1944 was significant for publications. During this year the British Embassy in Tehran published *Alam Zanan* (Women's Universe), a monthly journal that included interviews with prominent women such as Dr. Fatemeh Sayyah and also reported on the situation and the progress of women internationally in a comparative context.[144] The same year, Badrulmoluk Bamdad, a pioneer of the women's movement during the Pahlavi era, became the editor of the weekly *Zan Emruz* (Today's Woman). This journal was published in Tehran with the slogan, "Our path is the creation of a social revolution." *Zan Emruz* considered itself politically autonomous, although it openly supported the Iranian Women's Party. The articles in this weekly consisted of critiques of superstition and veiling, as well as arguments for the necessity of women's education. It also did political reporting and covered news from the parliament.[145] The monthly publication *Banu* (The Lady) was also begun in 1944 and lasted for three years. It was published by Nayereh Saidi. Sayyah wrote a famous article in *Banu* in 1946 titled, "Madam, if you were elected to the parliament, what would you do?" Supporting a woman's right to stand for election to the parliament more than a decade before Iranian women were granted the right to vote, she wrote:

> One should know that in the first election, women will constitute a small minority. (Even) in countries where women have gained their rights for years, their representation (political) is not considerable. Women need to show more solidarity than men in order to compensate their low numbers in comparison to their male counterparts. Even if they are members of different political parties, in the Parliament they should establish a women's committee (fraction) concerned only with women and children's interests.[146]

The monthly *Bidariy-e Ma* (Our Awakening) was published from 1944 to 1946 by the Society for Democratic Women. Linked to *Hezb Toudeh* (Tudeh Party) and *Jebheye Azad* (Freedom Front)[147] the slogan of the monthly was, "We also have rights in this house." The first two issues of the monthly published a legal critique of Article 9 of the Supplementary Fundamental Laws of 7 October 1907. This article stated, "All individuals are protected and

144 Parvin Paidar, *Women and the Political Process in Twentieth-Century Iran* (Cambridge: Cambridge University Press, 1995), 126.

145 Ibid.

146 Noushin Ahmadi Khorasani and Parvin Ardalan, *Senator: Faliyathaye Mehrangiz Manouchehrian ba Bastar Mobarezat Hughughi Zanan dar Iran (Senator: The Works of Senator Mehrangiz Manouchehrian for Legal Rights for Women)* (Tehran: Nashr Tose-e, 2003), 391.

147 Guity Nashat, "Women in Pre-Revolutionary Iran: A Historical Overview" in *Women and Revolution in Iran*, ed. Lois Beck and Guity Neshat (Boulder: Westview Replica Edition, 1983), 26.

safeguarded in respect to their lives, property, homes, and honor, from every kind of interferences, and none shall molest them save in such case and in such way as the laws of the land shall determine." *Bidariy-e Ma* raised questions about the implementation of Article 9 and how it protected the honor of women:

> For example if one is accused of madness, then that person's credibility comes under question. . . . If the countries' legislative assembly has placed women in the same level of mad people and has denied them the rights to vote and to be elected, then has it not offended their honor? . . .[148]

Veiling was discussed extensively in *Bidariy-e Ma*, as was women's equality, which the journal regarded as a prerequisite to national progress and democracy.[149] *Zanan Iran* (Iran's Women), edited by Sayyah, was particularly vocal about Iranian women's suffrage.[150] It was the organ of the Iranian Women's Party (*Hezb Zanan Iran*) founded in 1953 by Safiyeh Firuz. *Zanan Iran* was also one of the thirteen new women's publications established during Prime Minister Mossadegh's tenure in office.

From the 1953 coup up to the Islamic Revolution, some eighteen women's periodicals were published in Iran, mainly in the form of glossy magazines promoting some aspects of Western culture. The weekly magazine, *Ettelaat Banovan* (Women's Information), was first published by *Moasseseh Ettelaat* (Information Institution) and enjoyed widespread circulation. Paidar claims it "turned into the main officially approved women's magazine in Iran."[151] Among the magazine's activities were organizing journalism courses for improving the skills of the editorial board; encouraging women to pursue journalism; establishing women's societies; and introducing readers to successful women. *Ettelaat Banovan* was published through 1978. After a temporary seizure it continued under the editorship of Zahra Rahnavard in 1980. Thus, after the 1979 revolution, *Ettelaat,* which had been a Pahalvi state apparatus, became the state apparatus of the Islamic Republic.

148 Noushin Ahmadi Khorasani and Parvin Ardalan, *Senator: Faliyathaye Mehrangiz Manouchehrian ba bastar mobarezat hughughi zanan dar Iran* (Senator: The Works of Senator Mehrangiz Manouchehrian for Legal Rights for Women) (Tehran: Nashr Tose-e, 1382/2003), 390.

149 Parvin Ghodsizad, "Jarayed dar Iran (5)," online *Daneshnameh Jahan Eslam* 1, n.d., http://lib.eshia.ir/23019/1/5000 (accessed 29 July 2016).

150 Ibid.

151 Parvin Paidar, *Women and the Political Process in Twentieth-Century Iran* (Cambridge: Cambridge University Press, 1995), 137.

Another publication that ran the rapids of editorial change was *Zan-e Ruz* (Today's Woman). This was first published in 1964 under the management of Forough Mesbahzadeh and the editorship of Majid Davaami. *Zan-e Ruz* played an important part in the creation of Morteza Mutahhari's book, *The Rights of Women in Islam*, which many refer to as the ideological framework for the state's stance towards women. The book originated as a series of articles written by Mutahhari and published by *Zan-e Ruz* between 1966 and 1967. Like *Ettelaat Banovan*, *Zan-e Ruz* continued publication with a complete change of content and editorship. Shahlah Sherkat, who went on to be the famous editor of *Zanan* (Women), was first a post-revolutionary editor of *Zan-e Ruz*.

1979 to 2009: the rise and fall of women's print media

Magazines such as *Zan-e Ruz* and *Ettelaat Banovan* that remained part of the state apparatus after the 1979 revolution became organs of the Islamic Republic. They promoted the state ideology regarding women's gendered roles as mothers, daughters and wives. *Zan-e Ruz* became the cultural forum for conservative, statist women. According to Eftekhari, "This weekly was aimed specifically at a female readership and continued under the guidance of *Kayhan* publishing house. . . . Only women who were accepted by the regime were given a platform in the magazine, which explains why this publication is still around."[152] Nonetheless, as Meharngiz Kar writes, the magazine at times not only published "the views and interpretations of more moderate clerics such as Ayatollah Bojnurdi", but also "occasionally, criticized the lack of women's rights more explicitly and in stronger language".[153] One of the most striking developments among revolutionary Muslim women following the revolution was their vocal opposition to violations of their rights.[154] These violations included legal discrimination in the area of civil law, as well as legal discrimination in the penal code. Once again, women's magazines and publications became a forum for women to discuss social status and to debate reforms. These discussions and debates utilized both rights language and religious rhetoric.

The women's publications of the early 1990s, including *Payam-e Hajar* (Hagar's Message), *Farzaneh* (Wise) and *Zanan*, became forums for

152 Roza Eftekhari, "Zanan: Trials and Successes of a Feminist Magazine in Iran" in *Middle Eastern Women on the Move* (Washington, DC: Woodrow Willson International Centre for Scholarship, 2003), 16, online www.wilsoncenter.org/sites/default/files/MEP_women.pdf, (accessed 27 July 2016).

153 Mehranguiz Kar, "Women's Strategies in Iran From the 1979 Revolution to 1999," in *Globalization, Gender, and Religion: The Politics of Women's Rights in Catholic and Muslim Contexts*, ed. Jane Bayes and Nayereh Tohidi (New York: Palgrave, 2001), 185.

154 Ibid., 179.

reform-minded women and men to speak about women's rights and legal reforms within an Islamic framework. *Payam-e Hajar*, for instance, was founded by Azam Taleghani in 1979.[155] This was the first magazine that worked within the framework of Islam to raise questions about the necessity of reinterpreting Islamic laws to address gender equality.[156] Taleghani, a staunch activist for women's rights, once explored running for the presidency herself, but unsurprisingly was vetoed by the Guardian Council. Also noteworthy in this branch of magazines is the government-funded journal, *Payam-e Zan* (Woman's Message), which Afary refers to as "the primary organ of Islamist women in Iran".[157] A post-war publication, and similar to the others in its gender focus, *Payam-e Zan* differs in that it promotes gendered roles for women as mothers, wives and caregivers. Moreover, it regards "feminism as an expression of Western immorality . . .".[158] And then there is *Zanan*. Published for the first time in February 1992 under managing director Shahla Sherkat, *Zanan* is referred to by Roza Eftekhari as "the first independent journal after the Iranian Revolution that specifically dealt with women's issues".[159] The discussions taken up by the magazine extended to "socio-political, legal and economic issues from the viewpoint of women's interests".[160] It is important to note that Sherkat had previously been the managing director of *Zan-e Ruz*. The shift in Sherkat's allegiance is indicative of larger-scale social changes. After eight years of war underpinned by religious rhetoric, many thought there was a need for a more liberal religious discourse. Furthermore, new media were needed to meet the demands of the post-revolution generation. In an interview with

155 I worked for Azam Taleghani in Iran in 2004 for three months, where I obtained copies of *Payam-e Hajar*.

156 Azadeh Kian, "Women and Politics in Post-Islamist Iran: The Gender Conscious Drive to Change," *British Journal of Middle Eastern Studies* 24, no. 1 (1997), 81. Also personal interviews and work experiences with Azam Taleghani 2003 and 2004. I should also note that Taleghani ran Qur'anic interpretation meetings in her offices, which I sometimes attended when working for Taleghani in 2004. These meetings were frequented by a very mixed audience, made up of the young, old, wealthy, poor, educated and uneducated.

157 Taleghani's publication *Payam-e Hajar* was the first magazine that worked within the framework of Islam to raise questions about the necessity of reinterpreting Islamic laws. Taleghani uses Ayatollah Taleghani's teachings both in the reinterpretations published in *Payam-e Hajar* and in the weekly meetings she held to study and reinterpret the Qur'an.

158 Janet Afary, "Portraits of Two Islamist Women: Escape from Freedom or from Tradition?," *Critique: Critical Middle Eastern Studies* 10, no. 19 (2001), 52.

159 Roza Eftekhari, "Zanan: Trials and Successes of a Feminist Magazine in Iran" in *Middle Eastern Women on the Move* (Washington, DC: Woodrow Willson International Centre for Scholarship, 2003), 15, online www.wilsoncenter.org/sites/default/files/MEP_women.pdf, (accessed 27 July 2016).

160 Marcus Michaelsen, "Mapping Iran's Online Public: Politics and Culture in the Iranian Blogosphere," *Iranian Studies* 45, no. 2 (February 2012), 246.

Omid Memarian, Hossein Ghazian identifies a process of new identity formation in post-revolution and post-war Iran. *Zanan* was a response to, and a result of, these new identities being formed.[161] *Zanan* also differed from *Zan-e Ruz*, not only in its ideological underpinnings but also in its reach. It was directed more towards middle-class and university-educated women. The magazine was a pioneer in exploring religious modern thought about women.[162] Going through the archives of *Zanan*, one can find legal articles by the secular lawyer and activist Mehrangiz Kar, as well as articles by Hujjat ul-Islam Seyed Mohsen Saidzadeh, a *hawza*-educated clergy person, who criticized conservative interpretations of religious texts and offered reformist alternatives. *Zanan* was shut down after sixteen years of publication on January 1, 2008, by the order of the Media Supervision Committee of Iran's Ministry of Culture and Islamic Guidance.[163] The closure was prompted by *Zanan's* publication of a report titled *Koshte Mishavand ta Bokoshand* (They Die in Order to Kill), which focused on the Iranian martyrdom movement (*jonbesh-e eshtehadi*).[164] Noushin Ahmadi Khorasani refers to the closure of *Zanan* as the closure of the last "paper" forum for the Iranian women's movement.[165]

161 Omid Memarian, "Jame dar Entezari Radical va Tarsnak, Goftegoo ba Hossein Ghazian, Jame Shenas (Society in Anticipation Radicalism and Fear, a Conversation with the Sociologist Hossein Ghazian)," (6 February 2008), online www.ettelaat.net/08-februari/news.asp?id=26777, (accessed 27 July 2016).

162 The previously mentioned publications all engage with questions of women and religion. *Jens Dovom* (Second Sex), managed and edited by Noushin Ahmadi Khorasani from 1998 to 2001, represents a more secular type of feminist publication related to the later *Salnamah-ye Zanan-e Iran* (Iranian Women's Almanac) and *Fasl-e Zanan* (The Season of Women). For more on this vein see "Noushin Ahmadi Khorasani: Two Decades in the Struggle for Women's Rights," online https://tavaana.org/en/content/noushin-ahmadi-khorasani-two-decades-struggle-womens-rights, (accessed 9 January 2016).

163 *Zanan's* license was revoked sixteen years after its inception as according to news reports "Zanan had 'endangered the spiritual, mental and intellectual health of its readers, gave the impression of insecurity in society, and drew a dark image of the situation of women in Islamic society by publishing certain articles.'" See "Iran: Women's Rights Defenders Defy Repression," *MDE* 13/018/2008 (London: Amnesty International Publications, 2008), 3. M. Nissimov, Y. Mansharof and A. Savyon, "Iranian Women's Magazine Shut Down for Publishing Investigative Article on Martyrdom Movement," *Middle East Media Research Institute (MEMRI)*, Inquiry & Analysis no. 439 (May 2009), 4.

164 S. Shiva Zarabadi, "Koshte Mishavand ta Bokoshand (They Die in order to Kill)," *Zanan* 104 (January 2008), republished online http://pezhvakeiran.com/page1.php?id=399 (accessed 29 July 2016).

165 For a more detailed study of the content of *Zanan*, refer to Elham Gheytanchi, "Civil Society in Iran, Politics of Motherhood and the Public Sphere," *International Sociology* 16, no. 4 (December 2001), 570.

From paper to online media

With the rise of the Internet in Iran, websites, including personal weblogs dedicated to women's issues, mushroomed.[166] In cyberspace, Persian-language blogs offered areas to promote free expression "outside the confines of politically manipulated physical space".[167] The Internet also provided room for women's rights activists to disseminate information about women's rights. It allowed them to raise issues that would not have been published in the mainstream media. At least in its beginnings, women's online media enjoyed a freedom, which was unthinkable when compared with the confines of print media and state censorship of women's issues.[168] As Maryam Hosseinkhah asserts, "The women's movement's online presence was not solely for the purpose of dissemination of information. It was also seen as a mobilization and organizational tool. It played the role of a bridge between various ideologies and between women activists. . . ."[169] Hosseinkhah asserts that the fact that women's rights websites almost immediately became authoritative sources for the mainstream media on women's issues was partially due because many well-known figures, activists, lawyers, human rights and women's rights activists wrote for these websites.[170] In short, not only were these online spaces accessible and functional, but also they were credible. At the same time, women webloggers could also write anonymously on topics that might have proved taboo otherwise, all without the fear of being found out or censored, at least initially. As Amir-Ebrahimi notes, "Women, among the principal actors in the Iranian blogosphere, began to self-narrate and reveal their hidden selves."[171] The first Iranian women's online publication was *Zanan-e Iran* (Women of Iran), which began its activity in 2001. Soon thereafter the Iranian Feminist Tribune of *Markaz Farhangi-e Zanan* (Women's Cultural Center) was created.

166 For more on Iranian Persian-language blogging see: Elizabeth M. Bucar and Roja Fazaeli, "Free Speech in Weblogistan? The Off-Line Consequences of Online Communication," *International Journal of Middle East Studies* 40, no. 3 (August 2008), 403–419.

167 Fereshteh Nouraie-Simone, "Wings of Freedom: Iranian Women, Identity, and Cyberspace", in *On Shift in Ground: Muslim Women in the Global Era*, ed. F. Nouraie-Simon (New York: Feminist Press, 2005), 61–79.

168 Bucar and Fazaeli note that the arrest of webloggers in 2004, was as a consequence of their online actions. Although cyberspace initially provided a censorship-free forum, it eventually became partially regulated.

169 See also "Internet: Fazaye Jaygozing va Abzar Ertebati Jonbesh Zanan-e Iran," 8 March 2011, online www.dw.com/fa-ir/اینترنت-فضای-جایگزین-و-ابزار-ارتباطی-جنبش-زنان-ایران/a-6462058, (accessed 3 March 2016).

170 See also ibid.

171 Masserat Amir-Ebrahimi, "Transgression in Narration: The Loves of Iranian Women in Cyberspace," *Journal of Middle East Women's Studies* 4, no. 3 (Fall 2008), 101.

After the revolution the women's movement became enmeshed within religious and state rhetoric. Women who had power to reform discriminatory laws were those within the state apparatus. For example, in the era of the Islamic Republic these were women parliamentarians or women presidential advisors (women who in Chapter 2 I refer to as Islamic state-feminists).[172] During the reform era (1997–2004), much of the gender talk was intertwined with the politics of the reform movement. Women reformist parliamentarians, particularly in the sixth parliament (*majlis-e sheshom*), did fight for equal rights for women. When the conservatives took a majority of seats at the seventh parliament (*majlis-e haftom*) in 2004 and subsequently kept them in the eighth and ninth parliaments, there was a shift in the movement, away from political power dependencies and the conservative Islamic framework, towards autonomy and secularity. The shift in the women's movement away from a political power base has gone hand in hand with the movement's oppression and the arrest and exile of many of its activists. As Tohidi states, "women's struggle in today's Iran is primarily a cultural and legal one, which is fought in a historical context rather than a battlefield."[173] Women who are active in the movement, unlike past reformist political groups who used women's issues as political tools, are not seeking political power, but tangible solutions to women's problems, whether in Iran, in prison or in exile.

The One Million Signatures Campaign (OMSC) is an example of one of the newer incarnations of the Iranian women's movement. OMSC was based on the 2004 Moroccan model of family law reform,[174] and was unique in the extent of its mobilization and the support it enjoyed nationally and internationally. Writing near its beginning Tohidi noted, "this campaign seems to have surpassed ideological, sectarian and religious boundaries and limitations."[175] She also added, "(t)his movement has distanced itself from the more prevalent masculine and elitist perceptions that assume only a handful of avant-garde intellectuals, having discovered the 'Whole Truth' are the sole proprietors of solutions, who through personal sacrifice would impart the

172 Also refer to Roja Fazaeli, "Contemporary Iranian Feminism: Identity, Rights and Interpretations," *Muslim World Journal of Human Rights* 4, no. 1 (2007), 1–24.

173 Nayereh Tohidi, "Iran's Women's Rights Movement and the One Million Signatures Campaign," *Change for Equality*, (November 2006), republished online www.payvand.com/news/06/dec/1174.html (accessed 28 July 2016).

174 This entailed the reform of the Family Law or the Code of Personal Status *Mudawana*, which was based on Maliki jurisprudence and instituted a year after Morocco's independence in 1957. For a detailed study of recent law reform in Morocco see Fatima Sadiqi and Moha Ennaji, "The Feminization of Public Space: Women's Activism, the Family Law and Social Change in Morocco," *Journal of Middle East Women's Studies* 2, no. 2 (Spring 2006), 86–115.

175 Ibid.

knowledge, bring freedom and 'save the souls of the ignorant and oppressed masses.'"[176] The OMSC was "initiated by the younger generation of women's rights activists",[177] who aimed to collect one million signatures to demand an end to legal discrimination against women in Iranian laws.[178] The campaign was inaugurated following a peaceful protest on June 12, 2006, in Haft-e Tir Square in Tehran.[179] The campaigners aimed to identify women's needs and priorities in the process of signature collection with the hope of strengthening women's voices and promoting social change through their collaborative efforts. The campaign emphasized knowledge and dialogue promotion as precursors to democratic action.[180] OMSC became "a point of convergence among many groups and individual activists in different parts of Iran".[181]

The OMSC used human rights norms as a yardstick for its objective of attaining non-discrimination and equality between genders. Although the movement leaned towards secularity, there was also adequate Islamic justification for the campaign. As the campaign organizers affirmed:

> The demands of the Campaign are not in contradiction to Islamic principles: the demand to reform and change discriminatory laws is not in contradiction to Islamic principles and is in line with Iran's international commitments. Iran is a signatory to the UN Convention on Civil and Political Rights and as such, is required to eliminate all forms of discrimination. Based on these commitments, the government of Iran needs to take specific action in reforming laws that promote discrimination.[182]

According to the activists, "(a) million signatures supporting changes to discriminatory laws, will demonstrate to decision-makers and the public at large that a large segment of the Iranian population is in support of revising

176 Nayereh Tohidi, "Iran's Women's Rights Movement and the One Million Signatures Campaign," November 2006, online www.payvand.com/news/06/dec/1174.html, (accessed 31 March 2016).

177 Ibid.

178 "About 'One Million Signatures Demanding Changes to Discriminatory Laws'," *Change for Equality*, 28 August 2006, online http://we-change.org/site/english/spip.php?article18, (accessed 28 July 2016).

179 Ibid.

180 Ibid. On June 12, 2006, about 2,000 Iranian women participated in a sit-in to protest discriminatory laws against women, in particular they demanded change to the clauses in the Constitution which deny women's rights. See also, Mahsa Shekarloo, "Iran: Iranian Women take on the Constitution," *Women Living under Muslim Laws* (21 July 2005), online www.wluml.org/ar/node/2370, (accessed 28 July 2016).

181 "About 'One Million Signatures Demanding Changes to Discriminatory Laws'," *Change for Equality* (28 August 2006), online http://we-change.org/site/english/spip.php?article18, (accessed 28 July 2016).

182 Ibid.

discriminatory laws against women and that these demands are not limited to a small segment of society."[183] The OMSC also referred to the ongoing call for reform of these laws by religious scholars such as Ayatollah Saane'i and Ayatollah Bojnourdi, among others. Nonetheless, the campaign faced severe crackdowns and many of the activists were arrested, interrogated and threatened. Many of those arrested were charged with "being a threat to the national security". Women activists were accused of plotting a "velvet revolution" and being foreign agents.[184] After 2009, the public collection of signatures as well as other public aspects of the campaign ceased and by 2010 the campaign came to a halt. The cessation was due not only to pressures exerted on the activists by the state, but also related to the activists' choice to protest the Ahmadinejad presidency following the contested 2009 elections. There was little desire on the part of campaign activists to collect and present signatures to the *majlis* during the tenure of a government they deemed illegitimate and unelected.

The pendulum of the women's movement in Iran, as in many Islamic countries, swings back and forth between nominally private and public spheres. Even while female activists fight for equal rights in the public arena they are faced with inequality in their family lives. The spectrum of women's identities spans from public reformer to mother, wife, sister and daughter. When pressured by the government, male interrogators may leverage these later family-based categories of identity to force a confession, or submission to the state. They assume they have the power to grant a woman her own family's honor and thereby to push her back into what is understood as being a private and cloistered realm. In this way the natural pendulum of identity has become an injurious instrument of control in the hands of the Islamic government.

In response to this governmental need to control women and consolidate power, the OMSC was established as a public campaign that would seek results without seeking power. Ahmadi Khorasani argues that "in reality, the One Million Signatures Campaign was borne of a feminine imagination to resist the violence imposed on us by the riot police when they attacked our peaceful rally for equal legal rights on June 12, 2006, in Haft-e Tir Square."[185] The campaign's face-to-face strategy required women activists

183 Ibid.

184 See Parvin Ardalan, "Who Is Accused of Being a 'Threat to Civil Security?'," trans. Sussan Thamasebi, *Change for Equality*, 6 May 2007, online http://we-change.org/site/english/spip.php?article80, (accessed 28 July 2016).

185 Noushin Ahmadi Khorasani, "The Two Storytellers of the Women's Prison and the Imaginary Literature of the One Million Signatures Campaign," trans. D. Simin, *Change for Equality*, 28 April 2007, online www.we-change.org/english/spip.php?article74, (accessed 15 July 2011).

(as well as some of their male counterparts) to inspire and motivate the public one person at a time. This strategy required them to engage in rights-based dialogue with individuals in public spaces, as well as to go door to door and house to house to collect signatures. In this way, the OMSC troubled "the old school notion of public dominated male realm and the private sphere of women and family".[186] In response the government increased pressure. Threats to and arrests of campaigners were meant to strike fear into the hearts of activists so that they would retreat into their homes, the very place where gender discrimination can be most prevalent. Noushin Ahmadi Khorasani described the fear created by the state at that time in the following way: "our lives are consumed with fear. Fear of falling behind. Fear of a conservative government that wants to imprison us in our houses or flats or in cells."[187] When they did end up in prison, women from OMSC attempted to turn that punitive environment into a new platform for the campaign by sharing their ideas for equality with fellow prisoners and teaching them about international human rights. However, such instances of brave determination were pursued in spite of, not absent, the fear of repercussions, which was significant. Khorasani describes the effects of this fear on the campaigners:

> . . . since the inception of the Campaign five months ago, members of the Campaign have had the misfortune of experiencing a crisis of some sort on bi-weekly basis. As a result, we have been forced into a state of fear and anxiety, forced to comfort one another, forced to address the multiple crises at hand, and forced to constantly reassure one another that we are indeed not engaged in any sort of illegal activity – so why is it that we live in such fear? Are we asking for anything more than justice and our basic human rights?[188]

The fact that women are also traditionally the bearers of their families' honor in Iran created another type of fear within the family sphere. There was the scary prospect that the honor and identity women activists held as members of a family might be lost in the course of activism which itself sought the recovery of women's honor and identity. Thus, the women were

186 Fatima Sadiqi and Moha Ennaji, "The Feminization of Public Space: Women's Activism, the Family Law, and Social Change in Morocco," *Journal of Middle East Women's Studies* 2, no. 2 (Spring 2006), 86–114.

187 Noushin Ahmadi Khorasani, "Signed with an X," *New Internationalist, NI* 398 (March 2007), 8.

188 Noushin Ahmadi Khorasani, "Treating Us Like Criminals! Pressures Increase on Activities Involved in the One Million Signatures Campaign," trans. Sussan Tahmasebi, *Change for Equality* 19 (February 2007), online http://we-change.org/site/spip.php?article413, (accessed 28 July 2016).

surrounded by forces of state and family that destabilized their very sense of self. The relationship between state and family in Iran is complex. Valentine Moghadam argues that the "'Middle Eastern Muslim family has long been described as a patriarchal unit, and it has been noted that Muslim family laws have served to reinforce patriarchal gender relations and women's subordinate position within the family."[189] The family as defined in the Iranian Constitution is the primary unit of the society. Article 10 of the Constitution states that "since the family is the fundamental unit of Islamic society, all laws, regulations, and pertinent programmes must tend to facilitate the formation of a family, and to safeguard its sanctity and stability of family relations on the basis of the law and the ethics of Islam."[190] Moghadam continues, "Far from being an enclave, the family is vulnerable to the state, and the law and social policies that impinge upon it undermine the notion of separate spheres. Yet the haven ideology persists and is often strategically deployed by state authorities and dissidents alike."[191] The OMSC activists were pushed back into this "private" sphere by the state, yet this was also a space that continued to be regulated by the state. One of the activists described the dynamic in this way:

> When we are denied space to conduct our activities, we have no other choice but to squeeze into our own apartments and homes to hold training workshops. Inevitably the police come to warn our neighbours about the "suspicious" coming and goings in our apartments. You [referring to officials in charge of arrests and threats] try to sensitize our neighbours, so that perhaps they can carry out your duties in your stead.[192]

Parents of the younger activists were threatened and warned of their children's collaboration with the campaign and were asked to caution their daughters and to keep them in the house in this way:

> Local police stations are brought on as your collaborators, and they work to coerce and threaten parents, so that they can confront their children. You call the homes of Campaign members, and inform their parents

189 Valentine Moghadam and Fatima Sadiqi, "Women's Activism and the Public Sphere: An Introduction and Overview," *Journal of Middle East Women's Studies* 2, no. 2 (Spring 2006), 1–7.

190 Iranian Constitution, Article 10.

191 Valentine Moghadam, *Modernizing Women: Gender and Social Change in the Middle East* (Boulder, CO: Lynne Reinner Publishers, 2003), 118.

192 Noushin Ahmadi Khorasani, "Treating Us Like Criminals! Pressures Increase on Activities Involved in the One Million Signatures Campaign," trans. Sussan Tahmasebi, *Change for Equality* 19 (February 2007), online http://we-change.org/site/spip.php?article413, (accessed 28 July 2016).

> about the existence of lists – lists of persons who should be "advised" and lists of persons scheduled to be "arrested". Interestingly enough, the police emphasize that parents should not convey these "private" conversations to their daughters, rather they should advise them and guide them so that they are not deceived by others.[193]

With such threats the state assiduously infiltrated the private realm of the family and attempted to thwart or control the nerve centers of activism by inflaming the patriarchal sensitivities of the family.

Women activists in general, and especially those in patriarchal societies, are often threatened with the loss of honor, both their own and, by association, their family's. The classical patriarchal view is that women should be homemakers and that they should not be looking for equal rights, which could in turn lead to immorality or, in Mutahari's phrase, to sexual-communism.[194] For this reason, it is not surprising that in Iran a general tactic used by male interrogators of women's rights activists is to level an accusation of adultery (*zina*). To accuse a woman of adultery is to bestow the ultimate insult upon her. With this accusation the interrogator penetrates the activist's most private space and does so intentionally in order to insult her honor and the honor of her family.[195]

Nahla Abdu writes, "In the context of the colonial state, sexual abuse, harassment and torture are often used as a direct tool for enforcing women's submission, compliance and obedience; these are means enforced to quell women's participation in the resistance movement."[196] It is not only in colonial contexts that women's participation in resistance movements is quelled by such means. Any patriarchal society, in particular those in countries where the regimes are authoritarian or theocratic, may employ sexuality in a similar way. Any place where one's honor depends on one's perceived piety is a place where threats and acts of torture, abuse and harassment may be used to silence those who are perceived as being in opposition to the state. In these instances the state tries to control women's bodies and their sexuality as a way of exercising political control over the family and society at large.

Parvin Ardalan asserts that women's rights activists, "by virtue of their gender and the nature of their work", are positively discriminated against.

193 Ibid.

194 Morteza Mutahari, *Nezam-e Hughugh Zan dar Islam* (The Rights of Women in Islam), 45th ed. (Tehran: Sadra Publication, 2007).

195 I am not of the opinion that men have or should have any claim over women's honor; however, as reality prevails, in patriarchal societies such ownership is indeed claimed in this way.

196 Nahla Abdo, "Globalization, 'Culture Talk', and Palestinian Women Resistance," Draft Paper Presented at Trinity College Dublin (March 2007), 15.

This is true, but nonetheless understanding "the interaction of security forces with women's rights activists and the pressures they exerted on this sector" in Iran is complicated and in need of further analysis.[197] Iranian state authorities have used different techniques in their crackdown on women's rights activists. These include threats, raiding of houses and offices, public and private arrests, invitations to collaborate with security forces and interrogations of all sorts, some of which even "include tea and sweets".[198] Another technique used by the state is to create rumours and feelings of mistrust among activists. Ahmadi Khorasani explains this technique:

> . . . you start rumours about the ethical, financial and sexual misconduct of campaign members, about their uncontrollable desire for fame, their relations with foreigners, their perpetration for carrying out velvet revolutions, and other strange and bizarre behavior which seem somehow to surface of their own accord. Of course, there "does" not exist any formal and organized venue through which these rumours are spread. But with the help of these rumours, the public can come to understand that the rights, are in fact, terribly dreadful women starved for attention and fame, in search of asylum in the West.[199]

These strategies, from sticks and carrots to good cop/bad cop, are all different forms of patriarchal state control over women employed to weaken the women's movement. From the start of OMSC, many of its supporters were been interrogated, detained and imprisoned. To the dismay of the authorities the women activists who were imprisoned managed quickly to reshape and redefine the prison space by bringing other female prisoners in contact with the campaign language of rights and freedoms while simultaneously educating the broader public with stories from the women prisoners themselves that were unmediated by the state apparatus. This type of innovation activism, rendered in shorthand here as "prison narratives", confounded the public/private binary on which state control and coercion were premised.

197 Parvin Ardalan, "Who is Accused of Being a 'Threat to Civil Security?'," trans. Sussan Tahmasebi, *Change for Equality* (6 May 2007), online http://we-change.org/site/english/spip.php?article80, (accessed 28 July 2016).

198 I experienced similar tactics in my interrogations. On the first day I was asked to collaborate with the security, during another session I was accused of being an adulterer (*zina kar*). In a later session I was offered tea and sweets and was told that I should consider my interrogator a friend and evaluate who my real friends were.

199 Noushin Ahmadi Khorasani, "Treating Us Like Criminals! Pressures Increase on Activities Involved in the One Million Signatures Campaign," trans. Sussan Tahmasebi, *Change for Equality* (19 February 2007), online http://we-change.org/site/spip.php?article413, (accessed 28 July 2016).

The prison narratives are a mixture of loss and hope. They are powerful and personal. Many are told by women's rights activists who found themselves in the same space as women prisoners in the *band nasvan* (women's ward). These narratives, collected before the 2009 elections, shed a new light on the lives of women who had been entangled in a web of violent legal and cultural discrimination. Previously these women were very rarely talked about and even more rarely seen as victims. Yet the narratives portray these women as victims of a society where discriminatory laws, patriarchal forces and a culture of violence conspire both to criminalize them and to make them criminals. Nahid Keshavaraz, an activist who spent twelve days in Evin prison, describes the women's ward there as containing some 400 women. According to Keshavarz, those convicted of drug-related crimes make up the majority of women prisoners. After this category there are those considered to have committed an illicit sexual act. Third in number are those who have been charged with scams, such as bounced cheques, and fourth are women who have been charged with murder.[200] Narratives from other women prisons in Shiraz and Tabriz also paint a similar picture of the women's wards. Shahla Gholami, a women's rights and political activist from Tabriz who spent five years in Tabriz prison between 1989 and 1993 (as well as doing a month of time in 2007), describes the women's criminal ward (*nasvan jaraem*) of Tabriz prison as overcrowded and consisting of four rooms. In each room there are four or five triple bunk beds. However, because of the sheer number of prisoners (at least 200 women), many are forced to sleep on the floor next to one another. Shahla also describes the access to food and hygiene as being limited. Vegetables, fruits, milk and other food items, as well as soap, shampoo, toothbrushes and toothpaste, are not provided. Each prisoner may try to acquire these from the prison shop, which sells the items at a much higher price than what one would pay outside the prison walls. Each prisoner is allowed to shower once a week for ten minutes.[201]

Shahla also notes an alarming rise in the number of women prisoners in Tabriz's women's criminal ward who have been convicted of murder, half of whom have been accused of killing their husbands. These women constitute 40 per cent of the total number of prisoners in the ward.[202] The online narratives emerging from the women's movement have been predominantly

200 Nahid Keshavarz, "Zendan Evin Band Nasevan dar Nami Nazdik (Evin Prison's Women's Ward up Close)," *Zanestan* 23 (5 May 2007).

201 Shahnaz Gholami, "Zendan Zanan Tabriz, Nimeh Penhan (Women's Prison in Tabriz, the Hidden Half)," Second Edition, 17 October 2012, online www.iran-nabard.com/n328/zendan328.htm, (accessed 5 March 2016).

202 Ibid.

concerned with this last category of women: those charged with murder and awaiting the death penalty.

Maryam, a journalist and a woman's rights activist, is one interlocutor of these narratives. She is one of the thirty-three women who were arrested on 4 March 2007, while protesting the trial of five women's rights activists outside Branch 6 of the Revolutionary Court in Tehran. Maryam and two other young women were then transferred to a women's prison after protesting the lack of medical attention given to the arrested women activists. Maryam, who had previously visited the same prison as a journalist reporting on the condition of women's prisons in Iran,[203] describes her experience of incarceration in this way:

> I still do not believe that I am back at the women's prison, I am angry since they have separated the three of us from the others without any court case or legal reasoning, but I am so delighted to see the prison again that I have forgotten my anger. I am no more the young journalist who entered the prison with numerous previous arrangements. I am a prisoner, one of the 33 women, some of them are in solitary confinement. Our crime is their desire for equal rights.[204]

Maryam's narrative is emotionally charged. As a blogger she has used the Internet as a platform to make public the situation of women prisoners. Monireh Baradaran describes Maryam and her contemporaries as a new generation of political prisoners. Their prison experience is reflected in their writings. According to Baradaran, one of the distinctive traits of these online accounts is the freshness of their narration. The activists write these accounts on their personal weblogs a few days after they are released or, at times, even when they are in prison. The writings are then communicated to colleagues, friends and family, who in turn publish them. The following

203 Maryam Hosseinkhah, "Evin Az Negah-e Zendanian (Evin Through the Lens of Prisoners)," *Etemad-e Melli* (29 March 2007), republished online https://maryamhosseinkhah.wordpress.com/2007/03/29/evin-through-the-lens-of-prisoners/, (accessed 29th July 2016). See also Maryam Hosseinkhah and Solmaz Sharif, "Gozareshi Az Band Zana Zendan Evin: Jayee Shabih Khodesh (A Report from Women's Prison: A Place Like No Other)," *Etemad-e Melli* (27 February 2006), republished online http://pezhvakeiran.com/page1.php?id=399, (accessed 29 July 2016). Translations are my own.

204 Maryam Hosseinkhah, "Campein Yek Million Emza Dar Band Umoomiye Evin (The One Million Signature Campaign in Evin Women's Prison)," *Hawwa* (March 2007), online https://30salegiii.blogspot.co.uk/2007/03/blog-post.html, (accessed 29 July 2016). Translations are my own.

is an example of the type of narrative style that has become a hallmark of the campaign:

> We enter the room [cell] most of them wake up, only the 20-year-old Leila remains asleep. The rest are above 40 years and a few above 60. One by one, they open their eyes and they look at us as if they felt sorry for us being so young. They formed a circle around us. Seeking the moment, I began telling them about the Campaign and women's rights. They could not believe, the women whose noise of hammering fists they had heard earlier today are the same journalists, social workers and lawyers who work for women's rights. We tell them that many of the women who are now in solitary confinement are those working on the cases of Kobra Rahmanpour,[205] Ashraf Kolhar[206] and Akram Ghavidel.[207] To our surprise they tell us that the woman who body-searched us downstairs was Akram Ghavidel. Apparently prisoners who are well-behaved get to help in the daily running of the prison. This is unbelievable. Everything is like a movie. Outside these walls Asieh Amini works for Akram's freedom and this side of the prison Akram has to take Asieh to a solitary cell, search her and lock the door. I don't know whether to laugh or cry. When I tell Akram, she doesn't believe it. "The same woman who went and saw my child? Swear to god, I didn't recognize her . . .," Both our bodies tremble.[208]

In another interview, Asieh Amini,[209] a journalist and human rights activist whose campaigning on women's death penalty cases is well known, recalls the time she encountered Akram in prison:

> One of the strangest feelings that I've ever experienced was when a woman brought food for me and my friends in the cold cell where we

205 Kobra Rahmanpour, a twenty-six-year-old woman awaiting execution in Evin prison, "was sentenced to death for the premeditated murder of her mother-in-law in 2000". For more see: Amnesty International, "Iran: Fear of Imminent Execution, Kobra Rahmanpur," *Public AI* Index: MDE 13/041/2003, 15 December 2003.

206 Ashraf Kalhori, a 37-year-old mother of four, was sentenced to death by stoning after being charged with *zina* (adultery).

207 Another death row convict.

208 Maryam Hosseinkhah, "Sakenine Band Nasvan Evin; Zanani ke Hich az Ghanun Nemidand (The Inhabitants of Women's Prison in Evin; Women Who Know Nothing of Laws)," *Zenestan* (5 May 2007), online www.zanestan.es/issue23/07,05,05,12,46,00/, (accessed 28 July 2016).

209 Email interview with Asieh Amini, 10 November 2010.

> were being kept. I had a toothache and was not in a good mood. She closed the door and seconds later she opened the door to ask: is there an Asieh Amini in this room? I said what do you want from her with a frown. I am Asieh. She came inside the cell and said in a low voice (so that the prison guard cannot hear her), I am Akram. Akram Ghavidel. She threw herself in my arms and we both cried.

Asieh had worked three years on Akram's case trying to stop her execution. Another mark of these narratives is an attention to the contested nature of legal and religious knowledge in Iran as it sits alongside the process of women's rights education. Maryam depicts the women prisoners' lack of rights and their lack of knowledge of their rights:[210]

> Many of them are here for months, some for years, without knowing their fate. They don't know anything about the law. They have no lawyers and outside the prison walls there is no one who cares enough to follow up their cases. Some don't have families, some have been abandoned by their families, and some others have run away. I understand their pain with all of my being.[211]

Maryam continues:

> Everything is like a movie, a scary movie, but arresting. I had never even imagined that I could be in front of all these women, whose cases I am so familiar with and each of whose sentences (death) had at one point shaken me to the core. They were all there: Kobra Rahampour, Ashraf Kolhar, Akram Ghavidel, Shahla Jahed and many more whose names I didn't know. Their pain was the same old pain of not having rights and not knowing their rights. I told Kobra that there are many who are active in search of justice and freedom for her. She looked at me with kindness and said: I wish justice was executed for all women.[212]

Apart from a lack of knowledge of the law, the law itself is a hurdle for these women. Some were divorced by their husbands while in prison. Yet, when Maryam asks Akram why she killed her husband, Akram replies, "I wanted a divorce. But

210 See also Maryam Hosseinkhah, "Sakenine Band Nasvan Evin; Zanani ke Hich az Ghanun Nemidand (The Inhabitants of Women's Prison in Evin; Women Who Know Nothing of Laws)," *Zenestan* (5 May 2007), online www.zanestan.es/issue23/07,05,05,12,46,00/, (accessed 28 July 2016).

211 Ibid.

212 Ibid.

neither my husband nor the court granted me one."[213] The laws of divorce are much more favourable to men than to women. Where a man can easily divorce a woman, a woman can divorce a man only under restricted conditions.

Mahboubeh, another women's rights activist, writes about the women on death row whom she met in Evin prison:

> "Our husbands are lying in enclosed graves and we are in open graves. We too ceased to live the very day that we killed our husbands." These are the words of a woman who spends her nights on the three-story bed across from me. Her nights are filled with nightmares of the death of her husband – a husband she stabbed to death.
>
> This is Evin prison – the women's ward. Nahid and I do not fully comprehend what national security we have undermined, nonetheless charged as such we spend our days in limbo in the midst of all these women. Ten of the sixteen women with whom we have shared a cell for over a week, are here on charges of murdering their husbands. These women, having lost faith in a legal system that offers no hope and no protection, weave their days to the darkness of the night that lingers behind the tall walls of Evin. If our laws had the capacity to defend women charged with murder, they would not be here now, spending their time idly in waiting for the day that would swallow them [a term used by female inmates to describe execution day].
>
> These women, they all seem kind and patient to me. They are women forced into marriages they did not choose, women who were forcibly married off at the age of 13 and 14, women whose husbands were chosen by their fathers. One of these women was forced into marriage through physical violence bestowed upon her. She asks, "Why doesn't anyone listen to our problems or pains? Where was the judge when my husband forced me onto the streets, into prostitution, in an effort to earn enough money to support his habit of addiction? What is one to do? Which laws were meant to support me? Which laws were intended to save me? Why didn't the judge listen to my pleas? I grew weary. The law provided me with no refuge. I defended myself. Yes! I killed him![214]

According to Mahboubeh, many women have similar stories of being in abusive relationships, requesting a divorce not allowed by discriminatory laws and then deciding to take matters into their own hands. Their interest

213 Ibid.

214 Mahboubeh Hossein Zadeh, "All Women Are Victims, Not Just Those in Prison," trans. Sussan Tahmasebi, *Change for Equality* (14 April 2007), online http://we-change.org/site/english/spip.php?article62, (accessed 28 July 2016).

in taking an active part in OMSC, even from death row, demonstrates the extent of their passion for some form of justice. This is conveyed in the following quote from Mahboubeh's narrative:

> The female inmate who has now started to record her own experiences in a small diary, pulls me aside and asks: "Can I help you in collecting signatures for the Campaign?" She wants me to use whatever means possible to get her a signature form, so that women who are condemned to spend their days at Evin prison, too can have the opportunity to create change for others. So that with their individual signatures they can bring hope to other women. And this reminds me of the last question asked by my interrogator before I was brought here: "Your demands in the Campaign, including banning of polygamy, equal rights to blood money and testimony, are in contradiction to the foundations of Islamic jurisprudence and the foundations of the Islamic Regime. Given these facts, will you continue to ask for changes in the laws?" In response to this question, I wrote: "Yes! I know that our demands are not in contradiction to Islam." And today, after this experience, I am more determined than ever and I write: "I ask for changes to these discriminatory laws. I ask them in an effort to honor the dignity of all the women in my country."[215]

These narratives are clear indications of the extent to which discriminatory laws against women can negatively affect women's livelihood, driving them, in some extreme cases, even to murder. By depicting women prisoners' lack of knowledge about their rights, these narratives demonstrate the necessity of a grassroots reform movement in which women are educated about their rights. The OMSC, initiated by a new generation of feminist activists, brought to public attention the everyday realities of gender discrimination in Iran. With that focus on what has been lost by women over many years also came a strange sense of hope. Through the prison narratives and the reports of the campaign published on the Internet, discrimination previously faced by women in private became public, and hence became shared and shareable. A sense of solidarity was built up among women who were previously isolated from one another. The challenge remains how best to support this new solidarity so that the public spaces made and reclaimed by the movement will not be lost.

Many of the feminists mentioned in this discussion are now in exile from Iran following a crackdown on the women's movement and actions taken after the June 2009 presidential elections. Despite the persistence of ideological differences from earlier eras, some of which have already been described in the brief historical account of the Iranian women's movement, the feminists

215 Ibid.

involved in the OMSC came together to recognize a common goal: women's emancipation. In the next section I expand upon in detail some of the different categories of the feminists who make up Iranian women's rights activists.

Although the campaign is no longer active, women activists have since organized other, smaller, campaigns and vigils. On 22 October 2014 a vigil was organized in front of the *majlis* by a group of women's rights activists to protest a series of violent acid attacks in Isfahan. The activists used rights-based language such as "a safe city is my right" (*shahr amn haq man ast*) and "a safe street is my right," (*khiyaban amn haq man ast*) to voice their concerns.[216] Other campaigns, vigils and protests have been held around the ban on women's presence at sporting events.[217] In response the government has declared that the ban is rooted in religious opposition from *ulama* who do not deem women's presence at sporting events as appropriate.[218]

The "Campaign to Change the Male Face of the Parliament" (*Campaign Tagheer Chehreye Mardaneye Majlis*)[219] began its activity on 27 October 2015 to address the lack of elected women politicians in Iran, as well as the gender discriminatory laws passed by the ninth *majlis*. The campaign advocated for egalitarian-minded women to become members of the *majlis* in order to improve women's rights in Iran. The campaign's main goal was to increase women's participation in politics, with a focus on the 25 February 2016 general parliamentary elections.[220] According to the campaign, women have responsibilities across the society, from the private sphere of the family to the economic, social and cultural sectors of the public sphere. This includes service in elected office, which should reflect and be proportional to the country's gender demographics. To further the goals of the campaign, three committees were organized: Red Cards for Anti-Women Candidates (*Kart Ghermez baraye Candidahaye Zan Setiz*); I Will Be a Candidate (*Man Candida Mishavam*); and At Least 50 Seats for Women Seeking Equality (*Hadeaghal 50 Korsi Baraye Zanan Barabari Talab*).[221]

216 Akram Ehqaqi, "Tajamo-e Faalan-e Zanan dar Moghabel Majlis dar Hemayat az Ghorbanian Acid-pashi: Khyaban Amn Haq man Ast (Gathering of Women's Rights Activists in Front of the Parliament in Support of the Victims of Acid Attacks: A Safe Street is My Right)," 24 October 2014, online http://bidarzani.com/19207, (accessed 15 January 2016).

217 "Be Khoshonat Keshideh Shodan Tajamoh Mosalemat Amir Zanan dar Moghabel Varzeshgah Azadi (Maybe this Seat Belongs to a Woman: Violence at the Peaceful Assembly in Front of the Azadi Stadium)," (24 June 2014), online http://bidarzani.com/17488, (accessed 7 February 2016).

218 "Shoraye Tamin: Mamnoiat Hozoor Zanan dar Varzeshgah az Soye Shoraye Tamin Nabodeh Ast", online http://bidarzani.com/17617

219 "Darbareyeh Campain: Campaign: Be Soyeh Tagheer Chehreye Mardaneye Majlis", online www.women4parliament.org/کمپین-درباره/

220 Ibid.

221 Ibid.

2 Contemporary feminism in Iran

Definitions, narratives and identity

Introduction

On my return to Iran in 2003 and 2004 I found it helpful to devise a rubric of feminist types as a way of ordering and making sense of the women's movement in Iran at that time. The types I identified were Islamic state feminists, Islamic non-state feminists, Muslim feminists and secular feminists.[1] This section expands and builds upon those early arguments and observations about categories of feminism, and supplements them with interviews conducted with Iranian women's rights activists.[2] In the interviews some of the interviewees happily identified themselves as either Islamic or secular feminists; others disagreed with such categorizations, stating that these were labels primarily used by academics which have now become politicized.[3] Some of the interviewees offered other self-labels such as radical, socialist, liberal, modern thinker (*no andish*) or pragmatist (*amalgara*)[4] feminists.

1 See Roja Fazaeli, "Contemporary Iranian Feminism: Identity, Rights and Interpretations," *Muslim World Journal of Human Rights* 4, no. 1 (2007), article 8.

2 The Iranian journalist and women's rights activist, Maryam Hosseinkhah, helped me identify and interview an array of women's rights activists and academics inside and outside of Iran. We conducted thirty interviews in total. We used written questionnaires for interviewees living in Iran because phone conversations would have posed a threat to their personal security. The communications were mainly by email. Other interviews were conducted by phone or Skype and recorded. A number of interviews were carried out in person. We picked our interviewees carefully from a range of demographics (Tehran, Tabriz, Kermanshah, Rasht, Gorgan, Shiraz and Karaj) and ages (25–55). As well as interviewing well-known women's rights activists who feature regularly in Western academic writings, we also interviewed younger women and men who have transformed the face of the women's movement in the past five years both ideologically and demographically. The interviews were all conducted in Persian. The translations are all mine.

3 Also refer to Afshaneh Najmabadi, "(Un)Veiling Feminism," *Social Text* 64 18, no. 3 (Fall 2000), 32, where Najmabadi describes the politicized divide of secular/religious by the Islamic government.

4 Jelveh Javaheri in the interview defines a pragmatist (*amalgara*) feminist as a person who does not use solely one specific ideology but instead chooses a collection of views and thoughts which are useful depending on the time and the context we work in.

Although I realize the categories offered here are only four of many other possible groupings, I contend they remain important as tools to address the multiple power dynamics and dependencies at work in contemporary Iran.[5]

The struggle to define "Islamic feminism"

In Muslim-majority countries, the term "feminism" often has a negative connotation and is at times regarded as a Western concept. In Iran some of the confusion arises from the fact that the term "feminism" does not have a Farsi equivalent and is widely used "as a Western import into Farsi."[6] Much of the literature on Islamic feminism portrays it as newly invented. However, I argue that its underlying notions have existed for centuries and it is simply the term "Islamic feminism" that is a recent coinage.[7]

Since it found currency in the 1990s[8] the term "Islamic feminism" has been defined diversely according to context. I contend that no homogenous definition of the term exists and that it is not desirable to attempt to apply a single definition to all contexts. As Ziba Mir-Hosseini notes, "The problem lies both in the explicit issue of how the term is defined and in the implicit meanings it has acquired in its usage."[9] Margot Badran defines Islamic feminism as "a feminist discourse and practice articulated within an Islamic paradigm . . . which derives its understanding and mandate from the Qur'an, seeks rights and justice for women, and for men, in the totality of their existence."[10] According

5 I use the term "dependency" in this chapter to address the economic, social and ideological dependence of feminists in Islamic countries on one or more of the following institutions: state, family, funders or scholars. Dependencies may be negative or positive. This notion is comparable to Abdullahi An-Na'im's definition of "Human Rights Dependency" as cited in Abdullahi A. An-Na'im, "Human Rights in the Arab World: A Regional Perspective," *Human Rights Quarterly* 23 (2001), 702.

6 Parvin Paidar, "Gender and Democracy: The Encounter between Feminism and Reformism in Contemporary Iran," *Democracy, Governance and Human Rights*, Programme Paper No. 6 (United Nations Research Institute for Social Development, October 2001), 2. Shalah Sherkat also noted in the early 1990s that the term feminism was misunderstood by some parts of society and references to the word were "mixed with negative convictions." Cited in Hammed Shahidian, "'Islamic Feminism' Encounters 'Western Feminism': Towards An Indigenous Alternative?," Paper Presented to the Feminism and Globalization Seminar, Illinois State University (February 1998), 3. Shahidian himself states "a major obstacle before Iranian women has been the absence of a general knowledge of feminism and women's movement around the world." (Shahidian, 3).

7 See, for example, Shahrzad Mojab, "Theorizing the Politics of 'Islamic Feminism'," *Feminist Review* no. 69, The Realm of the Possible: Middle Eastern Women in Political and Social Spaces (Winter 2001), 124–146.

8 Ibid., 124.

9 Ziba Mir-Hosseini, "Beyond 'Islam' vs 'Feminism'," *IDS Bulletin, Special Issue: Gender, Rights and Religion at the Crossroads* 24, no. 1 (January 2001), 67.

10 Margot Badran, "Islamic Feminism: What's in a Name?," online www.feministezine.com/feminist/international/Islamic-Feminism-01.html, (accessed 5 March 2016).

to Badran, Islamic feminist discourse is "grounded in the Qur'an and other religious texts".[11] Badran's definition of Islamic feminism is predicated on the engagement of the scholar with a sacred text.[12] This is the common understanding of the term "Islamic feminism" conveyed in the literature produced in the past ten years.[13] However, I argue that the Iranian version of Islamic feminism differs from Badran's definition. Although the discourse of Islamic feminism in Iran is certainly articulated within the framework of Islam, it is grounded more in political Islam than in any attempt to exegete the Qur'anic text through an egalitarian lens. If we take Badran's definition of Islamic feminism, then Islamic feminism in Iran would not be a significant category. Although historically there have been a number of female *mujtahidas* in Iran, their works remain largely unknown and their exegetical works (i.e., works that carry out a detailed analysis of sacred texts within a faith framework) do not always represent an egalitarian or a feminist interpretation of the Qur'an and the *Sunna*.[14] Furthermore, observing the women's rights movement in Iran, it is clear that women activists and lobbyists, when needed, depend more on male religious authorities' views of women's issues than that of the women *mujtahidas*.[15]

11 Interview with Margot Badran, "Islamic Feminism Is a Universal, Discourse," online www.qantara.de/webcom/show_article.php/_c-307/_nr-26/i.html, (accessed 15 August 2011).

12 Examples of scholars who directly engage with text include Amina Wadud (b. 1952), Monir Gorji (b. 1940s), Mohsen Saidzadeh (b. 1958) and Asma Balras (b. 1950). However, not all the mentioned scholars consider themselves feminist.

See, for example, Mohsen Saidzadeh, (pseudonym Mina Yadegar Azadi), "Ejtehad va Marja'iyate Zanan (Ijtihad and Marja'iyat of Women)," *Zanan* 8 (1992), 24–33.

Amina Wadud, *Qur'an and Woman, Rereading the Sacred Text from a Woman's Perspective* (New York: Oxford University Press, 1999). Asma Barlas, *'Believing Women' in Islam, Unreading Patriarchal Interpretations of the Qur'an* (Austin, TX: University of Texas Press, 2004).

13 Freshteh Ahmadi, for example, writes that the basic methodologies of Islamic feminism are *ijtihad* and *tafsir*. Freshteh Ahmadi, "Islamic Feminism in Iran, Feminism in a New Islamic Context," *Journal of Feminist Studies in Religion* 22, no. 2 (2006), 36. Personal interview with Ziba Mir-Hosseini (Summer 2010).

14 See, for example, the works of Mujtahida Zohreh Sefati (b. early 1950s), Nosrat Amin (1886–1983), (Hajieh Khanom) Zinat ul-Sadaat Homayooni (b. 1917/18 –), Fariba Alasvand (b. 1967 –) and Masoumeh Golgiri (lecturer in Jama'at al-Zahra [all-female *hawza* in Qom]). See Mirjam Künkler and Roja Fazaeli, "The Life of Two Mujtahidas: Female Religious Authority in 20th Century Iran" in *Women, Leadership and Mosques: Changes in Contemporary Islamic Authority*, ed. Masooda Bano and Hilary Kalmbach (Leiden: Brill, 2011), 127–160. *Ya'dnamah-i Banu-yi Mujtahidah Nusrat al-Sadat Amin: mashhur bih Banu-yi Irani* (Isfahan: Markaz-i Mutala'at va Tahqiqat-i Farhangi, 1992).

It is interesting to note also that there have been debates on who has access to reinterpretation of Islamic texts; should one simply be educated or is it essential for one to have *hawza* training to reinterpret the Qur'an and the *hadith*?

15 There is only evidence in recent years of consultation with *mujtahida* Zohreh Sefati in reforming the age of marriage for boys and girls. See Mohammad Badiee, "Goftegu ba Faqih Pajuhandeh Banu Zohereh Sefāti (Interview with the Researcher Jurist, Lady Zohreh Sefati)," *Keyhan Farhangi*, no. 199 (April 2003), online www.noormags.com/View/Magazine/ViewPages.aspx?numberId=1131&ViewType=1&PageNo=8, (accessed 31 March 2016).

The Iranian feminist journal *Zanan*[16] has been credited by some as the platform where Islamic feminism in Iran was born. This is where Islamic feminists "offered Islamic readings of gender equality and justice".[17] My study of the archives of *Zanan*'s articles from 1992 until its closure in 2008 reveals that the main authors who offered egalitarian readings of Islamic texts were men.

One male clergyperson in particular played an important role in giving *Zanan* an Islamic feminist brand. Hujjat ul-Islam Sayed Mohsen Saidzadeh, a *hawza*-educated religious scholar,[18] began writing for *Zanan* under his wife's name: Mina Yadegar Azadi. He also wrote under his own name, as well as under a pseudonym: Zinat ul-Sadat Kermanshahi. Saidzadeh was arrested and defrocked in 1998 after publishing an article in the daily paper *Jameh* in 1998 that was critical of "the religious sayings and traditions that rationalize discrimination against women".[19] Since his release from prison, Saidzadeh has withdrawn from intellectual public life and no longer writes.[20]

Another journal, *Farzaneh Quarterly*, was established a year after *Zanan* in 1993. Farzaneh's scope of readership did not reach that of the *Zanan*'s. *Zanan*, as previously described, enjoyed a wide readership both inside and outside of Iran.[21] However, *Farzaneh* did draw a number of prominent authors. These

16 *Zanan*'s license was revoked after sixteen years after the publication began its work. According to news articles as cited in a report by Amnesty International, *Zanan* was accused of having "endangered the spiritual, mental and intellectual health of its readers, gave the impression of insecurity in society, and drew a dark image of the situation of women in Islamic society by publishing certain articles". See "Iran: Women's Rights Defenders Defy Repression," *MDE* 13/018/2008 (London: Amnesty International Publications, 2008), 3. Also refer to M. Nissimov, Y. Mansharof and A. Savyon, "Iranian Women's Magazine Shut Down for Publishing Investigative Article on Martyrdom Movement," *Middle East Media Research Institute (MEMRI)*, Inquiry & Analysis no. 439 (May 2009), 4, online www.memri.org/publicdocs/Zanan_IA_sm.pdf, (accessed 28 July 2016).

17 Margot Badran, "Engaging Islamic Feminism," in *Islamic Feminism: Current Perspectives*, ed. Annita Kynsilehto, Tampere Peace Research Institute, Occasional Paper No. 96 (2008), 30. Also refer to Roza Eftekhari, "Zanan: Trials and Successes of a Feminist Magazine in Iran" in *Islamic Feminism: Current Perspectives*, ed. Anitta Kynsilehto, Tampere Peace Research Institute, Occasional Paper No. 96 (2008), 19.

18 Saidzadeh began his religious education at the age of ten in Qa'in Seminary in Khurasan. Later at the age of fifteen he went to the seminary in Mashahad and at the age of twenty he left Mashhad for the *hawza* in Qom. A *hawza* educated Islamic scholar, Saidzadeh served as a judge from 1983–1986 in Kermanshash. He began writing on women's rights in Islam in 1988 for *Payam-e zan* (more right winged journal linked to the *hawza*) and later in 1992 for *Zanan*.

19 Mehrangiz Kar, "Women's Strategies in Iran" in *Globalization, Gender, and Religion: The Politics of Women's Rights in Catholic and Muslim Contexts*, ed. Jane H. Bayes and Esfahlano Tohidi (New York: Palgrave, 2001), 194.

20 Ziba Mir-Hosseini, *Islam and Gender: The Religious Debate in Contemporary Iran* (Princeton: Princeton University Press, 1999), 274.

21 Mahboubeh in her interview asserts that *Farzaneh* was more of an academic journal than *Zanan* was and had a more intellectual readership, as well as Islamic feminist backing.

included women such as Monir Gorji, an interpreter of the Qur'an and the sole female member of the Assembly of Experts for the Constitution,[22] and Massoumeh Ebtekar,[23] an academic and the former vice president (*moavenat riyasat*) of Iran. Gorji, in particular, was identified by others throughout my interviews as an example of an Islamic feminist in Iran, though it is not clear whether she herself identifies as such. After having spoken with her, attended her lectures and read her writings, it is not clear whether Gorji's views favour gender equality in all aspects, or rather if she believes in the complementarity of gender roles. Gorji works within a traditional Islamic framework. However, her disillusionment with the political power structure in Iran has led her to change her views considerably since the 1979 revolution.

Such changes are not uncommon. Another woman whose views have shifted for various reasons is Mahboubeh Abbasgholizasdeh. I met Abbasgholizadeh in 2003 at a course I attended on women's studies in Tehran. She gave an introductory lecture on Islamic and Muslim feminisms. She explained to us how immediately after the Islamic Revolution of 1979 she had affiliated with Islamic feminism. The identity, she told us, had been closely linked with her utter devotion to Ayatollah Khomeini at the time. Yet her identity began to shift as her understanding of women's rights in the context of Islam changed. By 2003 Abbasgholizasdeh self-identified as a Muslim feminist who attempted to reinterpret Islamic law through the use of dynamic *ijtihad*.[24] We met again in 2006 and she told me that in the interim she had become a secular feminist. When I interviewed Mahboubeh in 2010[25] I asked her to elaborate on the shifts in her feminist identity over the past thirty-one years. Mahboubeh told me that when she looked back, she realized that the labels she had used were no more than academic terms employed to describe the changes which religious and non-religious women went through during the revolution and in the years following in the Islamic Republic.

22 This is the Assembly which revised the Iranian Constitution at the inception of the 1979 Islamic Revolution.

23 Ebtekar was also the editor and the license holder for *Farzaneh*.

24 Mahboubeh defined dynamic *ijtihad* as means of interpreting Islamic texts to satisfy the needs of our time, entailing identification of those parts of the Qur'an that are historical and hence their interpretation is subject to change. In a more general sense, *ijtihad* is translated as independent reasoning but in its broader meaning *ijtihad* translates to exertion of oneself or putting in utmost effort in doing something. Most Shi'a jurists define *ijtihad* as "the capacity or ability to find what the law could possibly be through juristic speculation". Khurasani, M.M.K., *Kifayat al-Usul*, M. Baha'i, Al-Amili, *Zubdat al-Usul,* cited in Abu'l-Fadl Izzati, *An Introduction to Shi'i Islamic Law and Jurisprudence, with an Emphasis on the Authority of Human Reason as a Source of Law According to Shi'i Law* (Lahore, Pakistan: Ashraf Press, 1976), 89.

25 Interview was conducted with Maryam Hosseinkhah.

In her narrative it is clear that Abbasgholizasdeh's feminist identity formation was intertwined with the Islamic Revolution and influenced by revolutionary Islam as articulated by the ideologue Ali Shari'ati and by Ayatollah Khomeini. According to Mahboubeh, it was Shari'ati's book, *Fatima is Fatima* (*Fatemeh Fatemeh Ast*) that anchored a strong identity for her. Wearing the *hejab*, Mahboubeh elaborates, gave her a feeling of belonging, a sense of having entered into the domain of power. Women like Abbasgholizasdeh took part in the revolution to be part of the masses, not to address gender discrimination. They believed once the monarchy was abolished the rest would work itself out. However, soon after the inception of the Islamic Revolution they began to sense a different sort of change and became disillusioned. Abbasgholizasdeh talked about this change in her interview:

> For example, segregation started. At the start of the revolution meetings were mixed but eventually they became segregated. Women went to another room, chatting and breastfeeding their babies, while the men held meetings in another room. . . . Before the revolution one would not order the other to cook. Wife and husband treated each other equally. A year or two later everything changed.

Abbasgholizasdeh also talked about how Fatima, the daughter of Prophet Muhammad, who was portrayed as a strong revolutionary role model during the revolution, became "Fatima, the good wife and mother" after the inception of the Islamic republic. Women were politically sidelined and lost some of their public and private rights. Slowly these women came to think that, although the state called itself an Islamic Republic, its legislation and mores were not really Islamic. The laws were the interpretation of male clerics, and consequently favoured men. Slowly some of these women began to question their change in status from revolutionary women to good wives and mothers. This questioning brought a number of women to critically query what their duties were within the family and the public realm.

Abbasgholizasdeh recalls that during the first few years after the Islamic Revolution, small groups of women would gather and study to try to understand their gendered duties by reading Islamic texts (Qur'an and *Nahjul Balagheh*)[26] and Khomeini's writings (such as *Tahrir al-Vasileye Khomeini*).[27] In 1985 a group of women led by Gorji traveled to the UN

26 Translated as "Peake of Eloquence", *Nahjul Balagheh* is a collection of sermons, letters and sayings of Ali ibn Abi Tablib (first Shi'a imam) (b. 601 – d. 661).

27 Ruhollah Khomeini, *Tahrir al-Vasileye Khomeini* (Tehran: Entesharat-e Kazemeini, 1987).

Women's Conference in Nairobi.[28] In Nairobi they were faced with criticism regarding women's rights in Islam by other international participants and realized they had no argument with which to defend themselves. This was the first and perhaps one of the most important groups to set out to reread the Qur'an in order to be able to answer the international community's questions about the legitimacy of the Qur'an and of Islam itself. None of these women, according to Abbasgholizasdeh, had studied classical religious texts or had any *hawza* training. Yet this was arguably the beginning of Islamic feminist discourse in Iran.

As Afsaneh Najmabadi notes, "one of the problems with current discussions of Islam and feminism is ahistorical generlizations." Abbasgholizasdeh also elaborates on this point by stating "it is a mistake to look at Islamic feminists in Iran outside a historical context." It is important to be clear not only about the context and the history against which we theorize the meaning of Islamic feminism, but also about the role that Iranian politics and revolutionary ideals have played in forming the identities of the women and men who are now feminists in Iran. Women labelled "Islamic feminists" in Abbasgholizasdeh's narratives are, according to her, women who attempt a rereading of the Qur'an within the framework of *Shari'a*. However, their critique of the male-centric views does not go beyond the framework of political Islamism (*eslamgariy-e dini*). In short, Abbasgholizasdeh defines Islamic feminists in this context as "a group who in the framework of Islam and the Qur'an question their duties". She also defines Islamic feminists as "a group who question their duties within the framework of Islam and the Qur'an". Muslim feminists[29] by contrast, apart from reaching outside the Islamic framework, also take into consideration debates on cultural and social realities. They ask questions not only about their duties, but also about their rights.

When interviewees were asked to define Islamic feminism, they offered a number of responses, all of which further emphasized the diversity of ways in which the term was capable of being understood. Some stated that Islamic

28 The other delegates were: Ashraf Broujerdi (former deputy Minister of Justice [1997–2004]); Masoumeh Ebtekar (b. 1960, the first woman cabinet member during Khatami's government (1997–2004), known for her involvement in the Iran hostage crisis as the spokesperson for the hostage takers (1979); and Azam Taleghani (b. 1942), who was the only NGO representative from Iran at the conference. She is a former member of parliament (first parliament formed 1979) and heads *Jame-e Zanan Enghelab Eslami*, an NGO based in Tehran. She is also the daughter of the late Ayatollah Taleghani.

29 Both of these categories, Islamic feminism and Muslim feminism, are expanded on in the following sections.

feminism, as defined by Badran, has never existed in Iran. Kaveh Mozafari, an active member of the OMSC,[30] responded as follows:

> In reality, one can say no one with such a label is active in Iran; those who may be known as Islamic feminist, do not use this title themselves. Certainly, there are those who pay attention to the fabric of an Islamic society [in their activism] and, for example, call themselves Muslim feminist; however, the use of this title is not common in Iran. . . . Those referred to are in general reformist women who themselves believe in Islam, and who attempt to interpret Islam in a way that would help equality of men and women.[31]

This link between Islamic feminism and reformist women, or even more generally reformist thought, was also elaborated on by Abbasgholizasdeh both in her interview and in her writing.[32] Negar Rahbar, a twenty-four-year-old mechanical engineer and an active member of the One Million Signature campaign in the north of Iran, concurred, stating, "the Islamic feminists I know in Iran are either women who are close to the (reformist) government (*hokumat*) or are feminists who, although they have secular outlooks, believe that the way for obtaining [gender] equality in Iran is through the use of dynamic *fiqh*[33] (*feqh pooya*) and believe that secular movements in Iran do not yield any results."[34] Jelveh Javaheri's[35] discussion on Islamic feminism is also worth reviewing:

> In my opinion, this view [Islamic feminism] found potency in Iran in the 1990s when attention to difficulties faced by women in their daily lives prompted some women's rights activists and publications (with such inclinations), to turn to clearer interpretations (*tafasir-e roshantar*) of Islam for solving women's actual problems. Therefore, with presenting

30 As Sussan Tahmasebi writes, "The One Million Signatures Campaign officially launched on August 27, 2006, aims to collect one million signatures in support of a petition addressed to the Iranian Parliament asking for the revision and reform of current laws which discriminate against women." See Sussan Tahmasebi, "One Million Signatures Campaign: Answers to Your Most Frequently Asked Questions," 24 February 2008, online http://1millionchange.info/english/spip.php?article226, (accessed 18 February 2011).

31 Interview with Kaveh Mozafari (a social scientist and women's rights activist based in Iran), Summer 2010.

32 Mahboobeh Abbasgholizadeh, "The Experience of Islamic Feminism in Iran," trans. Haleh Ghorayshi, *Farzaneh (the Journal of women's Studies and Research in Iran and Muslim Countries)* 5, no. 10 (Winter 2000), 7–14.

33 Jurisprudence, which defines the rules and methodologies of Islamic laws.

34 Interview with Negar Rahbar, 24-year-old, B.A. in Mechanics, lives in Gorgan (the capital of Golestan Province, northern Iran), Summer 2010.

35 Interview with Jelveh Javaheri, thirty-three-year-old, B.A. Computer Science, M.A. Sociology, Tehran, Summer 2010.

> such interpretations, they challenged the discriminatory laws against women which have caused extensive damage to the lives of women and many social ills. And they demanded amelioration of women's status and the change in laws with reliance on these interpretations. Gradually, the rhetoric of "reform" (*eslah gari*) or "religious modern thinking" (*no anidishi-e dini*) found currency in the women's realm. . . . Some researchers regard such outlooks as "Islamic Feminism."

Javaheri adds that the term "Islamic feminism" has been a contentious one in Iran and that there is no consensus on its definition. Moreover, the observation has been made that some women's rights activists have been vehemently opposed to the usage of this term.

The interviewees emphasized numerous times that Islamic feminists do not constitute a homogenous group; rather they come from a variety of cultural, regional, socio-economic and educational backgrounds. As Mir-Hosseini states, "like other feminists, their positions are local, diverse, multiple and evolving."[36] In the case of Iran, certain groups who were identified as Islamic feminists have now changed their affiliation to Muslim feminists and some who regarded themselves as Muslim feminists are now calling themselves secular feminists, reaffirming the transitional nature of their identities.[37] As for the question of whether *only* those who engage in *ijtihad* to reinterpret the text in an egalitarian way can be referred to as Islamic feminists, it is notable that both Haleh Afshar and Ziba Mir-Hosseini write on Islamic feminism in Iran, but that neither claim Islamic feminists are *de facto* religious scholars. For Nayereh Tohidi, Islamic feminism has emerged "primarily in cities among highly educated middle-class Muslim women who . . . are unwilling to break away from their religious orientation and hold Islam as a significant component of their ethnic, cultural, or even national identity".[38] Islamic feminism in Iran, as expressed in this manner, does not depend solely or primarily on rigorous engagement with a text. Yet Haleh Afshar observes that among women activists in Muslim majority countries, none have been as successful as "those who have located their political action in the context of Islam and its teachings".[39] She reasons that, since the Islamic Republic of Iran prides itself on its adherence to what it defines as Islamic values, then "the believers have been better able to engage in positive discussion and extract 'Islamic'

36 Ibid.

37 It is noteworthy that the changes in the identity of these women are contingent upon their responses to the changing structures of power within the state.

38 Nayereh Tohidi, "'Islamic Feminism': Perils and Promises" in *Middle Eastern Women on the Move* (Washington: Woodrow Wilson International Centre for Scholars, 2003), 136, online www.wilsoncenter.org/topics/pubs/MEP_women.pdf#page=133, (accessed 18 February 2011).

39 Ibid.

measures which are liberating."[40] This meshes well with Mir-Hosseini's contention that after the 1979 Islamic Revolution there emerged "a gender discourse that is 'feminist' in its aspiration and demands, yet is 'Islamic' in its language and source of legitimacy. . . ."[41]

Islamic state feminists

Many of the *khate Imamis* (supporters of Khomeini) developed a unique gender perspective even before the revolution. They then fought in the war and demanded their "rightful place in the post-war society".[42] Some of these women became active in politics, either through affiliation with men in power or by way of unflinching support of the regime. These are the Islamic state feminists. As Azadeh Kian states, "they attempted to present a different reading of Islam and Islamic laws which would be more attentive to the condition of women".[43] They realized that the state's adherence to traditional Islam was rooted in the male-dominated state apparatus. The dependence of these women on the state and traditional Islamic ideology made their attempts less credible in some circles and more credible in others. Only a handful of women had seats in the first, second or third *majlis*. As Marziyyeh Dabbagh narrates, for women to try to pass any motion in the parliament, first and foremost they had to persuade their male colleagues of the validity of their argument. Most times their negotiations were to no avail.[44] These women, although they supported some women's causes, are better identified as part of the conservative religious network that lent its support to the *vilayat-i-faqih*.[45] Although they did not oppose women's presence in the public sphere, they still viewed a woman's main role as that of a mother and housewife.[46] These women remained loyal to the traditional Islamic framework even as some of them also came to realize that "the present laws and regulations concerning

40 Ibid., 197.

41 Ziba Mir-Hosseini, "The Quest for Gender Justice Emerging Feminist Voices in Islam," Presented at the conference: Reframing Islam, Irish Centre for Human Rights (National University of Ireland Galway, Ireland 2005).

42 Ibid.

43 Azadeh Kian, "Women and Politics in Post-Islamist Iran: The Gender Conscious Drive to Change," *British Journal of Middle Eastern Studies* 24, no. 1 (1997), 75.

44 Ibid., 79.

45 *Vilayat Al-Faqih* as Khomeini stated "advocates a guardianship-based political system, which relies upon a just and capable jurist, *faqih*, to assume the leadership of the government in the absence of an infallible Imam". See also Ibrahim A. Karawan, "Monarchs, Mullas, and Marshals: Islamic Regimes?," *Annals of the American Academy of Political Science* 524, Political Islam, (November 1993), 103–119, Sage Publications.

46 Zadeh Kian, "Women and Politics in Post-Islamist Iran: The Gender Conscious Drive to Change," *British Journal of Middle Eastern Studies* 24, no. 1 (1997), 75–80.

women do not reflect the promising slogans of the revolution in the realm of the family, politics and society."[47] Early state feminists worked to advance the case of the state as well as their own. Religious fundamentalist regimes, as Afary points out, often have a number of women in prominent positions in order to popularize and develop the regime's gender ideology.[48]

A new generation of Islamic state feminists emerged in the post-war era. Changing economic, social and demographic realities prompted the government to support a growing number of women professionals. In 1992 the number of women parliament members tripled from three to nine. Nine women were also elected to the 1995 parliament.[49] In the same year, women's affairs offices were established in each ministry and government agency, and numerous non-governmental or quasi-governmental organizations dealing with women's issues were created. The new women parliamentarians were more vocal on women's issues. They called for an end to patriarchy and anti-women attitudes.[50] In the latter part of 1990s a reform movement emerged that comprised largely students and women. Women's rights became one of the most debated issues in government circles. A new wave of more powerful state feminists were appointed to top governmental positions. Massoumeh Ebtekar was named as Khatami's vice president and put in charge of environmental affairs. Azam Nouri was appointed by Ayatollah Mohajerani as deputy culture minister for legal and parliamentary affairs. Zahra Shojaee was named as Iran's first director general for women's affairs and the advisor on women at the Centre for Women's Participation (*Markaz Mosharekate Zanan*).[51] These gender-conscious women pursued politics out of necessity. They are paradoxical by-products of the revolution,[52] attempting "to adapt Islam to the realities of a society in which women's social, economic and political activities have become an integral part".[53]

47 Angiz Kar, "Women's Strategies in Iran from the 1979 Revolution to 1999" in *Globalization, Gender, and Religion: The Politics of Women's Rights in Catholic and Muslim Contexts*, ed. Jone H. Bayes and Nayereh Tohidi (New York: Palgrave, November 2001), 181.

48 Janet Afary, "Portraits of Two Islamist Women: Escape from Freedom or from Tradition?" *Women Living under the Muslim Laws* 25 (2001), 3.

49 Valentine M. Moghadam, "Islamic Feminism and Its Discontents: Towards a Resolution of the Debate," *Signs: Journal of Women in Culture and Society* 27, no. 4 (2002), 1141.

50 Maryam Behrouzi's statement in Valentine M. Moghadam, "Islamic Feminism and Its Discontents: Towards a Resolution of the Debate," *Signs: Journal of Women in Culture and Society* 27, no. 4 (2002), 1141.

51 Ibid. Also personal interview with Zahra Shojaee, Summer 2003. It is also important to note that not all these women would accept a feminist categorization. However, as noted by Abbasgholizadeh in her interview, this is no more than an academic practice.

52 Ziba Mir-Hosseini, "Women and Politics in Post Khomeini Iran: Divorce, Veiling and Emerging Feminist Voices" in *Women and Politics in the Third World*, ed. Haleh Afshar (London: Routledge, 1996), 142–169.

53 Azadeh Kian, "Women and Politics in Post-Islamist Iran: The Gender Conscious Drive to Change," *British Journal of Middle Eastern Studies* 24, no. 1 (1997), 76.

In talking to some of these state feminists it is clear that they paint an idealized picture of Muslim women's lives. Their ideal is the veiled woman of the revolution, liberated from the fetters of Western consumerism and capitalism. She is the mother, wife, sister or child of a martyr who lives her life according to the Islamic creed and using Fatima[54] as her role model. Women's rights, as conceived by them, are complementary rather than equal to men's.

Islamic non-state feminists

The majority of the non-state Islamic feminists also supported Khomeini at the start of the revolution. However, a distinguishing characteristic of non-state feminists is their preference for civil society over the state apparatus. Azam Taleghani is a good example of an Islamic non-state feminist.[55] Taleghani is the daughter of the late Ayatollah Mahmoud Taleghani, a political prisoner during the Shah's reign, and a head of the Women's Association of the Islamic Revolution (*Jam-e Zanan Enghelab Eslami*).[56] She was a member of the interim parliament (first parliament), and her work on women's issues began after she served her term in the parliament. Although she remains involved in politics, Taleghani's women's rights activism is not confined to the state apparatus as would be the case with an Islamic state feminist.

Taleghani's publication *Payam-e Hajar* was the first magazine that worked within the framework of Islam to raise questions about the necessity of reinterpreting Islamic laws.[57] She used Ayatollah Taleghani's teachings both in work published in *Payam-e Hajar* and in the weekly meetings she held to study and reinterpret the Qur'an.[58] Her organization depended on voluntarism because of inadequate funding, which led her to explore foreign funding options and networks. Because of this, Taleghani's passport was confiscated during a round of arrests in the summer of 2004 and she and many of the people working for her were interrogated and harassed. Constant surveillance by government agents is the norm for non-state feminists and at times Taleghani has been prohibited from leaving the country to attend

54 The daughter of Prophet Muhammad and wife of Ali ibn Abi Talib, the first Shi'a imam.

55 I worked for Azam Taleghani as a volunteer in Summer 2004.

56 Other members of the Association included Fereshte Hashemi, Shahin Tabatabaii, Zahra Rahnavard and Gawhar Dastgheib. See Asef Bayat, "A Women's Non-Movement: What It Means to Be a Woman Activist in an Islamic State," *Comparative Studies of South Asia, Africa and the Middle East* 27, no. 1 (2007), 162.

57 Azadeh Kian, "Women and Politics in Post-Islamist Iran: The Gender Conscious Drive to Change," *British Journal of Middle Eastern Studies* 24, no. 1 (1997), 81. Also personal interviews and work experience with Azam Taleghani, 2003 and 2004.

58 While working for Mrs Taleghani, I attended some of these meetings, which were frequented by a very mixed audience, young, old, wealthy, poor, educated and uneducated.

conferences.[59] These are but some of the basic dependency-related difficulties Islamic non-state feminists continue to encounter in Iran.

Muslim feminists

While "Muslim feminism" is at times used interchangeably with "Islamic feminism",[60] it is helpful make a clear distinction between the two terms. The term "Muslim feminism" is used by some feminists in Iran who previously identified themselves as Islamic feminists but who now wish to separate themselves from the formality of the latter category. Muslim feminists, like Islamic feminists, seek to reform Islamic law using *ijtihad*. However, Islamic feminists confine their use of dynamic *ijtihad* as a tool for reform to the framework of traditional Islamic *fiqh*. Muslim feminists look for answers outside of this framework as well. According to a self-professed Muslim feminist, "one has to take into account some principle rules such as justice and equality, both of which are the essence of Qur'an."[61] For Muslim feminists, context is crucial when engaging with debates about dynamic *ijtihad*.

Muslim feminists criticize Islamic state and non-state feminists for not seeking reform outside the framework of Islam. As Mahboubeh elaborated in her interview, Islamic feminists question their duties within the framework of Islam, whereas Muslim feminists look for their rights both within the same framework and also outside of it. Muslim feminists, therefore, regard themselves as a new category of feminists situated between Islamic and secular feminists.

Secular feminists

Secular feminists are proponents of separating the state from religious institutions. They see such separation as an important condition for women to achieve gender equality.[62] Given the current situation, and the historical

59 It was later revealed that one of the government informants was a young woman who attended Mrs Taleghani's Qur'an classes.

60 See, for example, Azza M. Karam, *Women, Islamism and the State, Contemporary Feminism in Egypt* (London: Macmillan Press, 1998).

61 Group interview with Mahboubeh Abbasgholizadeh as part of the International Course on Islam and Human Rights, Summer 2004. See also Maryam Hosseinkhah, "Goftegoo va Shonudhayee darbareye Taarozat Hughugh-e Zan dar Islam ba Hughoghe Bashar," *Iranian Feminist Tribune* (October 2004), 1–4, online www.iftribune.com/news.asp?id=7&pass=19, Translation of this article is my own.

62 The definition of secularism used here is simplified for the purposes of this paper. For more on the state-religion relationship see Jeroen Temperman, "The Neutral State: Optional or Necessary?: A Triangular Analysis of State-Religion Identification, Democratization and Human Rights Compliance," *Religion and Human Rights* 1, no. 3 (2006), 269–305.

relationship between the state and the clergy in Iran, many secular feminists have concluded that even if Iran is secularized, the clergy will always maintain some power. Therefore, some secular feminists also support dynamic *ijtihad*.[63]

Previously, I have suggested that the majority of secular feminists went into exile after the revolution and that few secular feminist scholars remained in the country.[64] Although this is true to a certain extent, the 2010 interviews show a general trend of the feminist movement towards secularism. These women, although not all vocal at the beginning of the Islamization of the country, became more and more outspoken during the reform era, using women's magazines such as *Zanan* as a platform to voice their concerns. It is also imperative to note that the younger generation of feminist activists, who some refer to as the fifth generation of Iranian feminists,[65] lean more and more towards secularism both in their activism and their advocacy.

Categories of dependence

Leila Ahmed suggests that the early dominant voice of feminism in Muslim-majority countries in the early 1900s was intertwined with social tendencies towards Westernization and secularization. These tendencies according to Ahmed were discernible mainly in "the upper, upper-middle, and middle-middle classes",[66] which "promoted a feminism that assumed the desirability of progress toward Western-type societies".[67] These feminists' ideologies therefore depended largely on Western feminist ideology.[68] All categories of Iranian feminists, but in particular Muslim and secular feminists, are dependent on foreign funding, and are often subject to ideological dependencies as well. Because of their dependence on Western funding, protection and publicity, some of these feminists are labelled by the state as Western implants or immoral imports from the West; this undermines their

63 Secular feminists such as Mehrangiz Kar have written numerous articles in *Zana on* the subject.

64 Roja Fazaeli, "Contemporary Iranian Feminism: Identity, Rights and Interpretations," *Muslim World Journal of Human Rights* 4, no. 1 (September 2007), 1–24.

65 The term "fifth-generation Iranian feminist" was first cited in Noushin Ahmadi Khorasani (Irani, Shole [trans.]), "The "One Million Signature Campaign": Face-to-Face, Street-to-Street," *Change for Equality* (29 March 2007), republished online www.payvand.com/news/07/mar/1352.html (accessed 28 July 2016).

66 Leila Ahmed, *Women and Gender in Islam: Historical Roots of a Modern Debate* (New Haven & London: Yale University Press, 1992), 174.

67 Ibid.

68 It is important to note that "Western feminism" is a generalized label and that it represents a broad range of feminist ideologies. As with "Islamic feminism", the term "Western feminism" is also contextual and temporal in its definitions.

legitimacy.[69] However, it is crucial to note that across all feminist categories the Iranian women's movement in general is growing less and less inclined to accept foreign funding. OMSC, for instance, prided itself on not accepting any outside or government funding, precisely because of a desire to stay autonomous and independent.

Muslim and secular feminists are also less likely to seek funding from the government for their projects. This may lead to their activities being deemed anti-governmental. As a result, they are more likely to become targets of state crackdowns.[70] Some secular feminists argue that Islamic feminists and their expatriate academic supporters, either consciously or unintentionally, delegitimize their work on secular trends and social forces. They "maintain that the activities and goals of 'Islamic Feminism' are circumscribed and compromised, and that there cannot be improvements in women's status as long as Islamic Republic is in place".[71]

Yet, the murkiness of the boundaries dividing civil society and the state in Iran reveals the difficulties of feminist dependencies in other ways. Iranian feminist organizations, or groups labeled as women's rights organizations, face multi-faceted constraints on their work, as do other NGOs. These include an inadequate legal and regulatory environment, internal management problems, lack of professionalism, weak technical and financial capabilities, excessive government control and insufficient transparency. Most women's rights organizations that I worked with in Iran, if truly non-governmental, were incapable of tapping into international funds, not only because of lack of skills but also because of fear of prosecution by the government. These organizations' dependency on the government was based on the amount of funding and support they were willing to accept, or that the government was willing to give to them. It is well known that if women's rights organizations (or other NGOs) wish to be independent, they face scrutiny and prosecution from the government.[72] The irony remains that the Government Organized

69 Iranian women activists are becoming more and more careful and aware of where their funding is sourced as the government tends to take advantage of feminists' use of foreign funds to clamp down on them and to delegitimize them.

70 The crackdown on women's rights activists and the civil society in general has been more acute since the contested presidential elections of 12 June 2009. Since many women's rights activists have been exiled and a number of those who remained have been imprisoned. Nasrin Sotoudeh and Bahareh Hedayat. For example, the recent arrests of Iranian women's rights activist who are involved in the One Million Signatures Campaign to end legal discrimination against women.

71 Valentine M. Moghadam, "Islamic Feminism and Its Discontents: Towards a Resolution of the Debate," *Signs: Journal of Women in Culture and Society* 27, no. 4 (2002), 1142.

72 The extent of the scrutiny is, however, dependent on those in positions of power. For example, during Khatami's presidential term, civil society in general enjoyed more independence and the number of NGOs mushroomed throughout Iran. Yet, towards the end of Khatami's time, civil society came under attack.

Non-Governmental Organizations (GONGOs), which have links to the government, are able to get funding both from the government and foreign donors. Their dependence on the state makes them less likely to be targeted for scrutiny; at the same time they can also use foreign funds.

It is also difficult to be an Iranian feminist without negotiating some form or fashion of family dependency. In Iran the patriarchal model of the family still prevails. Certain articles of the Iranian Civil Law, coupled with the socio-cultural, religious and historical supports for patriarchy, legitimize the second-class status of women within the family. For example, Article 1105 of the Iranian Civil Code designates the husband the head of the household. Article 1114 of the Civil Code asserts that a woman is to live in the residence that the husband provides, unless the choice of selecting a residence is given to the woman. Immigration and passport regulation makes it necessary for a married woman to seek her husband's written permission to obtain a passport or to travel outside of the country. According to Article 1169 of the Civil Code, the mother of a child has priority in looking after her son until the age of two and her daughter until the age of seven. As soon as this period is over, the custody of the child shall go to the father. Taking into account the above laws, one can see the difficulties faced by feminists and women in general.

Deniz Kandiyoti writes that a certain kind of bargaining with patriarchy has to be undertaken by women strategizing to gain their rights in these contexts.[73] This has led to the formulation of a distinct type of gender discourse being undertaken by women in many Muslim-majority countries. Gerami and Lehnerer identify four strategies used by women to navigate and transform such fundamentalist frameworks. These include: *collaboration*, meaning actively supporting state policies designed to entrench a woman's primary role as that of domestic worker; *acquiescence*, meaning submission to discriminatory state policies; *cooptation*, meaning transitory manipulation of discriminatory state policies with an eye towards temporary melioration; and subversion, meaning the substantive and wholesale work of undermining these policies in hopes of their collapse.[74] Afary uses Erich Fromm's analysis and theories of fundamentalism to describe a collaborative strategy that certain women use:

> [A] decision to join these movements stems from a desire to both "escape from tradition" and "escape from freedom." Women who join right-wing Islamist movements gain a number of rights that the traditional

73 Deniz Kandyioti, "Bargaining With Patriarchy," *Gender and Society* 2, no. 3 (September 1988), 274–290.

74 Shahin Grami and Melody Lehnerer, "Women's Agency and Household Diplomacy, Negotiating Fundamentalism," *Gender and Society* 15, no. 4 (August 2001), 556–573.

> patriarchal society does not offer them. These privileges, however, come at a heavy cost to others, especially secular advocates of women's rights who have suffered immensely under the Islamic theocracy of Iran.[75]

Feminists of all sorts work within larger domestic and global structures where multi-layered dependencies complicate their work. In the context of Iran, Islamic state feminists, dependent on the powerful male-elite, seek rights not just within an Islamic framework, but within an Islamic framework that has been shaped by the state. Islamic non-state and Muslim feminists also look to an Islamic framework and try to extract notions of equality from alternative interpretations of Islamic texts. Yet the success of such an enterprise still depends to some extent on convincing the dominant male-clerics to adopt these feminized interpretations. Secular feminists tend to rely heavily on Western understandings of feminism, not only for theoretical moorings but also for financial support. Where these moorings are absent they can feel adrift. While such categories may help an academic analysis of a complex social movement, the feminist movement cannot and will not be confined by these categories, in part because the categories themselves are not, and cannot, be definite. They have the capacity to shift and change, just as do the women who live within, around, because of and despite them.

75 Janet Afary, "Portraits of Two Islamist Women: Escape from Freedom or from Tradition?" *Women Living under Muslim Laws* 25 (2001), 4.

3 Women's rights in Islam

An Iranian case study

Introduction

This chapter is a study of women's rights in Iran, with an emphasis on the legal provisions in the Iranian Civil Code. As Homa Hoodfar asserts, "The single most important area of Iranian women's concern is the Family Code, which, as it stands, effectively renders any legal gain women may have made in other areas futile."[1] The Iranian Civil Code was approved in three stages. Volume I on properties (articles 1–955) was enacted by the *majlis* in 1928. Volume II on persons (articles 956–1256) was enacted in 1934. Volume III on evidence in proving claims (articles 1257–1335) was enacted in 1935[2] during the rule of Reza Shah Phalavi (r. 1925–1941) as part of his modernization and secularization attempts "to reduce the judicial role of the clergy" and to establish "a centrally controlled legal system".[3] The Iranian Family Law was codified as a part of the Iranian Civil Code between 1928 and 1935. As Nikkie Keddie notes, that while the 1928 Civil Code "shows French influence, it largely restated shari'a principles, updated where modern exigencies required".[4] According to Hamid Bahrami Ahmadi, a number of *ulama* were

1 Homa Hoodfar, "Iranian Women at the Intersection of Citizenship and the Family Code: The Perils of 'Islamic Criteria'" in *Gender and Citizenship in the Middle East*, ed. Suad Joseph (Syracuse, NY: Syracuse University Press, 2000), 288.

2 M. A. R. Taleghaney (Trans.), *The Civil Code of Iran* (Littleton, Colorado: F. B. Rothman, 1995), xix–xxi.

3 Nikki R. Keddie; with a section by Yann Richard, *Modern Iran: Roots and Results of Revolution* (New Haven: Yale University Press, 2003), 89.

4 Ibid., 90. Apart from French influences, references are also made to Egyptian and Ottoman influences on the Iranian Civil Code. The family law provisions apart from *Imami fiqh* are said to have also been influenced by Swiss laws mainly because of the influence of one of the drafters, Dr. Matin Daftari, who had trained in law in Switzerland. See Hamid Baharami Ahmadi, "Tarikhche Tadvin Ghanoon Madani (The Drafting History of the Civil Law)," *Faslnameh Pajoheshi Daneshgah Imam Sadiq* no. 24 (Winter 2005), 33–51, online www.ensani.ir/storage/Files/20101111113036-146.pdf, (accessed 28 July 2016).

instrumental in the drafting of the Civil Code.[5] Thus a considerable part of the Civil Code is based on the traditional interpretation of Shi'a *ithna 'ashari* (*Jafari/Imami*) *fiqh* (jurisprudence).[6] Although the Civil Code was influenced greatly by the *ulama*, the Shah continued his secularization process, gradually attempting to diminish the power of the clergy. In 1929 a law restricted the role of religious courts to questions of marriage and divorce. Keddie notes as well that "only those who could pass examinations covering the new laws and modern subjects were allowed roles in the courts."[7] Yet, even so, it is the *ulama*'s interpretation of Shi'a *fiqh*, which to this day is enshrined as law, and which institutionalizes women's gendered roles.

The family law provisions of the Civil Code were largely discriminatory against women. Men had a near monopoly on unilateral divorce, the right to polygamous marriages and the right to custody of children after divorce.[8] As Hoodfar notes, during Reza Shah's reign few reforms were pushed through regarding the family law provisions, "apart from the civil legislation act, which required the registration of all marriages and divorces, and required that girls must reach the age of fifteen before marrying".[9] The Marriage Act of 1937[10]

5 The drafting process was in two stages. The family laws were drafted in the second stage, beginning in 1934. The *ulama* members of the first drafting committee included the *mujtahids* Seyed Mohammad Fatemi Qomi (b. 1873), Haj Seyed Nasr-u-lah Taqva (b. 1863), Sheikh Mohammad Reza Iravani (b. 1887), Sheikh Ali Baba Firoozkoohi (b. 1873) and Seyed Kazem Usar Tehrani (b. 1885); it is noteworthy that Seyed Tehrani, like the mentioned *ulama*, had a *hawza* education and numerous permissions of *ijtihad*, but he also spent time studying in Paris, and Seyed Mohsen Sadr (also known as Sard al-Ashraf) (b. 1868) held several posts in the government, including ministerial and senatorial positions. The sole layperson member of the first Civil Code-drafting committee was Seyed Mostafa Adl (b. 1879). The second committee included Seyed Mohammad Fatemi Qomi (b. 1873), Haj Seyed Nasr-u-lah Taqva (b. 1863), Sheikh Mohammad Brojourdi, Sheikh Asadulah Mamqani, Seyed Mohsen Sadr, Seyed Mohammad Reza Afjei, Javad Ameri and Matin Daftari. See Hamid Baharami Ahmadi, "Tarikhche Tadvin".

6 According to Hamid Barhami Ahamadi names some of the *Shi'a Imami fiqh* books which were referenced in drafting of the Civil Code including books by Najm ul-Din Jafar-ibn Hassan ibn Yahya (known as Muhaqiq Heli (b.1205–1277)), *Shariye ul-Islam fi Masael al-Halal va al-Haram*, n.d. Mohammad ibn Maki (known as Shahid Aval (b.1333–1384), Al-*Lamea* al-*Dameshghiye*, n.d. Sheikh Mohammad Hassan Najafi (known as Javaher (jewel) (b. 1785-), *Javaher-ul-kalam*, n.d., Ibid.

7 Nikki R. Keddie; with a section by Yann Richard, *Modern Iran: Roots and Results of Revolution* (New Haven: Yale University Press, 2003), 90.

8 Former (pre-1979) Iranian Civil Code Articles 1133, 1121, 1092, 1123, 1101, 1122, 1129.

9 Homa Hoodfar, "Iranian Women at the Intersection of Citizenship and the Family Code: The Perils of 'Islamic Criteria'" in *Gender and Citizenship in the Middle East*, ed. Suad Joseph (Syracuse, NY: Syracuse University Press, 2000), 287–313.

10 According to Parvin Paidar, "the most significant aspect of the Marriage Act was that it made registration of all marriages, divorces and deaths in the state notary offices compulsory, a function which had traditionally been performed by the Shii clergy." See Parvin Paidar, *Women and the Political Process in Twentieth-Century Iran* (Cambridge: Cambridge University Press, 1995), 111.

followed Reza Shah's contested "antiveiling policy of 1936",[11] which faced severe opposition by both women and the clergy, causing "repeated objections and even unrest".[12] The ban came to an end after Reza Shah's abdication in 1941.[13] It was only after Mohammad Reza Shah's White Revolution[14] that the Family Protection Act (FPA) was enacted in 1967 and further modified in 1975.[15] The FPA restricted polygamy by allowing a woman to divorce her husband if he took another wife without her consent, required that a man have a court permit before marrying a second wife, raised the age of marriage for girls[16] and allowed women both more access to divorce[17] and better access to the custody of children after divorce.[18] While the FPA did not provide blanket gender equality, it is still arguably, as Doreen Hinchcliffe states, "one of the most important statutes to be enacted in the Islamic world", at least with regard to women's rights.[19]

In 1979 the Islamic Republic of Iran embarked on a series of misogynistic laws and decrees in the name of Islam that limited the access of women to much of the public domain. The result was a new gendered identity for Iranian women that was defined by the Islamic Republic "through the family, the workforce, the educational system, and a symbolic manufacturing of an ideal Islamic female".[20] The 1967/1975 FPA was deemed un-Islamic and was abrogated. However, the FPA was never replaced or officially eliminated. There are therefore still loopholes in the legal system where the FPA may

11 Ibid.

12 Farzaneh Milani, *Veil and Words, the Emerging Voices of Iranian Women Writers* (Syracuse, NY: Syracuse University Press, 1992), 35.

13 Ibid.

14 For more on the White Revolution see Ali M. Ansari, *Modern Iran*, 2nd ed. (Essex: Pearson Education Limited, 2007), 187–212.

15 See Doreen Hinchcliff, "The Iranian Family Protection Act," *The International and Comparative Law Quarterly* 17, no. 2 (April 1968), 516–521. The 1967 FPA gave women more rights in the areas of law concerned with custody, polygamy and divorce among others.

16 First from nine to thirteen and later to eighteen, see Azadeh Kian-Thiébaut, "From Motherhood to Equal Rights Advocates: The Weakening of Patriarchal Order," *Iranian Studies* 38, no. 1 (1 March 2005), 3.

17 Both husband and wife needed to obtain a certificate of impossibility of reconciliation if they did not reach mutual consent. A wife could also divorce her husband in case of his failure to support her or if he remarried without her consent. See Ziba Mir Hosseini, *Marriage on Trial: Islamic Family Law in Iran and Morocco: A Study of Islamic Family Law* (London and New York: I.B. Tauris, 1997), 54.

18 Ibid. Refer to Parvin Paidar, *Women and the Political Process in Twentieth-Century Iran* (Cambridge: Cambridge University Press, 1995), 153–154.

19 Doreen Hinchcliff, "The Iranian Family Protection Act," *The International and Comparative Law Quarterly* 17, no. 2 (April 1968), 516.

20 Eliz Sansarian, "The Politics of Gender and Development in the Islamic Republic of Iran," *Journal of Developing Societies* 8 (1992), 62.

be applied.[21] Women were banned from working as judges,[22] and the legal age of marriage for girls was lowered to thirteen.[23] Girls were barred from technical and vocational schools and also from higher-education fields such as engineering, agriculture and mathematical sciences.[24] As Parvin Paidar notes, if "women were regarded as signifiers of national identity, their appearance, behaviour and position first had to be Islamized".[25] The veiled women became the public face of the revolution and represented the anti-Western sentiments of the regime.[26] These Muslim women were now required to recognize and assume their maternal and domestic duties.

Although some of these laws were gradually reformed, family laws[27] remain largely discriminatory against women. Iranian women were faced with the introduction of a new Family Protection Bill in 2012. The draft bill was first submitted to the cabinet (*heyat dolat*) by the judiciary on 22 July 2007.[28] After some changes by the cabinet, the bill was sent to the *majlis* for consideration. The bill was approved by the "legal and judicial commission" of the *majlis* in July 2008 but was not passed by the *majlis* in its entirety until March 2012. Consequently it was sent to the Guardian Council for approval. The bill was eventually approved after six years of debate between the *majlis* and the Guardian Council and was presented to the implementational organs of the government on 11 April 2013. The draft bill faced widespread criticism, often being referred to as the "Anti-Family Bill" by its critics as it was seen to further erode women's rights.[29] Despite strong opposition by

21 Interview with Maryam Hosseinkhah 24 October 2010.

22 Although women's ability to serve as judges is not explicated in the Qur'an, numerous *fatwas* by male Muslim scholars hold being a man as a condition for judgeship. For more see The Laws Governing the Appointment of Judges (ratified 1982). In 1995 this law was reformed allowing women to serve as advisory, assistant or research judges. See Hossein Mehrpour, *Mabahethi az Hughugh-e Zan az Manzar-e: Hughugh-e Dakheli, Mabani Feqhi va Mavazin Beinolmelal (Certain Issues on Women's Rights, from the View Point of: Domestic Law, Islamic Jurisprudence, Principles and International Criteria)* (Tehran: Etelaat, 2000), 37.

23 In 2002 the sixth parliament proposed that the age of marriage for boys and girls be increased to eighteen; however, this met fierce opposition from the Guardian and Expediency Councils.

24 Haideh Moghissi, *Feminism and Islamic Fundamentalism: The Limits of Postmodern Analysis* (London: Zed Books, 1999), 100.

25 Ibid., 3.

26 Eliz Sansarian, "The Politics of Gender and Development in the Islamic Republic of Iran," *Journal of Developing Societies* 8 (1992), 61.

27 There are also provisions in the Iranian penal code, that discriminate against women. However, it is outside the scope of this chapter to cover these.

28 "Dou Shora, Layehey-e Hemayat Khanevadeh," *Majlis Shoray-e Eslami, Doreyeh Hashtom*, Year 1, 2008, online http://rc.majlis.ir/fa/legal_draft/show/720519, (accessed 2 August 2016).

29 See, for example, "Stop Iranian Parliament from Ratifying an Anti-Family Bill," March 2010, online http://fairfamilylaw.in/spip.php?article413.

the women's movement, the enacted "Family Protection Law" still contains many discriminatory clauses against women. At the same time some of its more controversial articles were changed as a result of the intervention of women's rights advocates.[30] In fact, the extent to which civil society played a self-assigned supervisory role in these legislative debates is noteworthy. The smallest changes made to the draft bill were scrutinized closely by the women's coalition; this was one reason it took so long for the law to be passed.

The draft bill contained fifty-two articles. The enacted law contains fifty-eight articles. The most controversial and contested provisions of the draft bill were a subparagraph of article 22 and articles 23 and 25. As Irene Schneider notes, articles 23 and 25 "were not drawn up by the judiciary when drafting the Bill," but were added to the bill by the cabinet. All these articles were either removed or reframed in the 2012 bill, chiefly because of the lobbying of *majlis* by the women's coalition. The major changes to the articles are outlined in the following discussion.

The subparagraph of article 22 in its initial wording removed any official requirements for the registration of temporary marriage.[31] It stated "registration of temporary marriage shall be subject to Rules of Procedure to be approved by the minister of justice."[32] This subparagraph was eventually deleted,[33] and instead a subparagraph was added to article 16, specifying conditions for the registration of temporary marriage. In the 2013 law the clauses in relation to temporary marriage appear in article 21, which states:

> . . . the legal regime of the Islamic republic of Iran, in order to protect the centrality and stability of the family unit, supports permanent *nekah* (marriage) as the foundation of a family. Temporary marriage is subject to Shari'a law and the provisions of the Civil Code and its registration is mandatory in the following cases:
>
> 1 Where the wife becomes pregnant
> 2 Agreement between the spouses
> 3 Stipulated in the marriage contract

30 Afrooz Maghzi, "Women and the New Family Law," *BBC Persian, Nazeran Migoyand*, 30 April 2013, online www.bbc.co.uk/blogs/persian/viewpoints/2013/04/post-542.html.

31 The law before and after the 1979 revolution was quiet on this matter.

32 Article 22 of the Family Protection Bill cited in Elahe Amani, "From Bad to Worse and Beyond . . . Widespread Opposition to 'Iran's Family Protection Bill'," *Iran Women Solidarity*, Friday 15 August 2008, online www.iran-women-solidarity.net/spip.php?article430, (accessed 5 March 2016). See also "Gozaresh Shor Aval (the Report of the First Council): Gozaresh Commission Gahazei va Hughughi be Majlis Shoray-e Eslami (the Report of the Legal and Juridicial Commission to the Islamic Consultative Assembly)," *Majlis Shorya-e Eslami*, 31 July 2008, 8.

33 Article 22 has become article 20 in the 2012 bill.

The question remains as to whether this article benefits or harms women. On the one hand it protects children born out of wedlock, but it does not provide additional support for women contracting temporary marriage, who are not entitled to *nafaqa* (maintenance), *irth* (inheritance) or divorce.[34] The inclusion of articles on temporary marriage was challenged by the women's coalition. They demanded a restriction of laws pertaining to temporary marriage or a total prohibition of the custom.

Article 23, as it was first presented to the *majlis*, supported polygamous marriages, depending on the man's financial resources. It stated "marriage to a subsequent permanent wife shall depend on court authorization upon ascertainment of man's financial capability and undertaking to uphold justice among his wives."[35] This article was modified in December 2009 to allow a man to marry more than one wife pending ten conditions, including the permission of the first wife.[36] However, the article was removed from the 2012 bill. The article 23 enacted in the 2013 law deals with the health of the couple, in particular, transmittable diseases.[37] Although the article on polygamy was removed, the new law stays largely silent on the specifics of polygamous marriages. However, there are mentions of *ezdevj mojadad* (remarriage, refers to polygamous marriages) in article 4. Article 4 names *ezdevaj mojadad* as one of the eighteen issues that the family court has the competency to consider. Article 56 states that registry office approval and

34 See Maryam Hosseinkhah, "Eblagh Ghanoon Hemayat az Khanevadeh (Notification of the Family Protection Law)," *Radio Zamaneh*, 12 April 2014, online www.radiozamaneh.com/62674, (accessed 1 April 2016).

35 Article 23 Family Protection Bill cited in Elahe Amani, "From Bad to Worse and Beyond . . . Widespread Opposition to 'Iran's Family Protection Bill'," *Iran Women Solidarity*, Friday 15 August 2008, online www.iran-women-solidarity.net/spip.php?article430, (accessed 5 March 2016). See also "Gozaresh Shor Aval (the Report of the First Council): Gozaresh Commission Gahazei va Hughughi be Majlis Shoray-e Eslami (the Report of the Legal and Juridicial Commission to the Islamic Consultative Assembly)," *Majlis Shorya-e Eslami*, 31 July 2008, 8.

36 These are: "1. Permission from the first wife; 2. Inability of the wife to perform her marital duties; 3. Continued disobedience of the wife following a court order; 4. Madness or incurable disease; 5. Confirmed conviction to a year's custodial term or a cash fine the non-payment of which carries a year's custodial sentence; 6. Addiction that according to the court's judgement, impairs family life; 7. Unacceptable behaviour or relationships that cannot be tolerated by the husband, leading to the irrevocable breakdown of the marriage; 8. Abandoning marital life for six months; 9. Barren woman; 10. Absence of wife for one year." See "A statement by equal rights defenders in protest against article 23 of Family Protection Bill: "Prohibit Polygamy!" *Ta Ghanoon Barabar Khanevadeh*, 23 September 2010. Note, however, that condition no. 7 along with article 24 (regarding the amount of *mahr*) were deleted in the latest meeting of the private law committee of the *majlis*, See "Madeye 24 va band 7 madeye 23 layeheye hemayat az khanevadeh hazf shod," *Fars News*, 28 October 2010.

37 "Layehey-e Hemayat az Khanevadeh (Family Protection Bill)," *Majlis Shorya-e Eslami*, 2 April 2012, online http://rc.majlis.ir/fa/law/show/840814 (accessed 29 July 2016). See also the 2013 Family Protection Law Published (Ghanoon Hemayat Khanevadeh), online www.rooznamehrasmi.ir/laws/ShowLaw.aspx?Code=847, (accessed 5 March 2016).

recording of marriages, including *ezdevaj mojadad*, should be in accordance with existing laws.

Article 25 in the drafted bill imposed taxation on the amount of *mahr* received by the woman. The article read "at the time of registration of marriage, the Ministry of Economic Affairs and Finance is required to collect tax on unreasonable and higher-than-conventional marriage portions, in view of the condition of the couple and the national economic issues. . . ."[38] Article 25 was also removed from the 2012 bill. Article 22, the relevant article in the new law around questions of *mahr*, does not contain the taxation language.

Marriage: permanent and temporary

It is no coincidence that the most contentious sections of the 2013 Family Protection Law dealt with marriage and divorce. Marriage and divorce in Islam tend to be controversial subjects where women's rights are concerned. In Islam marriage is a form of contract.[39] According to Mir-Hosseini:

> . . . the disparity between men's and women's rights in Muslim societies was – and still is – sustained largely through rules that classical jurists devised for regulating the formation and termination of the marriage contract. In this respect, there is no major difference among the various *fiqh* schools: all share the same inner logic and conception of the family. If they differ it is in the way and the extent to which this conception is translated into legal rules.[40]

The contract of marriage in Islam is governed by Islamic contract law and is "subject to the same regulations as other contracts."[41] As in the Qur'an, where

38 Article 25 Family Protection Bill cited in Elahe Amani, "From Bad to Worse and Beyond . . . Widespread Opposition to 'Iran's Family Protection Bill'" *Iran Women Solidarity*, Friday 15 August 2008, online www.iran-women-solidarity.net/spip.php?article430, (accessed 5 March 2016). See also "Gozaresh Shor Aval (the Report of the First Council): Gozaresh Commission Gahazei va Hughughi be Majlis Shoray-e Eslami (the Report of the Legal and Juridicial Commission to the Islamic Consultative Assembly)," *Majlis Shorya-e Eslami*, 31 July 2008, 8.

39 Although many scholars deem marriage in Islam as a contract, there are those such as Ayatollah Murteza Mutahari who regard the contract of marriage in Islam as one different to other socio-economic contracts. A marriage contract, in his opinion, is regulated by nature and instinct and has its own distinct mechanism. For more see Morteza Mutahari, *Nezam-e Hughugh Zan dar Islam (The Rights of Women in Islam)*, 45th ed. (Tehran: Sadra Publication, 2007), 247–248.

40 Ziba Mir-Hosseini, "The Construction of Gender in Islamic Legal Thought and Strategies for Reform," *Hawwa* 1 (2003), 4.

41 Nayer Honarvar, "Behind the Veil: Women's Rights in Islamic Societies," *Journal of Family Law* 6 (1988), 368. See also Tamilla F. Ghodsi, "Tying a Slipknot: Temporary Marriages in Iran," *Michigan Journal of International Law*15 (1993–1994), 663. See Majid Khadduri, "Marriage in Islamic Law: The Modernist Viewpoints," *American Journal of Comparative Law* 26, no. 2 (1978), 213.

there are numerous verses which deal with marriage and divorce,[42] the Iranian Civil Code also has a number of provisions regulating the marriage contract based mainly on *imami* (*ithna 'ashari*) Shi'a *fiqh* including: the courtship and engagement of a suitable woman (articles 1034–1040); the age of marriage (articles 1041–1044); marriage restrictions (articles 1045–1061) and polygamy and temporary marriage (articles 1075–1077). The Iranian Civil Code recognizes both temporary (*mut'a* or *sigheh*) and permanent (*nekah*) marriage contracts. This creates an interesting and complicated notion of the family, as well as an expansive notion of legitimate sexual relations.[43]

According to Ayatollah Khomeini, "by means of a marriage contract, a woman becomes lawful to a man and this may be in two forms, permanent and nonpermanent".[44] Khomeini defines permanent and temporary marriages according to the duration of the contract:

> . . . the permanent contract is that in which the duration of matrimony is not specified and the woman who is contracted for in this form is called "permanent". The nonpermanent contract is that in which the duration of matrimony is specified. For example, the woman is contracted for a period of one hour or one day or one month or one year or more. The woman who is contracted for in this form is called "*mot'e*" [*mut'a*] or "*sigheh*".[45]

Similar to other Islamic contracts, for the marriage contract (temporary or permanent) to be valid an act of offer (*iijab*) is to be made by the woman and an act of acceptance (*ghabool*) is to be made by the man in the same session.[46] Haeri writes "an act of 'offer' involves uttering a ritualistic formula by the woman and 'acceptance' involves a similar formulaic reply by the husband."[47]

42 For verses on marriage see 2:221, 2:230, 2:235, 2:237, 4:4, 4:6, 4:23, 4:25, 5:5, 23:6, 24:30, 24:60, 25:54, 33:37, 33:50 and 60:10, and for divorce refer to verses 2:227, 2:229, 2.230, 2:231, 2:232, 2:236, 33:4, 33:37, 33:49, 58:2, 58:3, 65:1 and 66:5.

43 It is noteworthy that the Iranian government actively promotes both permanent and temporary marriages. Women's roles as mothers and procreators were in particular promoted during the Iran and Iraq War (1980–1988). During this time families were encouraged to have more children and, according to Eliz Sansarian, "several *ulama* declared abortion and most forms of birth control unIslamic". This led to an uncontrollable population growth and forced the government to change its policies on population control. Refer to Eliz Sansarian, "The Politics of Gender and Development in the Islamic Republic of Iran," *Journal of Developing Societies* 8 (1992), 61–62. See also Hooma Hoodfar, "Bargaining with Fundamentalism, Women and the Politics of Population Control in Iran," *Reproductive Health Matters* 8 (November 1996), 30–40.

44 Tamilla F. Ghodsi, "Tying a Slipknot: Temporary Marriages in Iran," *Michigan Journal of International Law* 15 (1993–1994), 645.

45 Ibid., 661.

46 Article 1062 Civil Code.

47 Shahla Haeri, *Laws of Desire: Temporary Marriage in Shi'i Iran* (Syracuse, NY: Syracuse University Press, 1989), 36.

It is important to note that a woman's consent in marriage is necessary for the marriage to be legal.[48] A virgin requires her father's (or guardian's) permission to be wed; however, in some cases she can refer to the court for permission to marry without the father's permission. These cases are contingent on the discretion of the judges.[49]

After consummation of marriage, according to different Islamic traditions, the husband and wife have their own particular rights and duties. These rights and duties complement each other but are not equal or similar. According to Sahereh Labriz and Shokofeh Shekary, the duties of spouses to each other are companionship (*hosn-e moasherat*),[50] cooperation in strengthening the family unit and bringing up children, and faithfulness. The husband in a permanent marriage is the head of the household and as such is required to pay *nafaqa* (maintenance) to the wife, and is required to engage in intercourse with his wife. The duty of the wife is to be obedient or submissive (*tamkin*) and live in her husband's house.[51]

In most Muslim-majority countries therefore, Iran included, the headship of a household is designated to the husband.[52] Pursuant to this, a woman has the duty to obey her husband. On the other hand, the man who is designated the head of the household is obliged to provide maintenance, or *nafaqa*, for his wife. Article 1107 of the Iranian Civil Code defines *nafaqa* as "the cost of maintenance which includes dwelling, clothing, food, furniture in proportion to the situation of the wife, on a reasonable basis, and provision of a servant if the wife is accustomed to have servants or if she needs one because of illness or defects of limbs." *Nafaqa* is therefore regarded by some as the right of the wife and the duty of the husband, whereas obedience is seen as the duty of the wife and the right of the husband. *Nafaqa* is, however, only the

48 Article 1070 Civil Code, although in practice forced or arranged marriages do still take place in some communities in Iran. The following two *ahadith* may be used when a women's consent to marriage is in question:

> Narrated by Abu Huraira:
>
> The Prophet said, "A matron should not be given in marriage except after consulting her; and a virgin should not be given in marriage except after her permission." The people asked, "O Allah's Apostle! How can we know her permission?" He said, "Her silence (indicates her permission)."
>
> Narrated by Khansa bint Khidam Al-Ansariya:
>
> That her father gave her in marriage when she was a matron and she disliked that marriage. So she went to Allah's Apostle and he declared that marriage invalid.

49 Article1043 Iranian Civil Code, reformed 1991.

50 Article 1103 Iranian Civil Code.

51 Shokofeh Shekary and Sahereh Labriz, "Tamkin (Submission)," *Zanan*, no. 1 (1992), 58. Translations of this article are my own.

52 Article 1105 of the Iranian Civil Code.

entitlement of a permanent wife. In a temporary marriage the husband is not obliged to pay *nafaqa* unless it has been stipulated in the prenuptial contract. This is significant as article 1129 of the Iranian Civil Code states:

> If the husband refuses to pay the cost of maintenance (*nafaqa*) of his wife, and if it is impossible to enforce a judgement of the court and to induce him to pay the expenses, the wife can refer to the judge applying for divorce and the judge will compel the husband to divorce her. The same stipulation will be binding in a case where the husband is unable to provide for the maintenance of the wife.

Although the civil code does not articulate the penalty for the non-payment of *nafaqa*, both the Iranian Penal Code and the 2013 Family Protection Act clearly define the consequence of the failure to pay *nafaqa*. Article 642 of the *tazirat* section (book five, chapter 19) of the Iranian criminal code asserts "Anyone who fails to pay his wife's *nafaqa* (maintenance), while he has the financial ability, subject to the wife's *tamkin* (obedience), or fails to pay other members of his family that he is legally responsible to pay their *nafaqa*, shall be sentenced by court to three months and one day to five months' imprisonment."[53] Article 53 of the 2012 Family Protection Act asserts that the non-payment of the *nafaq* to an obedient wife or other family members in need of *nafaq* is deemed criminal with reference to the aforementioned article.

Just as a husband's failure to provide *nafaqa* can establish a legal basis for divorce, lack of obedience can lead to financial penalties for the woman. A husband may refuse to pay *nafaqa* (maintenance) on basis of *nushuz* (disloyalty). This also can lead to a husband divorcing his wife. *Tamkin* is the Persian word regularly translated as duty, submission to or obedience. Mir-Hosseini pairs *tamkin* and *nafaqa* when discussing rights and duties:

> *Tamkin*—submission, defined as unhampered sexual access—is a man's right and thus a woman's duty; whereas *nafaqa*—maintenance, defined as shelter, food and clothing—is a woman's right and a man's duty. A woman becomes entitled to *nafaqa* only after consummation of the marriage, and she loses her claim if she is in a state of *Nushuz*.[54]

53 Islamic Penal Code of the Islamic Republic of Iran – Book Five, Iranian Human Rights Documentation Center, online http://iranhrdc.org/english/human-rights-documents/iranian-codes/1000000351-islamic-penal-code-of-the-islamic-republic-of-iran-book-five.html, (accessed 2 March 2016).

54 Ziba Mir-Hosseini, "The Construction of Gender in Islamic Legal Thought and Strategies for Reform," *Hawwa* 1 (2003), 4.

While the word *tamkin* is not explicitly referenced in the Iranian Civil Code, and definitions of *tamkin* vary depending on the *urf* (traditions) of the society in question, legal scholars such as Seyed Hassan Emami[55] and Majid Haeri[56] regard *tamkin* as solely the duty of the wife.[57] According to Shekary and Labriz, the word *tamkin* has a general (*om*) and a particular (*khas*) meaning in its legal definition. In its general, or *om*, definition *tamkin* is the acceptance of the husband's role as the head of the household. It entails respect for his opinions in the upbringing of the children and the running of financial and moral issues of the family. In its particular, or *khas*, definition *tamkin* translates to a woman's submission to intercourse unless there are lawful (*mashroo*) reasons to withdraw from it.[58]

Nushuz (disloyalty)

One of the more controversial verses in the Qur'an with regard to marriage and women's rights is 4:34.[59] According to some traditional translations and interpretations, the verse allows a man to beat his unruly or disloyal (*nasheze*)

55 Iranian Shi'a *Mujtahid Faqih* and legal scholar who studies in Najaf and Switzerland. He was appointed *Imam Jom'e* (the leader of the Friday prayers) of Tehran in 1954 during the reign of Muhammad Reza Shah Pahlavi.

56 Majid Haeri, *Ezdevaj va Talaq dar Eslam va Sayer Adyan* (Tehran: 1985), 77, cited in Shokofeh Shekary and Sahereh Labriz, "Tamkin (Submission)," *Zanan*, no. 1 (1992).

57 Hassan Emami, *Hughugh-e Madani (Civil Law)* (Tehran: Tehran University Publications, 1959), no. 4, 447.

58 *Tamkin* laws explicitly mandating a wife's obedience, apart from Iran, also exist in the Family Code of Algeria, Mali, Sudan and Yemen. Family code of Algeria, article 39, 1984; Marriage and Guardianship Code of Mali, article 32, 1962; Muslim Personal Act of Sudan, 1991; and Yemen's Personal Status Act No. 20, article 40, 1992.

59 Yufufalli's translation of this verse reads as follows:

> Men are the protectors and maintainers (*qawwamoona*) of women, because Allah has given the one more [*faddala*] (strength) than the other, and because they support them from their means. Therefore the righteous women [*qanitat*] are devoutly obedient, and guard in (the husband's) absence what Allah would have them guard. As to those women on whose part ye fear disloyalty (*nushuz*) and ill-conduct, admonish them (first), (Next), refuse to share their beds, (And last) beat them (lightly); but if they return to obedience, seek not against them Means (of annoyance): For Allah is Most High, great (above you all).

Amina Wadud's translation of the same verse is more egalitarian:

> Men are [*qawwamuna 'ala*] women, [on the basis] of what Allah has [preferred] (*faddala*) some of them over others, and [on the basis] of what they spend of their property (for the support of women). So good women are *qanitat*, guarding in secret that which Allah has guarded. As for those from whom you fear [*nushuz*], admonish them, banish them to beds apart, and scourge them. Then, if they obey you, seek not a way against them.

See Amina Wadud, *Qur'an and Woman, Rereading the Sacred Text from a Woman's Perspective* (New York: Oxford University Press, 1999), 70.

wife. Articles 1105, 1107 and 1129 of the Iranian Civil Code are understood to have stemmed from traditional interpretation of verse 4:34 of the Qur'an. According to some translations of this verse, men are maintainers of women and are given the right to beat those (wives) from whom they fear disloyalty (*nushuz*). The word *qawwamoona* from the verse is translated by some scholars as "in charge of"[60] or "managers of the affairs of".[61] Guardianship laws, which are discussed later in this chapter, have stemmed from such translations where men are deemed to be in charge of women's affairs. Yusufalli translates *qawwamoona* as "protectors and maintainers", whereas Aziza al-Hibri interprets *qawwamoona* as "moral guidance and caring". Al-Hibri also refers to the misuse of verse 4:34 by men in order to exercise authority over women, justifying their actions with "divinely ordained and inherent superiority".[62] The Shi'a *mujtahida* Nosrat Amin interprets *qawwamoona* to mean the "dominance of men over women" in her work *Makhzan al-Erfan*, with men also being understood as sustainers of women.[63]

The second part of verse 4:34 is likewise contentious.[64] Ayatollah Sanee'i was asked in an interview about the meaning of verse 4:34 and whether this implied that a man had the right to beat his wife. In response Sanee'i equated *nushuz* with a woman's unwillingness to have intercourse with her husband at his demand. The Ayatollah provided a three-step interpretation of the verse from the husband's perspective: 1. admonish them; 2. refuse to share their bed; 3. beat them as a form of foreplay. Sanee'i went on to explain that if the wife is not willing to have sex, "you ask her nicely. If she is still unwilling you tickle her a bit, and if she is still not willing then may be you lightly beat her with a *misvaak* as to tease her."[65] This interpretation, although less

60 Muhammad M. Pickthall, *The Glorious Qur'an: Text and Explanatory Translation* (New York: Muslim World League, 1977).

61 S. Abul A'la Maududi, *The Meaning of the Qur'an*, 13 vols, 6th ed., ed. A.A. Kamal and trans. Muhammad Akbar (Pakistan: Islamic Publication, 1982), 117.

62 Aziza Al-Hibri, "A Story of Islamic Herstory: Or How Did We Ever Get into This Mess?" *Women and Islam: Women's Studies International Forum Magazine* 5 (1982), 218. Also cited in Amina Wadud, *Qur'an and Woman, Rereading the Sacred Text from a Woman's Perspective* (New York: Oxford University Press, 1999), 71–72.

63 Nosrat Amin, *Makhzan al-Erfan*, online www.banooyeirani.ir/index.php?option=com_content&task=blogcategory&id=134&Itemid=165, (accessed 5 March 2016).

64 Nawal H. Ammar, "Wife Battery in Islam: A Comprehensive Understanding of Interpretations," *Violence against Women* 13, no. 5 (May 2007), 516–526. Ammar distinguishes four different schools of interpretations of verse 4:34. The first school permits wife-beating, the second permits wife-beating but with some consideration for her safety, the third school regards wife-beating as unacceptable in general but permissible under some circumstances and the fourth believes that the verse has been misinterpreted and in no situation is wife-beating allowed.

65 Group interview with Ayatollah Sanee'i, Qom, May 2004 as a part of a course on Islam and Human Rights, organized by the House of Culture and Sustainable Development, Tehran. See also Maryam Hosseinkhah, "Gofto va Shonudhayee darbareye Taarozat Hughugh Zan dar Islam

violent on the whole, still permits beating and regards submission to sexual intercourse as the wife's duty. It is important to note that some studies point to wife-beating as the most common form of violence against women in Muslim-majority communities.[66] This reality demands a thorough reformation of both law and society.

Contracting the contract

Given that marriage is a contract in Islam, there are conditions that can be stipulated before the marriage contract is signed. However, in most Islamic countries, given that patriarchy is the social norm, "women negotiate marriage contracts from unequal bargaining positions".[67] Although enshrined in the law in Iran (Civil Code Article 1119), this practice of negotiating conditions is rarely used.[68] Women more often forgo their right to stipulating certain conditions because of social pressure. Therefore, in Iran women regularly lose certain civil rights once they become married. These include the right to travel, the right to choose their place of domicile (Civil Code Article 1114) and the right to work (Civil Code Article 1117).[69] In other words, they lose particular aspects of their "individuality, autonomy and independence".[70] This is of special concern when the minimum age of marriage is

---

ba Hughoghe Bashar," *Iranian Feminist Tribune* (9 October 2004), republished online https://web.archive.org/web/20050210211959/http://iftribune.com/news.asp?id=7&pass=19, (accessed 29 July 2016). Translation of this article is my own. *Misvaak* translates to toothbrush, but what Sanee'i is referring to is the natural toothbrush *salvadora Persica*.

66 See, for example, Nawal H. Ammar, "Wife Battery in Islam: A Comprehensive Understanding of Interpretations," *Violence against Women* 13, no. 5 (May 2007), 516.

67 Tamilla F. Ghodsi, "Tying a Slipknot: Temporary Marriages in Iran," *Michigan Journal of International Law* 15 (1993–1994), 645. It is also important to note as Aziza Al-Hibri does that "the rise of patriarchy in the Muslim world was not historically an isolated event." The Byzantine and Persian empires based on patriarchal hierarchies greatly influenced the Muslim-Arab patriarchy. For more see Azizah Al-Hibri, "Islam, Law and Custom: Redefining Muslim Women's Rights," *American University International Law Review* 12, no. 1 (1997), 3.

68 In 1987 a new national marriage contract and family law was introduced in which the marriage registrar was obliged to present the contract to both parties. See Homa Hoodfar, "Iranian Women at the Intersection of Citizenship and the Family Code: The Perils of 'Islamic Criteria'" in *Gender and Citizenship in the Middle East*, ed. Suad Joseph (Syracuse, NY: Syracuse University Press, 2000), 310. For a translated version of the Iranian marriage contract, refer to Arzoo Oslanoo, *The Politics of Women's Rights in Iran* (Princeton and Oxford: Princeton University Press, 2009), Appendix. See also Maryam Hosseinkhah, "Shoroot Zemn Aqd ra Framoosh Nakonid (Do Not Forget the Prenuptual Conditions)," *Etemaad* (19 September 2007), 8, online www.magiran.com/npview.asp?ID=1485203, (accessed 29 July 2016).

69 Article 1117 of the Civil Code does not articulate a blanket ban by husbands on women's access to the workforce; rather, it states that a husband may ban his wife from working from certain technical jobs if they deem to conflict with family life or his or her dignity.

70 Azadeh Kian-Thiébaut, "From Motherhood to Equal Rights Advocates: The Weakening of Patriarchal Order," *Iranian Studies* 38, no. 1 (1 March 2005), 46.

low. Most traditionalist interpretations of the Qur'an hold the age of maturity for girls to be nine lunar years and fifteen lunar years for boys. These ages are also regarded by some as the minimum age of marriage and also of criminal responsibility.[71] Some religious scholars believe, however, that the age of puberty for girls begins with the start of their monthly periods. Ayatollah Jannaati issued the following *fatwa* regarding the age of puberty for girls: "Puberty in girls begins with the start of their monthly period. If for medical reasons they do not have monthly periods, they should then refer to the period of their female family members and accordingly set the age of puberty for themselves."[72] In 2000 a bill was passed by the sixth *majlis* (parliament) which proposed that the minimum age of marriage for girls and boys be raised to eighteen years of age,[73] with a provision that if a girl of fifteen wishes to marry, she could acquire a permit from the court. The bill was vetoed by the Guardian Council (*Shoray-e Negahban*), yet the *majlis* did not revoke the law. This led to a dispute with the Expediency Council (*Shoray-e Maslehat-e Nezam*).[74] Consequently on 22 June 2002 the law was reformed in the following way after an endorsement by the Expediency Council: "Marriage of a girl less than the age of 13 and a boy less than the age of 15 is dependent on the consent of their guardian and also contingent

71 These ages differ depending on the state's legislations; for example, in Bangladesh, the Kyrgyz Republic and Turkey (sixteen, with court permission), the age of marriage is eighteen. In Indonesia if under age twenty-one, both parties require the permission of their parents (minimum age for marriage is sixteen for girls and nineteen for boys). For details on age of marriage in Muslim-majority countries, see "Knowing Our Rights: Women, Family, Laws and Customs in the Muslim World," (Women Living under Muslim Laws, 2006), online www.wluml.org/sites/wluml.org/files/import/english/pubs/pdf/knowing%20our%20rights/kor_2006_en.pdf, (accessed 5 March 2016).

72 Mohammad Ibrahim Jannaati, "Fataway-e Montakheb (Selected Fatwas)," *The Official Website of Ayatollah Jannaati*, online http://jannaati.com/far/index.php?page=6, (accessed 28 July 2016). Translation of the *fatwa* is my own.

73 In accordance with the International Convention on the Rights of the Child (ICRC) to which Iran is a party, Article 1 of ICRC states "For the purposes of the present Convention, a child means every human being below the age of eighteen years unless the law applicable to the child, majority is attained earlier." Iran ratified ICRC on 13 July 1994, with no reservation. International Convention on the Rights of the Child, G.A. res. 44/25, annex 44 U.N. GAOR Supp. (No. 49) at 167, U.N. Doc. A/44/49 (1989), entered into force 2 September 1990 (ICRC from hereinafter).

74 It is imperative to note that Zohreh Sefāti, a female *mujtahida*, was consulted by the Expediency Council to ascertain the age of maturity. As Künkler and Fazaeli write, Sefāti differentiates between the age of *taklif* (duty – where one is obliged to perform her/his religious duties) and the age of marriage. She believes that the age of *taklif* should remain the same (nine for girls and fifteen for boys), basing her assumptions on a number of *ravayat*. Refer to Mirjam Künkler and Roja Fazaeli, "The Life of Two Mujtahidas: Female Religious Authority in 20th Century Iran" in *Women, Leadership and Mosques: Changes in Contemporary Islamic Authority*, ed. Masooda Bano and Hilary Kalmbach (The Hague: Brill, 2011), 127–160.

on the court (*be sharte raayat maslehat ba tashkhise dadgahe saleh*)."[75] It is imperative to note that a previously unmarried girl (virgin) who is above the age of thirteen needs the permission of her guardian (her father, or paternal grandfather in the case of a father's death) to marry.[76] If the guardian does not give her permission and does not clarify his reasons, the girl can subsequently seek a court permit to marry her chosen partner. However, the permission is contingent on the discretion of the judge and is difficult to obtain.[77]

Mahr

Mahr (bride price or the gift to the bride)[78] is another fundamental part of an Islamic marriage contract which is thought to have pre-Islamic roots.[79] *Mahr* is a sum (it could also be property) which is traditionally negotiated by the parents of the bride and groom, but is intended as a gift to the bride for the marriage. Although the sum of *mahr* is legally agreed to during the contracting of the marriage, in practice the amount is agreed to as a prerequisite of the marriage. Ebadi defines *mahr* "as the asset, which becomes that of a woman after a permanent or temporary marriage".[80] According to Article 1078 of the Iranian Civil Code, whatever is taxable and can be owned can be proposed as *mahr*.[81] Although the woman is entitled to ask for her *mahr*

75 Shirin Ebadi, *Huqu-e Zan Dar Ghavanin-e Jomhoriye Islamiy-e Iran (Women's Rights, in the Laws of the Islamic Republic of Iran)* (Tehran: Ganje Danesh Publication, 2002). Translations are my own.

76 Haleh Afshar citing Khomeini writes "According to Khomeini the only practical way of curbing the destructive powers of women is to marry them young and make sure that they have their first menstruation in the husband's house". Haleh Afshar, "Behind the Veil: The Public and Private Faces of Khomeini's Policies on Iranian Women" in *Women and Islam, Critical Concepts in Sociology*, Vol. III, Women's Movements in Muslim Societies, ed. Haideh Moghissi (London and New York: Routledge, 2005), 78.

77 Iranian Civil Code Article 1043, article 1044 is also notable as it states that in the absence of a guardian where the girl is unable to get his permission for marriage and the girl is in need of marriage then she could take necessary measures (court permit) to marry. See Shirin Ebadi, *Huqu-e Zan Dar Ghavanin-e Jomhoriye Islamiy-e Iran (Women's Rights, in the Laws of the Islamic Republic of Iran)* (Tehran: Ganje Danesh Publication, 2002), 110–111. Also note that a man who marries a girl under the age of thirteen without her guardian's permission is liable to 6 months to 2 years' imprisonment (Article 646 former Iranian Islamic Criminal Code).

78 The Arabic *mahr* and Persian *mehriye* are used interchangeably in this text.

79 See, for example, Murteza Mutahari, *Nezam-e Hughugh Zan dar Islam (The Rights of Women in Islam)*, 45th ed. (Tehran: Sadra Publishers, June 2007), 180–184.

80 Shirin Ebadi, *Huqu-e Zan Dar Ghavanin-e Jomhoriye Islamiy-e Iran (Women's Rights, in the Laws of the Islamic Republic of Iran)* (Tehran: Ganje Danesh Publication, 2002), 103.

81 According to Ebadi, conceptual romanticisms such as the loving heart of the husband or the first spring breeze, which are not taxable, are not accounted as *mahr*. Ibid.

anytime after the marriage,[82] it usually is not demanded unless the couple decides to divorce. Instead, this Qur'anic injunction is followed:

> And give the women (on marriage) their dower[83] as a free gift; but if they, of their own good pleasure, remit any part of it to you, Take it and enjoy it with right good cheer.[84]

Ebadi categorizes two types of *mahr*. The first is *mahr al-mesmi*, in which the *mahr* is agreed upon during the contracting of the marriage, and the second is *mahr ul-mesl*, which is the amount the bride is entitled to where no amount of *mahr* has been previously specified. As Ghodsi writes, for some "brideprice is perceived to be the consideration given for the object of the sale, the woman."[85] Haeri continues this logic when she contends ". . . *nekah* is a contract for the ownership, *tamlik*, of the use of [the] vagina."[86] Nonetheless, article 1092 of the Iranian Civil Code makes clear that a woman is entitled to half of her *mahr* in the event of a divorce before the consummation of marriage, thereby lessening, if only slightly, the woman's status as *milk* (possession).

Regarding amount, Article 22 of the 2013 family protection law states:

> If the amount of *mehriye*[87] during the contracting of *aqd* is one hundred and ten gold coins (*sekey-e tamam bahar azadi*), its being claimed (by the wife) will be subject to Article 2 of laws enforcing financial convictions (*ghanoon ejray-e mahkomiyathay-e mali*). If the *mehriye* is more than this amount, in case of a surplus, the criteria of payment of *mehriye* will depend on the husband's solvency. The observance of the regulations of calculating *mehriye* at the present rate is compulsory.[88]

82 Iranian Civil Code 1082.

83 Dower here is *mahr*.

84 Qur'an 4:4. Another Qur'anic verse on *mahr* states the following:

> "But if ye decide to take one wife in place of another, even if ye had given the latter a whole treasure for dower, Take not the least bit of it back: Would ye take it by slander and manifest wrong?" (4:20)

85 Tamilla F. Ghodsi, "Tying a Slipknot: Temporary Marriages in Iran," *Michigan Journal of International Law*15 (1993–1994), 665.

86 Shahla Haeri, *Laws of Desire: Temporary Marriage in Shi'i Iran* (Syracuse, NY: Syracuse University Press, 1989), 34.

87 *Mehriye* is the Persian for *mahr*.

88 See also the 2013 Family Protection Law (Ghanoon Hemayat Khanevadeh), online www.rooznamehrasmi.ir/laws/ShowLaw.aspx?Code=847, (accessed 5 March 2016).

Therefore, a man who is not able to pay a *mehriye* of more than 110 gold coins will not be imprisoned under the sentence set out in Article 2 of the law enforcing financial convictions.[89]

Whether *mahr* is seen as brideprice or a gift to the bride, it has become a bargaining chip and a sign of prestige; the higher the *mahr*, the more prestige a family gains. This has become problematic for younger men who wish to enter a marriage contract as at times the *mahr* stipulated is incredibly high. Sometimes this *mahr* is regarded as a form of protection for women against divorce. If a man wishes to divorce his wife he has to pay her *mahr*, and some believe that if the *mahr* is too high then he will forgo the divorce. The *mahr* is also considered as financial support for a woman after a divorce. In a group interview with Ayatollah Saane'i[90] a young Iranian man asked the ayatollah how he might marry a woman he loved, but whose *mahr* was beyond his means. The ayatollah answered that the young man should not try to wed someone above his social and financial status. Saane'i's statement is in line with Article 1091 of the Iranian Civil Code, which states: "in the fixing of the reasonable marriage portion, the status of the wife in respect to her family's station, and other circumstances and peculiarities concerning her in comparison with her equals and relatives, and also the customs of the locality, et cetera, must be considered."[91] To regulate the amount of *mahr*, Iranian Civil Code Article 1085 was amended in 1998 and an equation based on rate of inflation was introduced to calculate *mahr*.[92]

89 "Laws Enforcing Financial Convictions," online www.dadkhahi.net/law/Ghavanin/Ghavaninn_Madani/Ganoon_nahve_ejraye_mahkomiyathaye_mali.htm

90 As a part of a course on Islam and Human Rights, organized by the House of Culture and Sustainable Development, Tehran, we visited the house of Ayatollah Saane'i in Qom in May 2004. The proceeding of the first interview is published in See also Maryam Hosseinkhah, "Goftegoo va Shonudhayee darbareye Taarozat Hughugh-e Zan dar Islam ba Hughoghe Bashar," *Iranian Feminist Tribune* (9 October 2004).

91 Articles 1078 to 1102 of the Iranian Civil Code also deal with the issue of *mahr*. Article 1082 states that "immediately after the performance of the marriage ceremony the wife becomes the owner of the marriage portion (*mahr*) and can dispose of it in any way and manner that she may like." As mentioned earlier, it is unlikely that a woman would ask for her *mahr* before a divorce. Consequently, Article 1085 declares that "so long as the marriage portion (*mahr*) is not delivered to her, the wife can refuse to fulfil the duties which she has to her husband, provided that the marriage portion is payable at once. This refusal does not debar her from right of maintenance expenses."

92 The equation is the amount of *mahr* at the time of the wedding multiplied by the indicator number in the previous year divided by the indicator number at the time of the wedding, the result of which equals the present value of the *mahr*. The indicators are correlated to the amount of inflation. For a table of indicator values from 1936 to 2001 see Shirin Ebadi, *Huqu-e Zan Dar Ghavanin-e Jomhoriye Islamiy-e Iran (Women's Rights, in the Laws of the Islamic Republic of Iran)* (Tehran: Ganje Danesh Publication, 2002), 108. As previously mentioned, Article 25 of the Family Protection Bill 2007 imposes tax on the amount of *mahr* received by the woman.

Irs *(Inheritance)*

The laws of inheritance in Iran are based on the principle that the share of inheritance of a man is twice that of a woman.[93] Article 906 of the Civil Code holds that:

> If the deceased has left no living children, and no living children's children of whatever degree, either of the parents, if alone, takes the whole estate; and if the father and mother of the deceased are both alive, the mother takes one-third and the father two-thirds. But if the mother comes after someone else, one-sixth of the estate belongs to the mother and the rest to the father.

Article 907 also states that:

> If the deceased leaves no parents, but has one or more children, the estate will be divided as follows: If the offspring consists of only one, whether son or daughter, the whole of the estate belongs to that child. If there are several children, but all are sons or all daughters, the estate will be divided equally among them. If there are several children, some being sons and some daughters each son takes twice as much as each daughter.

Articles 892, 911, 920 and 923, under different terms, affirm that the inheritance of a woman is half that of a man. These laws often justify their basis with the Qur'anic verse 4:11:[94]

> Allah (thus) directs you as regards your Children's (Inheritance): to the male, a portion equal to that of two females: if only daughters, two or more, their share is two-thirds of the inheritance; if only one, her share is a half. For parents, a sixth share of the inheritance to each, if the deceased left children; if no children, and the parents are the (only) heirs, the mother has a third; if the deceased Left brothers (or sisters) the mother has a sixth. (The distribution in all cases ('s) after the payment of legacies and debts. Ye know not whether your parents or your children are nearest to you in benefit. These are settled portions ordained by Allah; and Allah is All-knowing, All-wise.

93 It is important to note here that Shi'a and Sunni scholars' view on inheritance differs significantly. For more see A.A.A. Fayzee, *Outlines of Muhammadan Law*, 4th ed. (Oxford: Oxford University Press, 1974). See also Muhammad Ja'far Ja'fari Langarudi, *Irs (Inheritance)*, 2 Vols. (Tehran: Amir Kabir Press, 1978).

94 See also Qur'an 4:10, 4:11 and 4:12.

This verse, although discriminatory against women, should also be read in historical context. At the time of its writing it represented a significant improvement in women's status, challenging a social norm in which no share of family inheritance was given to women.

Articles 940 to 948 of the Iranian Civil Code relate to questions of inheritance for permanently married spouses. In 2004 the Guardian Council rejected the idea of any amendments to these articles. However, after issuance of a *fatwa* by the Supreme Leader Ayatollah Khamenei affirming women's entitlement to inherit land, buildings and trees, some of these articles were amended in 2009, and Article 947 was repealed in 2011. Before the amendments and repeal the husband could inherit all of the wife's estate, while the wife was only able to inherit movable properties and the price of buildings and trees. Following the amendments the wife can inherit movable and immovable properties, but the inheritance laws are still largely written in favour of the husband. Of note, it is only in permanent marriages where the spouses inherit from each other. In temporary marriages they do not.

Temporary marriages

Mut'a, also known as *sigheh*, or temporary marriage,[95] is a practice that is supported by the majority of the Shi'a *imami ulama*.[96] The Arabic term *mut'a* translates to "enjoyment, pleasure, delight".[97] *Mut'a*, like permanent *nekah* (marriage), is a form of contract and requires "an act of *ijab* (offer) made by the woman and *Ghabul* (acceptance) made by the man".[98] The contract itself can last any period of *ajal* (time) as long as the period has been stipulated in the marriage contract. Murata explains that "there is no upper or lower limit to the duration of the time period. In other words, any time period is permissible, so long as both sides are aware of the situation and are satisfied."[99] It is

95 Please note that the terms *mut'a, sigheh* and *ezdevaj-e movaghat* are used interchangeably.

96 While this applies for the majority of the *Shi'a imami ulama*, the practice of *mut'a* is strongly prohibited for the *Shi'a Ismailis* of South Africa. *Mut'a* is also thought to be practiced by *Sunnis*. Temporary marriages have also been reported between women from poor Egyptian families and wealthy Arabs from the Gulf region; also in Algeria there are reported kidnappings of women under the pretext of temporary marriage. Refer to Mohamed Y. Mattar, "Trafficking in Persons, Especially Women and Children, in Countries of the Middle East: The Scope of the Problem and the Appropriate Legislative Responses," *Fordham International Law Journal* 26 (2003), 721–60. See J.P. Mills, "The Custom of Temporary Marriage among the Eastern Angami Nagas of Assam," *Man* 37 (August 1937), 122–123.

97 Sachiki Murata, *Izdiwaj-I muwaqqat (Mut'a Sigheh) (Temporary Marriage in Islamic Law)* (Tehran: Hamdami, 1979). Refer to Chapter 2 on the four pillars of *mut'a*.

98 Shahla Haeri, *Laws of Desire: Temporary Marriage in Shi'i Iran* (Syracuse, NY: Syracuse University Press, 1989), 51.

99 Sachiki Murata, *Izdiwaj-I muwaqqat (Mut'a Sigheh) (Temporary Marriage in Islamic Law)* (Tehran: Hamdami, 1979). Refer to Chapter 2 on the four pillars of *mut'a*.

generally believed that *mut'a* can last anywhere from one hour to ninety-nine years.[100] In contrast to permanent marriage, there is no need for witnesses while contracting *mut'a*. Therefore, two individuals of the opposite sex can perform *mut'a* themselves as long as they are aware of the terms of the contract. The contract terminates at the end of the specified duration, making divorce redundant. However, as noted by both Ghodsi and Haeri, "the revision or a unilateral termination by the temporary husband can also terminate the contract."[101]

According to Murteza Mutahari,[102] there is *ijma* (consensus) among Islamic scholars that *mut'a* was permitted by Muhammad when men were far from their wives and in discomfort.[103] However, some Sunni scholars suggest that the practice was prohibited by Muhammad at a later stage of his life.[104] *Mut'a* was also prohibited by the second Caliph Umar. The Shi'a scholar Mutahari perceives Umar's prohibition to have been politically motivated rather than legally grounded, and therefore considers it a temporary ruling rather than a binding precedent. Umar is said to have feared the dispersion of *sahab* (companions) in the newly conquered Islamic state and was of the opinion that the *sahab* should not enter into blood relationships with the newly converted Muslims before these converts acquired an Islamic education.[105] He therefore prohibited them from contracting temporary marriages. Other Shi'a clergy have interpreted Umar's banning of *mut'a* as "a personal vendetta against Imam Ali, who had allegedly made a short-term contract of *mut'a* marriage with Umar's sister".[106] Therefore, *mut'a* has been a contentious

100 See, for example, Shahla Haeri, *Laws of Desire: Temporary Marriage in Shi'i Iran* (Syracuse, NY: Syracuse University Press, 1989), 2. *Also,* Yusuf Sanee'i (Ayatollah), "A Selection of Islamic Laws," trans. Muhammad Yasser Kimyaei Far, online http://saanei9.tk/pictures/books/pdf/mon-ahkam-en.pdf, (accessed 28 July 2016), 121.

101 Tamilla F. Ghodsi, "Tying a Slipknot: Temporary Marriages in Iran," *Michigan Journal of International Law* 15 (1993–1994), 645. Shahla Haeri, *Laws of Desire: Temporary Marriage in Shi'i Iran* (Syracuse, NY: Syracuse University Press, 1989), 53.

102 Ayatollah Mutahari's views on temporary marriage are particularly important as his book, *The Rights of Women in Islam*, is regarded as the cornerstone of the Islamic Republic's policy on women. For more see Murteza Mutahari, *Nezam-e Hughugh-e Zan dar Islam (The Rights of Women in Islam)*, 45th ed. (Tehran: Sadra Publishers, June 2007).

103 A *hadith* credited to 'Abdullah ibn-i Mas'ud documented in Mussallam states, "We had gone to war. No Woman with us. We asked the Prophet to allow us to castrate ourselves. The Prophet did not permit that, but instructed us to *mut'a* women for a piece of clothe and a specified period." Cited in Shahla Haeri, *Laws of Desire: Temporary Marriage in Shi'i Iran* (Syracuse, NY: Syracuse University Press, 1989), 81.

104 Morteza Mutahari, *Nezam-e Hughugh-e Zan dar Islam (The Rights of Women in Islam)*, 45th ed. (Tehran: Sadra Publication, 2007), 66–67. Translation is my own. See also English edition Murteza Mutahhari, *The Rights of Women in Islam*, 51–52.

105 Ibid.

106 Dr. Hujjat al-Islam Anvari cited in Shahla Haeri, *Laws of Desire: Temporary Marriage in Shi'i Iran* (Syracuse, NY: Syracuse University Press, 1989), 183.

and much debated topic between Shi'as and Sunnis. Presently *mut'a* is lawful in the *ithna 'ashari* (*jafari*) tradition, but not permitted by other *madhahib* (schools of Islamic jurisprudence). Shi'a Muslims employ many *ahadith*, in particular from Imam Ja'far-e Sadiq, in favour of *mut'a*.[107] Sunni Muslims also have a number of *ahadith* in the collections of *Sahih* Bukhari and *Sahih* Muslim that support the banning of *mut'a*.[108] Umar's prohibition has legal standing for Sunni Muslims to this date. Shi'a imams, on the other hand, have sustained the practice of *mut'a* according to their *ahadith*. Today it remains widely supported by Shi'a clergy and consequently by the Iranian state.[109]

The Islamic Republic's support of *mut'a* is enshrined in the Iranian Civil Code where it is both defined and regulated.[110] This is not to say that *mut'a* was illegal before the revolution. Nasir al-Din Shah of the Qajar dynasty reportedly had *sigheh* wives who he took on his travels.[111] However, it was only after the Islamic Revolution that *mut'a* became a more public practice supported by the government.

Haeri demonstrates that *mut'a* in Iran was practiced widely in the holy cities of Qom and Mashahd because of the many pilgrims there.[112] In fact, many Shi'a clerics are very positively disposed towards the institution of

107 For example, Imam Sadiq reportedly stated that "every drop of the ablution water transforms into seventy angels who will then testify on the Day of Judgement on behalf of he who has practiced *mut'a*." He is also reputed to have said, "I never dissimulate, taqiyyih, on the subject of *mut'a*." See Ibid., 7. See also Sadiq Ardistani, *Islam va Masa'il-I Jinsi va Zanashui (Islam and Sexual and Marital Issues)* (Tehran: Khizir Press, n.d.), 236. See also Hasan Muhammad, "Izdivaj-I Muvaqqat dar Islam va Savab-i an (Temporary Marriage and Its Reward)" in *Izdivaj-I Muvaqqat dar Islam (Temporary Marriage in Islam)*, ed. Tabataba'i et al. (Qom: Imam Sadiq Press, 1985), 144–147. See also Ali Qa'imi, *Tashkil-I Khanivadih dar Islam (Creating Family in Islam)* (Qom: Dar al Tabliqat-I Islami Press, 1974), 297.

108 For example, there are a few *ahadith* that relate the practice of *mut'a* to that of eating donkey's flesh. See Sahih Bukhari, Volume 7, Book 67, Number 432. Also Sahih Bukhari, Volume 9, Book 86, Numbers 90 and 91. See also Sahih Muslim, Book 008, Numbers 3266 and 3267. Interestingly one such *hadith* is said to have been attributed to Imam Ali who in the Shi'a tradition is regarded as a proponent of temporary marriage: "Malik narrated this hadith on the authority of the same chain of transmitters that 'Ali b. Abi Talib said to a person: You are a person led astray; Allah's Messenger (may peace be upon him) forbade us (to do *mut'a*), as is stated in the *hadith* transmitted on the authority of Yahya b. Malik." See Sahih Muslim, Book 008, Numbers 3264 and 3267.

109 Ibid.

110 Articles 1075, 1076, 1077, 1096, 1097, 1098 and 1099 of the Iranian Civil Code deal with temporary marriage.

111 Shahla Haeri, *Laws of Desire: Temporary Marriage in Shi'i Iran* (Syracuse, NY: Syracuse University Press, 1989), 82.

112 Ibid.

temporary marriage. Murteza Mutahari, like Ali Shari'ati,[113] contends both men and women have more freedom in a temporary marriage than in a permanent marriage. He states "one of the brilliant laws of the *Jafari* school of thought—which is the established tradition in our country—is that marriage can be established in two ways: permanently and temporarily."[114] Mutahari regarded temporary marriage as "'free' of limits (*hudud*) and obligation (*quyud*)".[115] This freedom has positive and negative consequences for women's rights. Whereas in a permanent marriage the man is automatically designated head of the household, in temporary marriage the couple may agree otherwise, for example, if a man is not financially capable of providing for the woman or the woman does not want to use the man's money. While in a permanent marriage, the husband and wife automatically inherit from each other, the same is not true in the case of temporary marriage.[116] Whereas in a permanent marriage neither of the spouses is allowed to use contraception without the permission of the other, in temporary marriage such permissions are not necessary. Nonetheless, a child born out of a *sigheh* contract is legitimate and has the same rights as a child born in a permanent marriage.[117]

Mutahari and his clerical followers believe that nullification of *mut'a* would entail "hundreds of evils".[118] In response to an article in *Zan-e Ruz* where an author opposing *mut'a* stated that *mut'a* was not only contrary to human dignity but also to the Universal Declaration of Human Rights,[119] Mutahari responded that when young men and women were not able to get married at an early age the only solution was temporary marriage. Mutahari asserts, "If you ask a boy student of eighteen years of age whose sexual ardour is naturally at its height to get married permanently, people would laugh at you."[120]

113 Shari'ati and Mutahari regard *mut'a* to be the only solution for young people's sexual needs. See Ali Shari'ati, "Seminar-e Zanan (Women's Conference)" in *Zan (Woman) Fatimeh Fatimeh ast (Fatima Is Fatima), Majmoeye asar (A Collection of Writings)*, 20th ed., ed. Ali Shari'ati (Tehran: Chapakhsh Publications, 1998), 266.

114 Morteza Mutahari, *Nezam-e Hughugh-e Zan dar Islam (The Rights of Women in Islam)*, 45th ed. (Tehran: Sadra Publication, 2007), 48. Translation is my own. See also English edition Murteza Mutahhari, *The Rights of Women in Islam*, 26.

115 Ibid.

116 Ibid., 48.

117 Ibid., 49. The *idda* period also differs for permanent and temporary marriages. The time for *idda* for the first is three period cycles and for the second is two period cycles, or forty-five days.

118 Ibid., 27.

119 Universal Declaration of Human Rights, G.A. res. 217A (III), U.N. Doc A/810 at 71 (1948) (UDHR).

120 Murteza Mutahari, *Nezam-e Hughugh-e Zan dar Islam (The Rights of Women in Islam)*, 45th ed. (Tehran: Sadra Publication, 2007), 29.

He also asks, "is nature prepared to delay the advent of puberty till we complete our education, and bring our sexual instinct to a standstill, because our modern way of life does not permit us to marry at sixteen or seventeen years of age?"[121] Continuing with this logic Mutahari sets up two alternatives as straw men to his argument for temporary marriage. One is what Mutahari refers to as sexual communism. The other is celibacy.

According to Mutahari, sexual communism occurs when young boys and girls are left to their vices such that "we may allow a boy to have unlawful sexual relations with hundreds of girls, and allow a girl to have unlawful relations with tens of boys and have so many abortions."[122] Mutahari adds that the equal freedom given to boys and girls in the spirit of the Universal Declaration of Human Rights (UDHR) is what he regards as sexual communism. "We say this, because, according to so many persons lacking foresight, the spirit of the Universal Declaration of Human Rights is that when a women and a man are about to leap into the valley of Gehenna, they should leap together, hand in hand, shoulder to shoulder."[123] Mutahari's criticism of the notion of equality, as enshrined in the UDHR, stems from his belief that men and women differ both physically and mentally. Mutahari additionally brings into question the piety of men and women who partake in sexual relations without any form of marriage and who later wish to contract a permanent marriage. According to his definition, a person who has contracted temporary marriages, no matter the number, may remain pious. Therefore, the only positive solution which both appeases the sexual needs of Iran's youth and keeps them within certain moral bounds, according to Mutahari, is temporary marriage.[124]

His views are supported by many prominent figures. Hashemi Rafsanjani, at the time the Iranian president, declared the following in a famous *namaaz-e jumah* (Friday prayers) in 1990:

> Take, for example, the sexual instinct that God has given us. Some think that if we abstain from satisfying our needs and deprive ourselves from sexual gratification, then this is very good. Well, this is not so. It is wrong. It is anti-Islamic. . . . If we had a healthy society, then the situation of all these widows we now have [women widowed in the Iran-Iraq War] would be very different. Then, when they [widows] felt the [sexual] need, *niaz*, they could approach one of their friends or relatives from a position of confidence and invite him to marry them temporarily,

121 Ibid., 30.
122 Ibid.
123 Ibid., 30.
124 Ibid.

> *ezdevaj-e movaqqat*. This they could do without being ashamed or ostracized by others.[125]

Ayatollah Bojnourdi has similarly said, ". . . when you are hungry would you accept if someone asks you to endure? Islam has ascertained temporary marriage based on contract for such cases. This rule is of course logical and it is for this reason that Islam accepts it."[126] According to Ghodsi, "the government views this form of marriage as a pragmatic way for individuals to satisfy their sexual desires within legal confines."[127] She adds that "legal control of individuals' sexual relations, officials believe, will promote family stability and ultimately social harmony."[128] Tamilla Ghodsi also believes that the government's support of *mut'a* demonstrates the regime's invasive use of law "as a method of social control, a characteristic which has parallels in the West".[129]

Yet women's rights activists are divided regarding *mut'a*. For the majority it is a practice that leads to misuse and mistreatment of women, which should be prohibited. Mehrangiz Kar, for instance, states that Iranian laws concerning temporary marriage are in contrast to the international human rights treaties to which Iran is a party,[130] and have no part in the formation

125 Hasehmi Rafsanjani cited in Shahla Haeri, "Temporary Marriage: An Islamic Discourse on Female Sexuality in Iran" in *In the Eye of Storm: Women in Post Revolutionary Iran*, ed. Mahnaz Afkhami and Erika Friedl (Syracuse, NY: Syracuse University Press, 1994), 98.

126 Cited in Roya Karimi Majd, "Zanan Movaghat Gozareshi Andar Hekayat Ezdevaj Ba Modat-e Maloom (Temporary Wives, a Report on Temporary Marriage)," *Meydaan* (9 July 2007), online http://meydaan.com/news.aspx?nid=977, (accessed 2 August 2016).

127 Tamilla F. Ghodsi, "Tying a Slipknot: Temporary Marriages in Iran," *Michigan Journal of International Law* 15 (1993–1994), 645.

128 Ibid.

129 Ibid., 647.

130 (1) International Convention on the Elimination of All Forms of Racial Discrimination, U.N. Doc. 660 U.N.T.S. 195, entered into force Jan. 4, 1969 (ICERD hereinafter). ICERD was ratified by Iran on 29 August 1968 and Iran ratified amendment to the article 8 of ICERD on Nov 05.

(2) International Covenant on Civil and Political Rights, G.A. res. 2200A (XXI), 21 U.N. GAOR Supp. (No. 16) at 52, UN. Doc. A/6316 (1966), 999 U.N.T.S. 171, entered into force March 23, 1976 (ICCPR hereinafter). ICCPR ratified by Iran 24 Jun 1975.

(3) International Covenant on Economic Social and Cultural Rights, G.A. res. 2200A (XXI), 21 U.N. GAOR Supp. (No. 16) at 49, U.N. Doc. A/6316 (1966), 993 U.N.T.S. 3, entered into force Jan. 3, 1976 (hereinafter ICESCR). ICESCR was ratified by Iran on 24 June 1975.

(4) International Convention on the Rights of the Child, G.A. res. 44/25, annex 44 U.N. GAOR Supp. (No. 49) at 167, U.N. Doc. A/44/49 (1989), entered into force Sept. 2, 1990 (ICRC from hereinafter). Iran ratified ICRC on 13 July 1994, ICRC amendment re: article 43 (2) was ratified by Iran on 13 November 2001.

(4.1) Optional Protocol to the Convention on the Rights of the Child on the Sale of Children, Child Prostitution and Child Pornography, G.A. Res. 54/263, Annex II, 54 U.N. GAOR Supp. (No. 49) at 6 U.N. Doc. A/54/49, Vol. III (2000), entered into force January 18, 2000, ratified by Iran on 26 September 2007.

of the family unit.[131] However, there are a few women's rights activists who are of a different opinion. Some regard *mut'a* as a loophole for individuals to have relationships that are otherwise criminalized under Iranian laws. Others contend that by contracting *mut'a* a woman is able to live with a chosen partner lawfully without worrying about the legal consequences, whether the partnership is of a sexual nature or solely for cohabitation. A well-known feminist and editor of *Zanan* magazine, Shahla Sherkat, makes four points in favour of *mut'a*: "First, relations between young men and women will become a little bit freer. Second, they can satisfy their sexual needs. Third, sex will become depoliticized. Fourth, they will use up some of the energy they are putting into street demonstrations. Finally, our society's obsession with virginity will disappear."[132]

However, studies and reports, such as those carried out by Ghodsi, Gelareh Asayesh,[133] Jane Khatib-Chahidi[134] and Trudy Rubin,[135] indicate that the practice of *mut'a* is not socially accepted, even if it is legally sanctioned. In an interview, Ziba Mir-Hosseini affirmed, "Temporary marriage is not accepted by the [Iranian] society. Research shows that women who enter temporary marriages do so due to poverty and men who take a *sigheh* wife do not respect them and regard them as objects of sexual fulfilment. The patriarchal structure of Iranian society has given men an advantage in such relations."[136] Yet, in an earlier study, Haeri, after interviewing Iranian *sigheh* women, came to the conclusion that poverty (although the main factor) was not the sole reason women contracted temporary marriage. She suggested they did so for a variety of reasons, including sexual need and love.[137] Regardless of the variety of factors for temporary marriage contacts, and despite the fact that the practice is socially frowned upon, according to Haeri the Iranian government "has made an orchestrated effort to educate

131 Mehrangiz Kar, "Hughugh-e Zan-e Sighe-i (The Rights of a *Sigheh* Wife)," online www.mehrangizkar.net/archives/000135.php, (accessed 20 April 2008).

132 Shahla Sherkat cited in Elaine Sciolino, "Love Finds a Way in Iran: 'Temporary Marriage'," *The New York Times* (4 October 2000), online www.nytimes.com/2000/10/04/world/love-finds-a-way-in-iran-temporary-marriage.html?pagewanted=all, (accessed 29 July 2016).

133 Gelareh Asayesh, "Iran: The Rules of Courtship," *Toronto Star*, 4 February 1991, 31.

134 Jane Khatib-Chahidi, "Sexual Prohibitions, Shared Space and Fictive Marriage in Shi'ite Iran" in *Women and Space: Ground Rules and Social Maps*, ed. Shirley Ardener (Oxford and New York: Berg, 1993), 126.

135 Trudy Rubin, "Women Still Getting Arrested for Improper Dress in Iran," *Gazette* (Montreal) (6 July 1991).

136 Zahra Saeid Zadeh, "Goft-o Goo ba Ziba Mir-Hosseini: Bar Khalaf-e Hameye Donya be Samte Mard Salari Pish Miravim (A Dialogue with Ziba Mir-Hosseini: Unlike the Rest of the World We Move Towards Patriarchy)," *Meydaan*, 30 August 2007, online http://meydaan.com/ShowArticle.aspx?arid=347, (accessed 2 August 2016).

137 Shahla Haeri, *Laws of Desire: Temporary Marriage in Shi'i Iran* (Syracuse, NY: Syracuse University Press, 1989), 7.

the public of the specifics of the institution [of *sigheh*], its divine roots, its contemporary relevance, emphasizing its positive effects for the individual and social moral health."[138]

New medium for mut'a

While Haeri was able expertly to detail the dynamics of governmental support for temporary marriage in her 1986 work, she could not be expected to have anticipated the role that the Internet would come to play in the facilitation of *mut'a*. While the holy shrines are still famous places for meeting temporary spouses,[139] as Internet usage[140] has increased dramatically, so too has this medium's role in the *mut'a* process. Persian is a popular online language;[141] as of 2016 there were more than twenty-five active Persian-language websites where men and women can meet to propose temporary marriages.[142] These websites tend to have large user bases, with some claiming upwards of 30,000 members.[143] Unlike political blogs, which are scrutinized

138 Ibid.

139 Ibid., 11.

140 For more on Persian blogging, read Elizabeth Bucar and Roja Fazaeli, "Free Speech in Weblogistan? The Off-Line Consequences of On-Line Discourse," *International Journal of Middle-Eastern Studies* 40 (July 2008), 403–419. See also Khodadad Rezakhani, "Editorials without Editors: How Weblogs Are Changing the Iranian Youth Community in the Web," posted 2003, online www.iranologie.com/ewe.htm (accessed 29 February 2008). Alfred Hermida, "Web Gives a Voice to Iranian Women," *BBC Online News*, 17 June 2002, online http://news.bbc.co.uk/2/hi/science/nature/2044802.stm, (accessed 29 July 2016). Mehdi Jami, "Iranian Blogs Take on the Election," *BBC News* (17 June 2005), online http://news.bbc.co.uk/2/hi/middle_east/4099380.stm, (accessed 29 July 2016). Fereshteh Nouraie-Simone, "Wings of Freedom: Iranian Women, Identity, and Cyberspace" in *On Shifting Ground: Muslim Women in the Global Era*, ed. Freshteh Nouraie-Simone (New York: The Feminist Press, 2005), 61–79; Amir Ebrahimi, "Performance in Everyday Life and the Rediscovery of the 'Self' in Iranian Weblogs," *Bad Jens* (September 2004), online www.badjens.com/rediscovery.html, (accessed March 2006); Nasrin Alavi, *We Are Iran: The Persian Blogs* (Brooklyn, NY: Soft Skull Press, 2005).

141 Pardis Mahdavi, "Meeting, Mating, and Cheating Online in Iran," *ISIM Review* 19 (Spring 2007), 18–19.

142 Examples include: "Ezdevaj Movaghat va Ijad-e Taadol dar Farhang Jensiy-e Jame-e (Temporary Marriage and the Creation of a Cultural Sexual Harmony in the Society)," online www.movaghati.com and "Ezdevaj-e Movaghat dar Hughugh-e Madaniy-e Jomhoriye Eslamiy-e Iran (Temporary Marriage and Civil Laws in Iran)," online www.busc.blogsky.com, (accessed 1 April 2016).

"Ahkam ya Ravesh Ezdevaje Movaghat (Rules or Ways to Temporary Marriage)," online http://ravesh.blogsky.com/

143 Elahe Habibi, "Agar Sigheh Mishavi off Bogzar (If You Want to Contract Sigheh go Offline)," *Meydaan* (7 September 2007), online: http://meydaan.com/news.aspx?nid=978, (accessed 2 August 2016).

and constantly filtered,[144] these sites enjoy the support of the government.[145] The Internet sites for temporary marriage (*ezdevaje movaghat*) tend to cite both the Qur'an and *ahadith* to support their project.[146] One site claims that "*sigheh* can balance the sexual culture of the society."[147] Another, *Peyvand ezdevaj-e movaghat*, claims, "The main goal of this site is to promote the custom of marriage (temporary or permanent). We aim to preserve the God pleasing traditions of Prophet, Islam and the Imams and want to have a part in cleansing the society of sins and pollutions."[148]

To investigate the contents of these sites, including postings made by both females and males interested in contracting *mut'a*, I joined the site *peyvand ezdevaj-e movaghat* under a pseudonym. Visitors to the site are asked to provide personal details, including name, gender, province, place of residence (city), email address, age and marital status. Optionally one can also state the requirements one is looking for in a temporary spouse. The site provides several other services, such as message forwarding to any of its 15,000 members. Each message costs 1,000 toomans, which is payable to the site's account. The following are examples of public entries by men on the site:[149]

Entry 1.

Hello, I am an engineer and own my own company. I am 175 cm in height and weigh 69 kilos. I am interested in having a *sigheh* relationship with a respectable lady for 6 months and I can pay three million toomans in *mahr*.

144 Women's websites such as the Iranian Feminist Tribune, online www.iftribune.com; Zanestan (Women-estan), online www.zanstan.com and Change for Equality, online www.change4equality.com are constantly filtered, as are weblogs of some of the activists and journalists; for more on the arrest of webloggers in 2004 see Elizabeth Bucar and Roja Fazaeli, "Free Speech in Weblogistan? The Off-Line Consequences of On-Line Discourse," *International Journal of Middle-Eastern Studies* 40 (July 2008).

145 Mahdavi notes that "young Iranians increasingly use the Internet and cyberspace to explore relationships and engage in forms of cultural consumption prohibited by the regime." See Pardis Mahdavi, "Meeting, Mating, and Cheating Online in Iran," *ISIM Review* 19 (Spring 2007), 18–19.

146 Examples of verses cited on these sites include: "O ye who believe! make not unlawful the good things which Allah hath made lawful for you, but commit no excess: for Allah loveth not those given to excess" (5:86) and "O Prophet! why holdest thou to be forbidden that which Allah has made lawful to thee? Thou seekest to please thy consort. But Allah is oft-forgiving, most merciful." (66:1).

147 Elahe Habibi, "Agar Sigheh Mishavi off Bogzar (If You Want to Contract Sigheh go Offline)," *Meydaan* (September 2007), online http://meydaan.com/news.aspx?nid=978, (accessed 2 August 2016).

148 "Peyvand Ezdevaj-e Movaghat (Joined in Temporary Marriage)," online http://join.30gh.com/about.php, (accessed 2 May 2008).

149 All translations are mine.

Entry 2.

Hello, my name is Muhammad; I am 41 years old and am from Gorgan. Due to my wife's cancer I am faced with problems when it comes to sex. Therefore, I would like to contract a temporary marriage with a respectable lady and in the case of compatibility I will propose permanent marriage. I am a civil servant and earn seven hundred thousand toomans a month. I accept replies from respectable ladies who contact me with conditions and the amount of *mahr* required.

These are examples of entries by women:

Entry 1.

I like us to be friends first and to like each other. Men who are lewd, *harze,* make me sick. I am beautiful, have a good body, wear nice clothes, am educated and live with my parents. I am looking for a long-term relationship, which is clean and baggage-free. Those of you who are looking for passing relationships don't contact me. My *mehriye* (*mahr*) is five hundred thousand toomans a month.

Entry 2.

Hello, my name is Sussan. I am 23 years old and from a city in the south of Iran. At the moment I am a student in Tehran and to cover my expenses I am willing to temporarily marry a suitable person. I should stress that I am still a virgin and it is necessary that I remain one. It is also necessary to state that my father passed away 13 years ago. As for looks I am rather beautiful and have a good body. Also I am a firm believer in religion. I have already contracted temporary marriage three times and am in *idda* of my previous marriage. My *idda'* is over on 9th of Tir when I could remarry. Rules:

1 The *aqd* (the formal contracting of marriage) should be registered at a formal registry office;
2 My *mahr* is two hundred thousand a month to which the three months *idda* is added. This means *mahr* for one month is eight hundred thousand, two months is one million, three months one million and two hundred thousands and four months is one million four hundred thousand;
3 The maximum period of marriage is 4 months (I also need to rest);
4 The total amount of *mahr* has to be paid once the marriage is contracts (during *aqd*);

5 My *mahr* in order to give away my virginity is 1,000 golden coins, this will be recorded at the registry office during the signing of contract (this is to indicate how important this issue is to me);
6 To have had a HIV/AIDS test previous to marriage;
7 After the end of the contract we will not know each other and I do not want to be hassled.[150]

Roya Karimi observes, "distinguishing the line between prostitution and temporary marriage is not an easy task, not for the woman, not for the man, and not even for the specialists."[151] Prostitution is illegal in all Islamic countries, including Iran. For this reason the legality of *mut'a* is yet another paradox of Iranian society and legislation. The line that separates temporary marriage and prostitution in Iran is a narrow one. It is drawn at precisely the point where women put a price on their "pious" sexual relationship and men buy this "piety" to gain rewards in the hereafter.

Polygamy

Men in many Muslim-majority countries are permitted to take up to four wives.[152] Nicholas Awde explains that multiple marriages were historically contracted "for a variety of reasons: some from personal affinity, some to widows with no one to turn to, while others were politically motivated to create or maintain alliances."[153] The *ijma* (consensus) of the *fuqaha* (Islamic scholars) in the Shi'a tradition is that men are allowed to contract up to four simultaneous permanent marriages, but that there is no limitation on the number of temporary wives they can marry. The law of polygamy is rooted in the following Qur'anic verse:

> If ye fear that ye shall not be able to deal justly with the orphans, marry women of your choice, two or three or four; but if ye fear that ye shall

150 All the entries are from the website "Ezdevaj-e Movaghat (Temporary Marriage)," online www.30gh.com

151 Roya Karimi Majd, "Zanan Movaghat Gozareshi Andar Hekayat Ezdevaj Ba Modat-e Maloom (Temporary Wives, a Report on Temporary Marriage)," *Meydaan* (9 July 2007), online http://meydaan.com/news.aspx?nid=977 (accessed 2 August 2016).

152 Except for Tunisia, Turkey, Tajikistan, Uzbekistan and the Kyrgyz Republic. Article 18 of the Personal Status Act (*Ahval Shakhsiy-e*) in Tunisia criminalizes polygamy. Those who engage in polygamy, if convicted, will serve a one-year prison sentence and have to pay a fine of 240,000 Tunisian Francs. Also, Article 21 of the same act asserts that if a second marriage takes place before the termination of the first, then it is considered to be null in Turkey. It is also noteworthy that in most cases (apart from Shi'a *ithna 'ashari fiqh*) having more than four wives is not permitted.

153 Nicholas Awde, *Women in Islam: An Anthology from the Qur'an and Hadith* (London: Routledge, 1999), 10.

> not be able to deal justly (with them), then only one, or (a captive) that your right hands possess, that will be more suitable, to prevent you from doing injustice.[154]

It is widely agreed, in particular among feminist scholars that the foregoing verse was revealed in connection to the treatment of orphan girls. Even Amin, whose writings are more conservative, holds this view. Amina Wadud notes that a solution to the mismanagement of the orphan's wealth[155] was marriage to the female orphan. She states "on the one hand, the Qur'an limited this number to four, and on the other hand, the economic responsibility of maintaining the wife would counterbalance the access to the wealth of the orphaned female through the responsibility of management."[156] Like Wadud, Ayatollah Bojnurdi also recognizes justice to be the main concern of verse 4:3. Bojnurdi explains that Islamic *ahkam* (judgements) and *ghavanin* (laws) are based on *edalat-e ejtemai* (social justice) and morality; if a judgement contradicts social justice then it is not Islamic.[157] According to Bojnurdi, polygamy is only permitted when it is regarded as just. If the society and the culture do not regard polygamy as just, then it should be forbidden, unless the wife is sick or cannot bear a child.[158]

Ali Shari'ati, at a conference on women, while admitting that the law of polygamy was often misused for sexual gratification of men, believed that it should be permitted in some specific circumstances, for example, when war had left behind many widows and orphans. He used the Algerian War of Independence (1954–1962) as an example. According to Shari'ati, the heads of the Algerian Popular Front instructed members who had survived the war to marry the wives of those members who had died. Survivors who already had wives were encouraged to marry a second wife. This was not done to appease the laws of God, Shari'ati stated, but rather was the necessity of a specific time. Polygamy in this instance, he concluded, was introduced to solve a particular social problem rather than to satisfy self-indulgence.[159]

154 Qur'an 4:3.
155 Qur'an 4:2.
156 Amina Wadud, *Inside the Gender Jihad, Women's Reform in Islam* (Oxford: One World, 2006), 83.
157 Parvin Bakhtiarnejad, "Ayatollah Mousavi Bojnurdi: Chand Hamsari ba Edalat-e Ejtemai dar Tanaqoz ast," *Taqheer baray-e Barabari* (27 Aban 1358), online www.we-change.org/spip.php?article158
158 Ibid.
159 Ali Shari'ati, "Seminar-e Zanan (Women's Conference)" in *Zan (Woman) Fatimeh Fatimeh ast (Fatima Is Fatima), Majmoeye asar (A Collection of Writings)*, 20th ed., ed. Ali Shari'ati (Tehran: Chapakhsh Publications, 1998), 263–266.

A *fatwa* decreed by Ayatollah Saane'i in 2007 places a further limitation on polygamy. Saane'i's *fatwa* declares: "Marriage of a man to a second wife without the first wife's permission is against a reasonable life and goes against the Qur'anic principle of justice, which is the condition for a second marriage."[160] According to Saane'i a second marriage without the first wife's permission should be deemed unlawful. Although there is no single article in the Iranian Civil Code that specifically permits men to have more than one wife, a collection of articles hint at the legality of men engaging in polygamy. For example, Article 942 of the Civil Code, addressing matters of inheritance, states "if there be more than one wife, the fourth or eighth part, which belongs to the wife, will be divided equally among them."[161] The 1967 civil registry laws (*thabth ahval*) also oblige the registrar to record the number of simultaneous marriages in the notarized copy of a birth certificate. Furthermore, one of the jurisdictions of the Iranian family law courts (established in 1997) includes issuing permission for polygamy to men.[162]

Divorce

Unlike many contracts, where either party has the right to terminate, the termination of an Islamic marriage contract (in permanent marriages) is by and large the domain of the man. In classical *fiqh* the act *of talaq* (repudiation) is that whereby the husband divorces his wife at will without cause or recourse to a court of law. This is allowable as long as the husband is an adult (i.e., has reached the age of maturity) and is sane. Repudiation can be carried out orally or in written form when the wife is in a period of purity (i.e., when she is not menstruating) and "when no intercourse has taken place between the parties since her last menstruation".[163] Another form of divorce is known as *khul*. As

160 Yusuf Sanee'i, "Takid-e Mojadad-e Hazrat-e Ayatollah Uzma Saane'i: Ezdevaj-e Mojadad-e Mard Bedoon-e Rezayat-e Hamsar Aval Haram Ast va Khalaf-e Edalat Ast (Ayatollah's Sanee'i's Emphasis: Polygamy without the Permission of the First Wife Is Haram and Unjust)," *Grand Ayatollah Saanei's Official Website*, online www.saanei.org/page.php?pg=showdialog&id=124&lang=fa, (accessed 27 May 2008).

161 Iranian Civil Code, Article 429. Also Article 1047 (3) forbids the marriage of "a man with females of descent from his wife, no matter of what degree no exception being made even if the woman is a foster – relation, provided that the husband and wife have already consummated the marriage." The mentioned article clearly legitimizes a man having more than one wife. See also Shirin Ebadi, *Huqu-e Zan Dar Ghavanin-e Jomhoriye Islamiy-e Iran (Women's Rights, in the Laws of the Islamic Republic of Iran)* (Tehran: Ganje Danesh Publication, 2002), 121.

162 Ziba Amiri, "Chand Hamsari, az Nokhostin Sang Banaye Ghanoon ta Konoon" in *Zanan va Ghavaneen Tabiz Amiz dar Iran, Chand Hamsari*, ed. Parvin Ardalan, Narges Tayebat and Firoozeh Mohajer, online www.chage4equality.com, 35.

163 Doreen Hichcliffe, "Divorce in the Muslim World," *Features*, May 2000, 63.

Mir-Hosseini defines it, *khul* is "a separation claimed by the wife as a result of her extreme reluctance (*ikrah*) towards her husband, and the essential element is the payment of compensation (*'awad*) to her husband, in return for her release."[164] Doreen Hinchcliffe remarks, "*khul* is merely a variant on the *talaq* where the husband receives financial or other compensation from his wife in return for divorcing her."[165] This financial compensation is usually in the form of the wife forgoing her *mahr*.[166] Occasionally the *qadi* (judge) is entrusted with the termination of marriage after litigation in the Shari'a court on the initiative of one of the two spouses in the case of *tafriq* (judicial divorce), or a third party in the case of *faskh* (judicial dissolution).[167] Thus, in a *khul* divorce, if the wife fails to secure her husband's consent, she has the choice of referring to a court where she is at the mercy of a judge's discretion. *Tafriq* (also known as *tatliq*) has become a juristic outlet through "which a woman can obtain a court divorce in the contemporary Muslim world."[168]

In Iran, according to Article 1133 of the Civil Code, "a man can divorce his wife at will."[169] This means that the husband will not need his permanent wife's permission, the permission of the court or any concrete reason to divorce his wife. The Civil Code enshrines two types of divorce: *baen* (irrevocable), in which a husband cannot renounce his intention of divorcing his wife (Article 1144), and *rajee* (revocable), in which a man can go back to his wife (Article 1145).[170] Limitations on when a husband is not permitted to repudiate his wife are covered by Articles 1140 to 1142 of the Civil

164 Ziba Mir-Hosseini, "The Construction of Gender in Islamic Legal Thought and Strategies for Reform," *Hawwa* 1 (2003), 7.

165 Doreen Hichcliffe, "Divorce in the Muslim World," *Features*, May 2000, 64.

166 For more on divorce in the Muslim world and in different schools of thought, refer to Lynn Welchman, *Beyond the Code, Muslim Family Law and the Shar'i Judiciary in the Palestinian West Bank* (The Hague: Kluwer Academic Publishers Group, 2000), 247–280. See also Lucy Carroll, "Qur'an 2:229: 'A Charter Granting to the Wife?' Judicial Khul' in Pakistan," *Islamic Law and Society* 3, no. 1 E.J. Brill, Leiden, (1996), 91–126. Also refer to Dawoud El-Alami, "Remedy or Device? The System of Khul and the Effects of Its Incorporation into Egyptian Personal Status Law," *Yearbook of Islamic and Middle Eastern Law* 6 (1999–2000), 134–139. Noel Coulson, "Regulation of Sexual Behaviour under Traditional Islamic Law" in *Society and Sexes in Medieval Islam*, ed. Afaf Lufti Al-Sayyid Marsot (Malibu: Unenda Publication, 1977), 63–68.

167 Ziba Mir-Hosseini, "The Construction of Gender in Islamic Legal Thought and Strategies for Reform," *Hawwa* 1 (2003), 8.

168 Ibid.

169 The following article, 1134, requires that "the divorce must be performed in the actual form of utterance and in the presence of at least two just men who must hear the actual form of divorce." Also, *talaq* is defined in two ways in the Civil Code, *baen* and *rajee*.

170 Article 1145: A divorce is irrevocable in the following instances: 1. A divorce performed before the occurrence of matrimonial relations; 2. A divorce of a wife who is incapable of conception; and 3. (a) A divorce which a wife achieves by giving a consideration to her husband and (*khul'a*) and (b) a divorce by mutual consent (*mubarat*), as long as the wife has not demanded the return of the consideration.

Code. These articles are mainly concerned with the wife's menstrual cycle and whether she is pregnant. The period of *idda* "for a divorce or for the dissolution of a marriage consists of three consecutive monthly cycles of a woman unless the woman concerned, though of child-bearing age, has no monthly period, in which case the period of *idda* will be three months."[171] These laws are based on a literal interpretation of Qur'an 2.228.[172] The waiting period historically was deemed necessary to ascertain paternity, should any child be conceived. However, this waiting period is now questionable, as paternity can be determined by genetic testing.

Women have more limited access to divorce. Mehrpour names three instances in which a woman can divorce her husband. One is the case of a *khul*, as previously mentioned, which is dealt with in Article 1146 of the Civil Code, which states: "A *khul* divorce occurs when the wife obtains a divorce owing to dislike of her husband, against property which she cedes to the husband. The property in question may consist of the original marriage portion, or the monetary equivalent thereof, whether more or less than the marriage portion." A woman can also seek a divorce in a situation where mutual dislike exists between the spouses. This type of divorce is known as *mubarat* and is dealt with in Article 1147. Another path to divorce exists when a woman goes to court and proves one of the following conditional articles from the Civil Code to be true:

- If the husband refuses to pay the cost of maintenance of his wife (*nafaqa*), and if it is impossible to enforce a judgement of the court and to induce him to pay the expenses, the wife can refer to the judge applying for divorce and the judge will compel the husband to divorce her (Article 1129).
- When it is proved to the court that the continuation of the marriage causes difficult and undesirable conditions, the judge can for the sake of avoiding harm and difficulty compel the husband to divorce his wife. If this cannot be done, then the divorce will be made on the permission of the Islamic judge (Article 1130).
- If a man has been for four years continuously absent with unknown whereabouts, his wife can apply for a divorce (Article 1029).

Finally, a woman can ask for the right to divorce in the prenuptial agreement in accordance with Article 1119 of the Civil Code.

171 Iranian Civil Code Article 1151. Also note that Articles 1148 to 1157 of the Iranian Civil Code deal with the issue of *idda*.

172 "Divorced women shall wait concerning themselves for three monthly periods. Nor is it lawful for them to hide what Allah Hath created in their wombs, if they have faith in Allah and the Last Day. And their husbands have the better right to take them back in that period, if they wish for reconciliation. And women shall have rights similar to the rights against them, according to what is equitable; but men have a degree (of advantage) over them. And Allah is exalted in Power, Wise." Qur'an 2:228.

Hezanat (custody)

Hezanat (custody) is the responsibility of both parents while they are married and live together.[173] However, as mentioned in Article 1169 of the Iranian Civil Code, if the parents divorce, then the custody of a child (male or female) is given to the mother for the first two years following birth. After this period, custody of boys devolves to the father. Girls remain in the custody of their mother until they reach seven years of age. This law was amended in 2004 so that a mother could have custody of both sons and daughters for up to seven years.

Initial reforms to custody laws in the Islamic Republic of Iran were the result of a need to address the situation of the children of those men who died during the Iran and Iraq War. The first and second *majlis* passed laws in January 1982 and August 1985, respectively, which stated that the custody of minors, in cases where fathers had the status of martyrs, should be awarded to their mothers.[174] However, custodianship arguments have not only been limited to cases affected by wartime circumstances. In this regard, actions taken by the women's movement form a noteworthy part of this extended reform process. One such action was led by the Nobel Peace Laureate Shirin Ebadi following the death of an eight-year-old girl, Arin, who was violently killed by her father, stepmother and stepbrother in September 1997. Ebadi was the attorney representing Arin's mother. With the help of members of the Society for the Protection of the Rights of the Child (*Anjoman Hemayat az Hughoogh-e Koodakan*), Ebadi planned a memorial service for Arin during which protests were made against existing custodial laws. Ebadi recounts the event as follows:

> We sent a notice in to the newspaper on behalf of the Society for the Protection of the Rights of the Child that read, "Hereby we announce that a memorial gathering for the young bud, Arin, whose petals have been ripped off, will be held in al Qadir mosque." Each mosque has a preacher. We told the mosque that we would pay their preacher, but that we would bring our own preacher to do the memorial. My husband's uncle is a clergyperson. We went to him and explained the situation and asked him to preach at this event and to explain what had happened to the child. We wanted him to say "don't hit your children," and to

173 Article 1168 of the Iranian Civil Code.

174 "Ghavanin Khanevadeh dar Iran az Ebtedaye Enghelab Eslami ta Konoon – Infography (Iranian Family Laws from the Islamic Revolution up to Now – Infography)," *Paygah Tahlili Khabari Khanevadeh va Zanan*, 7 November 2012, online http://mehrkhane.com/fa/news/4436/اینفوگرافی-تاکنون-اسلامی-انقلاب-ابتدای-از-ایران-در-خانواده-قوانین, (accessed 1 April 2016).

> underscore that the law should protect children. We wanted him to make the point that if this child was with her mother then this would not have happened. . . . He agreed. Meanwhile, the funeral for a mother of one of our members took place. Whatever was left of the dates, halva, etc. . . . from the funeral we brought with us for the memorial. And in the three days we had left we told each member of the society to bring at least four people with them to the memorial. . . . We made a petition for people to sign, which stated that the law should be changed and that custody should be given to mothers. The memorial became very crowded and journalists from all around attended . . . At the end of the gathering I jumped to the microphone on the women's side and said, "What caused this child's death was the law. If the law was fair then the child would have been with her mother and would not have been killed by her cruel father and stepmother. It is not important that the murderer should be executed, but what's important is to avoid future crimes. Therefore, those who agree that custodial laws should be reformed, in a sign of protest, should take the white flowers from the baskets that have been provided, rip off the petals and throw them in the street!" Maryam Zandi, the famous photographer, was there and she started shouting, "The Law should be reformed." The crowd followed her and ripped the petals off of the white flowers which we had brought from the funeral; they kept shouting slogans, and some were crying . . .[175]

This is an example of the type of campaign action that the women's movement has used to pursue reform in the law. According to Shadi Sadr, this particular event was the start of a process that led to the enactment of a law against child abuse and the 2004 reform of custodial laws.

Article 1170 of the Iranian Civil Code states that, if the mother becomes insane or marries another man while she is the custodian of the children, then the custody will be transferred to the man. While there is no Qur'anic basis for custody laws, the *hadith* literature is favourable to women.[176] The Iranian Civil Code is less so. In cases where the mother is given custody and wishes to take the child/children outside the country, she needs the written permission of her husband. She can only take her children abroad freely when she is the legal guardian of her children.[177] In all cases, however, according to Article

175 Shirin Ebadi.

176 For example, a *hadith* narrated by Ibn 'Umar reads: A man and his wife had a case of Lian (*ormula'ana*) during the lifetime of the Prophet and the man denied the paternity of her child. The Prophet gave his verdict for their separation (divorce) and then the child was regarded as belonging to the wife only. *Sahih* Bukhari, Volume 8, Book 80, Number 740.

177 Shirin Ebadi, *Huqu-e Zan Dar Ghavanin-e Jomhoriye Islamiy-e Iran (Women's Rights, in the Laws of the Islamic Republic of Iran)* (Tehran: Ganje Danesh Publication, 2002), 129.

1173 of the Iranian Civil Code, which was ratified by the *majlis* in 1997, if the physical health or moral education of the child is endangered as a result of the carelessness or moral degradation of the custodial father or the mother, then the court can take any decision appropriate for the custody of the child on the request of relatives, a guardian or the public prosecutor.

Vilayat (guardianship)

According to Article 1181 of the Iranian Civil Code the guardianship of children, including authority over finances, rests with the father or the paternal grandfather. This guardianship is termed *vilayat-e ghahri* (natural guardianship). A mother's right to guardianship is even less than that of a stranger's. It is the public prosecutor who nominates a candidate for guardianship when the *valiy-e ghahri* (natural guardian) is incapacitated.[178] The long-term implications of guardianship are significant as a *bakere* (virgin) requires her *vali's* permission to get married.[179]

Other limitations on marriage

There are a number of limitations on interfaith marriages in Islam.[180] Marriage between men and women of different traditions within Islam is permitted. In Iran a man is also permitted to marry women of the book (Christian, Jewish and Zoroastrian). However, a woman is prohibited from marrying a non-Muslim. Article 1059 of the Iranian Civil Code states that "marriage of a Muslim woman with a non-Muslim is not allowed." Those in support of this law reason that Islam is passed down from the father and hence, if a Muslim woman marries a non-Muslim man, then the link is broken and the religious identity is lost.

Conclusion

In the years preceding the Islamic Revolution of 1979, religion tended to be regarded as a private affair in Iran. It was not enforced by the state; if not chosen the state did not seek punishment. After the revolution, a different face of

178 Articles 1181 to 1192 of the Iranian Civil Code deal with guardianship.

179 Refer to Mehrangiz Kar et Homa Hoodfar, "La Loi sur le Status Personnell telle que Définie par la République Islamique d'Iran: Une Evaluation," *Les frontières mouvantes du mariage et du divorce dans les communautés musulmanes. Grabels: Women Living under Muslim Laws, 1996, (Programme Femmes et Loi dans le Monde Musulman: Dossier Spécial)*, Dossier Spécial no. 1 (1996), 26.

180 For more on interfaith marriage in Islam, see Abdullahi An-Na'im (ed.), *Inter-Religious Marriage among Muslims: Negotiating Religious and Social Identity in Family and Community* (New Delhi: Global Media Publications, 2005).

Islam emerged in Iran, particularly for women. As Ziba Mir-Hosseini writes, "It was no longer enough to believe; one had to wear one's beliefs in the form of *hejab*."[181] In Muslim-majority countries like Iran, especially where Arabic is not an official language, individuals routinely depend on the interpretation of male clergy to understand the Qur'an, the *hadith* and the duties of religious practice in Islam. These are also the interpretations that most often find their way into state laws. In a post-revolutionary Iran the form of Islam that expanded rapidly into the public realm was shaped by male-dominated Qur'anic *tafsir* and *hadith* interpretations. For such reasons it is important, as Nikkie Keddie notes, not to "overemphasize Qur'an's certain role in the position of women."[182] At the same time, the status of women in Muslim-majority societies is not solely contingent upon interpretations of religious texts, but also on conditional factors such as politics and economics and their impact on law. In Iran, as in most Muslim-majority countries, family law is one area of the law that clearly and regularly discriminates against women. These laws are all too often vehemently defended in legislative chambers, where men form a majority, as being based on Islamic laws, customs and norms. In such contexts where Qur'anic textual arguments for equality are ignored, overlooked or unknown and social, political and legal norms are pegged to masculine forms and privileges, reform-minded women's movements are needed and necessary, if women's rights are to be realized and advanced.

181 Ziba Mir-Hosseini, "The Quest for Gender Justice Emerging Feminist Voices in Islam," Presented at the conference, Reframing Islam, Irish Centre for Human Rights (National University of Ireland Galway, Ireland 2005), 1.

182 Nikki R. Keddie; with a section by Yann Richard, *Modern Iran: Roots and Results of Revolution* (New Haven: Yale University Press, 2003).

4 Human rights, Islam and the debate around CEDAW

Introduction

Inspiration for reform, as well as its execution, can come from many places. In the summer of 2004 the idea of human rights was spreading like wildfire across NGOs and semi-governmental organizations in Tehran and other Iranian cities. At the time I was working for a Tehran-based NGO, the House of Culture and Sustainable Development (HCSD), doing research for a book on Iranian civil society organizations. These organizations had grown in an unprecedented fashion since the reformist president Khatami came to power in 1997. The newly fashionable "human rights question" was immediately linked for women's rights advocates with questions around the UN Convention on the Elimination of All Forms of Discrimination against Women (CEDAW). The latter was a hot topic given that in the previous year, 2003, the Iranian *majlis* had authorized the ratification of CEDAW only for the authorization to be vetoed by the *Shoray-e Negahaban* (Guardian Council) on the grounds that it was contradictory to Islam. The dispute between *majlis* and *Shoray-e Negahban* on the ratification of CEDAW was brought to the *Shoray-e Maslehat-e Nezam* (Expediency Council), where the decision remains, untaken and dormant. Women's rights activists in 2004 were hopeful that they could convince the state to ratify CEDAW soon, particularly given that they had the backing of the *majlis*. It was in this context that my house was raided and my possessions, including my notes, interview tapes and laptop were confiscated by the intelligence agency of the Iranian Interior Ministry (*vezarat keshvar*). When everything was given back to me three months later, the tapes and the computer had been wiped clean of all information. I was left with the notes I had taken during my interviews on Iranian civil society organizations and my memories. In 2010 I decided to revisit the question of CEDAW with Iranian women's rights activists through a series of interviews. I conducted these with the help of Maryam Hosseinkhah and included in them some of the same women I had previously met with in 2004. During the course of these interviews I noticed that the hope that Iran would imminently ratify CEDAW, palpable in 2004, had faded considerably in the intervening years.

The debate around Iran's non-ratification of CEDAW extends beyond Iran's borders and is part of a larger debate about how Muslim-majority countries engage with international human rights law, particularly as it pertains to women. Many Muslim-majority countries criticize what they term the "Western nature of human rights".[1] Within this critical framework the human rights discourse is understood to be a continuation of colonial and imperial action. While, as Naz Modirzadeh notes, the human rights movement "is so large, so diverse, and so complex that a critique of the discourse as a whole is almost impossible",[2] it is also the case, as Shadi Mokhtari asserts, that "in the post-September 11th period, there is an unmistakable popular disillusionment with the promise of human rights and international law in the Middle East."[3] This disillusionment and the faded hope for Iranian ratification of CEDAW are two sides of the same coin.

The first part of this chapter is a discussion of the different approaches to the debates surrounding the relationship between Islamic laws and international human rights law. Next a background to CEDAW is given, with a particular focus on Muslim-majority countries, their engagement in the drafting of the Convention and their ensuing critique of its provisions.[4] The following section investigates the engagement and non-engagement of Islamic countries with the human rights regime. The sheer number of reservations to CEDAW by Muslim-majority countries is one of the main focuses of this section. The question of whether Iran should become a party to CEDAW is then revisited.

1 See, for example, Adamantia Pollis and Peter Schwab, "Human Rights: A Western Construct with Limited Applicability" in *Human Rights: Cultural and Ideological Perspectives*, ed. Adamantia Pollis and Peter Schwab (New York: Praeger, 1979), 1–18. See also Samuel P. Huntington, *The Clash of Civilizations and the Remaking of World Order* (New York: Simon & Schuster, 1996), 70–72.

2 Naz K. Modirzadeh, "Taking Islamic Law Seriously: INGOs and the Battle for Muslim Hearts and Minds," *Harvard Human Rights Journal* 19 (2006), 19.

3 See Shadi Mokhtari, "Human Rights in the Post-September 11th Era: Between Hegemony and Emancipation," *Muslim World Journal of Human Rights* 3, no. 1 (2006), 6.

4 Although the UN conferences on women, and in particular the fourth world conference on women (1995), which adopted the Beijing Declaration and Platform for Action, are of outmost importance when discussing women's rights, in this study CEDAW will be the only women-specific provision which is discussed. It is nonetheless important, as Jessica Neuwirth notes, that "the public pressure mobilized by the Beijing World Conference on Women and its aftermath has been more effective than the legal obligation of CEDAW in narrowing the gap between the rhetoric and the reality of sex equality before the law, but the gap remains substantial." Jessica Neuwirth, "Inequality before the Law: Holding States Accountable for Sex Discriminatory Laws under the Convention on the Elimination of All Forms of Discrimination against Women and Through the Beijing Platform for Action," *Harvard Human Rights Journal* 18 (2005), 19–54.

Different approaches to the human rights and Islam debate

Niaz Shah outlines what he refers to as four major approaches to the debates on Islam and human rights.[5] These are the secular, non-compatible, reconciliatory and interpretive approaches. The secular approach, Shah argues, is used by scholars, such as Reza Afshari,[6] who advocate strict adherence to the Universal Declaration of Human Rights (UDHR) and to international human rights standards in general. The non-compatible approach is employed by Islamic governments and conservative Muslim scholars. The argument made by the non-compatibilists is that the international human rights system is a hegemonic tool of the West and a new form of Western imperialism. The third approach is that of reconciliation, whose proponents "argue that Islamic human rights norms are compatible with international standards in many respects and that where they conflict, those areas could be reformulated and reconciled with international standards."[7] According to Shah, scholars such as Abdullahi An-Na'im,[8] Mahmood Monshipour[9] and Bassam Tibi,[10] are in this category. The fourth approach is the interpretive approach. Those aligned with this approach believe that Islamic law is reformable through reinterpretation of the divine text of the Qur'an. Shah argues that this group of reformers is not trying to reconcile Islamic and international human rights standards, but rather prove that the Qur'an "is a living text and can be reinterpreted to meet contemporary needs of given Muslim societies".[11]

As helpful as these categories are to engaging in the debate, Shah makes some sweeping generalizations. Many of the generalizations are the result of conflating Islam as a faith with Islam as a socio-political and legal system. Shah

5 Niaz A. Shah, "Women's Human Rights in the Koran: An Interpretive Approach," *Human Rights Quarterly* 28, no. 4 (November 2006), 868–903.

6 Reza Afshari, "An Essay on Islamic Cultural Relativism in the Discourse of Human Rights," *Human Rights Quarterly* 16, no. 2 (May 1994), 235–276.

7 Niaz A. Shah, "Women's Human Rights in the Koran: An Interpretive Approach," *Human Rights Quarterly* 28, no. 4 (November 2006), 875.

8 See, for example, Abdullahi An-Na'im, "The Interdependence of Religion, Secularism, and Human Rights," *Symposium Talking Peace with Gods, Part 2, Common Knowledge* 11, no. 1 (2005), 23–48 and Abdullahi An-Na'im, "'The Best of Times' and 'the Worst of Times': Human Agency and Human Rights in Islamic Societies," *Muslim World Journal of Human Rights* 1, no. 1 (2004), article 5.

9 See, for example, Mahmood Monshipour, *Islamism, Secularism and Human Rights in the Middle-East* (Boulder, CO: Lynne Reinner, 1998). Mahmood Monshipour, "State Prerogatives, Civil Society, and Liberalization: The Paradoxes of the Late Twentieth Century in the Third World," *Ethics & International Affairs* 11, no. 1 (March 1997), 233–251. See also Mahmood Monshipour, *Democratization, Liberalization and Human Rights in the Third World* (Boulder, CO: Lynn Reinner, 1995).

10 Bassam Tibi, *The Challenge of Fundamentalism: Political Islam and the New World Disorder* (CA: University of California Press, 2002).

11 Niaz A. Shah, "Women's Human Rights in the Koran: An Interpretive Approach," *Human Rights Quarterly* 28, no. 4 (November 2006), 881.

falters in his analysis where he fails to realize that any reinterpretation of Islam, however "Islamic" it be, will not, and cannot, be incorporated into the politics of a country where Islam is used as an instrument of repression. In such places, reform-minded interpreters of the Qur'an are regarded as dissidents whenever their reforms do not satisfy the ends of the government in power. As al-Hibri notes, this dynamic is compounded by the fact that "the international community appears to have readily embraced the patriarchal interpretations of Islam as authoritative."[12] It is also difficult to discuss the correlation between Islamic law and human rights without taking into account other related issues such as "world power and jostling for position, the post-Cold War issues of competition, and the post-Cold War drive for hegemonic dominance."[13] In short, Muslim-majority countries' compliance with the human rights regime and their ratification of international conventions do not depend solely on the compatibility or incompatibility of two systems of law.

A brief background to CEDAW

The Convention on the Elimination of All Forms of Discrimination against Women (CEDAW) was adopted by the General Assembly of the United Nations in 1979.[14] CEDAW is often called the international *Magna Carta*, or Bill of Rights, for women.[15] The text of the Convention includes attributes from the Universal Declaration of Human Rights (UDHR),[16] the International Covenant on Civil and Political Rights (ICCPR),[17] the International Covenant on Economic, Social and Cultural Rights (ICESCR)[18] and

12 Azizah Al-Hibri, "Islam, Law and Custom: Redefining Muslim Women's Rights," *American University International Law Review* 12, no. 1 (1997), 3.

13 Khaled Abou El Fadl, "A Distinctly Islamic View of Human Rights, Does It Exist and Is It Compatible with the Universal Declaration of Human Rights?" in *Islam and Human Rights, Advancing a U.S.-Muslim Dialogue*, ed. Shirin Hunter and Homa Malir (Washington, DC: The Centre for Strategic and International Studies, 2005), 29.

14 Convention on the Elimination of All Forms of Discrimination against Women, G.A. res. 34/180, 34 U.N. GAOR Supp. (No. 46) at 193, U.N. Doc. A/34/46, entered into force 3 September 1981 (CEDAW).

15 1975 was declared the United Nations International Women's Year; subsequently the World Conference in Mexico (1975) was held on a variety of topics relating to women's specific needs. The Mexico conference recommended the convening of a second conference to be held in Copenhagen in 1980, The World Conference of the United Nations Decade for Women: Equality, Development and Peace (1976–1985).

16 Universal Declaration of Human Rights, G.A. res. 217A (III), U.N. Doc A/810 at 71 (1948) (UDHR).

17 International Covenant on Civil and Political Rights, G.A. res. 2200A (XXI), 21 U.N. GAOR Supp. (No. 16) at 52, U.N. Doc. A/6316 (1966), 999 U.N.T.S. 171, entered into force 23 March 1976 (ICCPR).

18 International Covenant on Economic, Social and Cultural Rights, G.A. res. 2200A (XXI), 21 U.N. GAOR Supp. (No. 16) at 49, U.N. Doc. A/6316 (1966), 993 U.N.T.S. 3, entered into force 3 January 1976 (ICESCR).

International Labour Organization (ILO) conventions.[19] CEDAW's origins are further linked to the Convention on the Political Rights of Women and the Nationality of Married Women.[20]

Initially a Declaration on the Elimination of Discrimination against Women[21] was prepared by working groups within the Commission on the Status of Women (CSW) in 1976. The drafting work within the CSW was encouraged by the World Plan of Action for the Implementation of the Objectives of the International Women's Year, adopted by the World Conference of the International Women's Year held in Mexico City in 1975.[22] This action plan called for a Convention on the Elimination of Discrimination against Women, with effective procedures for its implementation. This all in turn influenced the drafting of the Convention by a working group of the Third Committee of the General Assembly from 1977 to 1979. However, the Convention did not come into force until 1981 after its 20th ratification.[23]

The principle of non-discrimination on the basis of sex is clearly enshrined in international law in UDHR, ICESCR and ICCPR. However, these instruments fail to address women's rights effectively. The Covenants are mainly concerned with discriminatory "actions by public agencies, whereas

19 Such as ILO Convention Concerning the Employment of Women before and after Childbirth (Geneva: ILO, 1919), ILO Convention C3, 38 UNTS 23, entered into force 1921, revised 1952. See also ILO Convention Concerning Employment of Women during the Night (Washington: ILO, 1919), entered into force 1921, revised 1934 by Convention No. 41 and in 1948 by Convention No. 89. ILO Convention Concerning Maternity Protection (revised) (Geneva: ILO, 1952), ILO Convention C103, 214 UNTS 321, entered into force 7 September 1955. For a complete list of ILO conventions refer to, online www.ilo.org/ilolex/english/convdisp1.htm.

20 Sally Engle Merry, *Human Rights and Gender Violence: Translating Law into Local Justice* (Chicago: University of Chicago Press, 2006), 74.

21 Declaration on Elimination of Discrimination against Women, U.N. Doc. G.A. res 22/2263, 1976.

Also cited in Jessica Neuwirth, "Inequality before the Law: Holding States Accountable for Sex Discriminatory Laws under the Convention on Elimination of All Forms of Discrimination against Women and Through the Beijing Platform for Action," *Harvard Human Rights Journal* 18 (2005), 22.

22 See "Report of the World Conference of the International Women's Year, Mexico City, 19 June–2 July 1975," *Studies in Family Planning* 8, no. 1 (1977), 23. See also "Report of the World Conference of IWY, Mexico City," June–July 1975, U.N. Doc. E/Conf.66/34 (76.IV.1), 1976; "Report of the World Conference of the U.N. Decade for Women: Equality, Development and Peace," Copenhagen, July 1980; U.N. Doc. A/CONF.94/35 (80.IV.3), 1980; "Report of the World Conference to Review and Appraise the Achievements of the U.N. Decade for Women, Nairobi, July 1985," U.N. Doc. A/CONF.116/28/Rev.1 (85.IV.10), 1986.

23 See also "Implementation of Article 21 of the Convention on the Elimination of All Forms of Discrimination against Women," Committee on the Elimination of Discrimination against Women, U.N. Doc. CEDAW/C/1995/4, 16 November 1994. See also "The Situation in the Middle East," U.N. Doc. A/RES/38/180 (A-E), 19 December 1983.

discrimination against women occurs in the private as well as the public arena".[24] Therefore, CEDAW breaks the barriers of the "rights hierarchy" by guaranteeing enjoyment of equality in civil, political, economic, social and cultural contexts. It "codifies the existing gender-specific and general human rights instruments containing guarantees of freedom from discrimination on the basis of sex, although it adds some significant new provisions".[25] Discrimination against women is defined in Article 1 of the Convention and is the thread that runs through the Convention's substantive provisions:[26]

> **Article 1**
>
> For the purposes of the present Convention, the term "discrimination against women" shall mean any distinction, exclusion or restriction made on the basis of sex which has the effect or purpose of impairing or nullifying the recognition, enjoyment or exercise by women, irrespective of their marital status, on a basis of equality of men and women, of human rights and fundamental freedoms in political, economic, social, cultural, civil or any other field.

The Convention progresses beyond earlier human rights conventions by addressing the pervasive and systematic nature of discrimination against women and identifies the need to confront the social causes of women's inequality by addressing "all forms" of discrimination that women suffer. The Convention is thereby able to address the particular nature of women's disadvantages.[27]

There are a number of different ways to view the Convention. It may be viewed as a political manifestation declaring the rights of women to equality and non-discrimination, as an international legal instrument, as a treaty and point of reference or as a framework for policy making, lobbying and social activism.[28] This study addresses the Convention as all of the foregoing,

24 Elizabeth Evatt, "Finding a Voice for Women's Rights: The Early Days of CEDAW," *The George Washington International Law Review* 34, no. rev. 515 (2002–2003), 516.

25 Andrew Byrnes, "The Convention on the Elimination of All Forms of Discrimination against Women" in *Human Rights of Women, International Instruments and African Experiences*, ed. Wolfgang Benedek, Esther Mayambala Kisaakye and Gerd Oberleitner (London and New York: Zed Books, 2002), 120.

26 Ibid., 124.

27 Rebecca Cook, "Women's International Human Rights Law: The Way Forward," *Human Rights Quarterly* 15 (1993), 233.

28 Andrew Byrnes, "The Convention on the Elimination of All Forms of Discrimination against Women" in *Human Rights of Women, International Instruments and African Experiences*, ed. Wolfgang Benedek, Esther M. Kisaakye and Gerd Kisaakye (London and New York: Zed Books, 2002), 120.

recognizing that CEDAW "is the most prominent international normative instrument to identify the special concerns of women".[29]

Critiques of CEDAW

The Convention has faced a wide array of criticism. Charlesworth et al., in the early 1990s, suggested that the terms of the Convention and the manner in which member states accepted it "prompt us to ask whether it offers a real or chimerical possibility of change".[30] The content of the Convention and the work of the Committee have also been criticized broadly. Kaufman and Lindquist locate their criticism in the term CEDAW itself: "The title of the women's convention itself arguably presupposes a male standard to the extent that it calls for the Elimination of Discrimination against Women, attempting to bring women into the male world through the removal of legal constraints."[31]

This statement is in line with Charlesworth's general criticism of international law and her argument "that international law implicitly excludes women by assuming a male norm. In other words, international law is built on the understanding that 'whatever is true of men, or makes sense to them . . . automatically suffices for women.' "[32] Another major critique of CEDAW is the sheer number of reservations entered on ratification by Muslim-majority countries. Schöpp-Schilling argues, "[t]hese reservations are one of the reasons that the right to non-discrimination on the grounds of sex still has not reached the status of customary international law, in contrast with the right to non-discrimination on the grounds of race."[33] The Convention allows for a wide scope of interpretation. While specifically naming the "political, economic, social, cultural and civil" fields, it goes further by adding "or any other field".[34] This wide scope of interpretation has led to an increase in the number of reservations,[35] which is discussed further in the following sections.

29 Hilary Charlesworth, Christine Chinkin and Shelly Wright, "Feminist Approaches to International Law," *American Journal of International Law* 85, no. 4 (October 1991), 631.

30 Ibid.

31 N.H. Kaufman and S.A. Lindquist, "Critiquing Gender-Neutral Treaty Language: The Convention on the Elimination of All Forms of Discrimination against Women" in *Women's Rights, Human Rights, International Feminist Perspectives*, ed. J. Peters and A. Wolper (London: Routledge, 1995), 114–125.

32 Hilary Charlesworth, "Feminist Ambivalence about International Law," *International Legal Theory* 11 (2005), 6.

33 Hanna Beate Schöpp-Schillin, "Treaty Body Reform: The Case of the Committee on the Elimination of Discrimination against Women," *Human Rights Law Review* 7, no. 1 (2007), 213.

34 CEDAW, article 1.

35 Hanna Beate Schöpp-Schilling, "Reservations to the Convention on the Elimination of All Forms of Discrimination against Women: An Unresolved Issue or (No) New Development?" in *Reservations to Human Rights Treaties and the Vienna Convention Regime, Conflict, Harmony or Reconciliation*, ed. Ineta Ziemele (Leiden: Martinus Nijhoff Publishers, 2004), 3–41.

Compared with other international conventions, especially ICERD and ICCPR, CEDAW has a much weaker implementation procedure, and the specialized nature of CEDAW has been used by the "mainstream" human rights bodies to ignore, or minimize, women's perspectives. Since the Committee on the Elimination of All Forms of Discrimination (hereafter the Committee, or the CEDAW Committee) is the body to deal with these specific gender issues, other bodies are relieved of this task. The Committee's move to Geneva in 2008 was meant to encourage closer cooperation between the Committee and other human rights treaty bodies.[36]

CEDAW Committee and the optional protocol

The CEDAW Committee is the supervisory mechanism established by CEDAW. It is modelled on earlier treaty bodies such as the Human Rights Committee. The Committee was established under Article 17 of the Convention for "the purpose of considering the progress made in the implementation for the Convention", with the main part of the task being the examination of the reports submitted by state parties in accordance with Article 18 of the Convention.[37] CEDAW provides for the establishment of a Committee of twenty-three experts who are elected by the state parties to serve in their personal capacity. They are chosen from a wide variety of geographical backgrounds[38] and are expected to be "of high moral standing and competence in the field covered by the Convention".[39] However, as Elizabeth Evatt recalls, in its early years many of the Committee members were in government services and some were even diplomats and ambassadors.[40] The independence of the Committee was therefore compromised, and conflicts of interests arose. In addition, a provision in the Committee's rules allowed members to have advisers. This provision further undermined the Committee's independence.[41]

The Committee has faced many hurdles since its establishment. The Committee was located in Vienna from 1982 to 1993 as part of the Centre for the Advancement of Women and the Centre for Social Development and Humanitarian Affairs. The Committee was then moved to New York in 1993

36 Ibid.

37 CEDAW, article 17.

38 Andrew Byrnes, "The Convention on the Elimination of All Forms of Discrimination against Women," in *Human Rights of Women, International Instruments and African Experiences*, ed. Wolfgang Benedek, Esther M. Kisaakye and Gerd Kisaakye(London and New York: Zed Books, 2002), 129.

39 CEDAW, article 17.

40 Evatt, "Finding a Voice for Women's Rights: The Early Days of CEDAW," *The George Washington International Law Review* 34, no. rev. 515 (2002–2003), 522.

41 Ibid., 524.

and on 1 January 2008 relocated to Geneva.[42] This relocation finally enabled the Committee to have the same support structure and services as those provided for other human rights treaty bodies. The move was also essential in order to accommodate the treaty bodies' reform agenda for "a harmonized and integrated human rights treaty bodies system".[43]

The reporting provisions of CEDAW require state parties to detail the steps they have taken to implement the goals of the Convention.[44] The reporting procedure was initially the only monitoring or enforcement procedure established under the Convention. The procedure has been widely criticized. Criticisms have addressed the length of time that the Committee takes to deal with submitted reports as well as a disconnect between the reporting procedure and political will. Like other UN treaty bodies, the Committee has limited power to compel states to obey.[45] However, since the coming into force of the Optional Protocol to the Convention[46] on 22 December 2000, the Committee has been able to consider communications submitted by individuals, or groups of individuals, on violations of the Convention by state parties to the Convention and the Optional Protocol. The Optional Protocol

42 See the Resolutions adopted by the General Assembly, U.N. Doc. A/RES/60/230.1995. and U.N. Doc. G.A. Res/60/230, March 2006.

43 Hanna Beate Schöpp-Schilling, "Treaty Body Reform: The Case of the Committee on the Elimination of Discrimination against Women," *Human Rights Law Review* 7, no. 1 (2007), 210. See also Philip Alston, "Effective Implementation of International Instruments on Human Rights, Including Reporting Obligations under International Instruments on Human Rights, Initial Report of the Secretary General's Independent Expert," 8 November 1989, U.N. Doc. A/44/668. See also "Interim Report on Updates Study by Mr Philip Alston," 22 April 1993, U.N. Doc. A/Conf.157/PC/62/Add.11/Rev.1. Refer also to Philip Alston, "Effective Functioning of the United Nations Human Rights Treaty System," 27 March 1996, E/CN4/1997/74. Also refer to "Concept Paper on the High Commissioner's Proposal for a Unified Standing Treaty Body," 14 March 2006, U.N. Doc. HRI/MC/2006/CRP.1 ('Concept Paper'). See also "Report of the Chairpersons of the Human Rights Treaty Bodies on Their Eighteenth Meeting," 25 September 2006, A/61/385. See also "Report of the Secretary-General, Strengthening of the United Nations: An Agenda for Further Change," 9 September 2002, U.N. Doc. A/57/387. Also, "Plan of Action Submitted by the United Nations High Commissioner for Human Rights. Annex to in Larger Freedom: Towards Development, Security and Human Rights for All, Report of the Secretary General," 26 May 2005, U.N. Doc. A/59/2005/Add.3. Refer to Anne Bayefsky, *The UN Human Rights Treaty System: Universality at the Crossroads* (Ardsley, NY: Transnational Publishers, 2001).

44 For a detailed account of the Committee's reporting procedure refer to "Compilation of Guidelines on the Form and Content to be Submitted by States Parties to the International Human Rights Treaties," U.N. Doc. HRI/GEN/2/Rev. 1/Add.2, 5 May 2003.

45 Sally Engle Merry, *Human Rights and Gender Violence: Translating International Law into Local Justice* (Chicago: The University of Chicago Press, 2006), 72. See also Rosemary Foot, *Rights Beyond Borders: The Global Community and the Struggle over Human Rights in China* (Oxford: Oxford University Press, 2000), 269–270.

46 Optional Protocol to the Convention on the Elimination of Discrimination against Women, G.A. res. 54/4, annex, 54 U.N. GAOR Sup. (No. 49) at 5, U.N. Doc. A/54/49 (Vol. 1) (2000), entered into force December 22, 2000.

also entitles the Committee to inquire on its own volition into grave or systematic violations of the Convention by states parties that have accepted this procedure. Thus far,[47] 104 states are party to the Optional Protocol.

Under Article 20(1) of CEDAW the Committee is to meet for "a period of not more than two weeks annually in order to consider the reports submitted in accordance with Article 18".[48] This period turned out to be a gross underestimation of the meeting time needed by the Committee and is less than that provided for other treaty bodies.[49] For many years, this provision severely hampered the work of the Committee. The short time frame for reporting made it difficult for the Committee to examine reports and report to the General Assembly in good time. Inevitably there was a backlog in work. The brevity of the Committee's working time has been addressed by an amendment to Article 20(1). While this has not yet been ratified, there has been an "allotment of additional working time by the General Assembly over the years, culminating in a measure allowing for three sessions of three weeks each for 2006 and 2007, including holding three of these sessions in two chambers".[50] For these reasons "the Committee seems to be finally on an equal footing with other treaty bodies that face a similar amount of work, such as the [Committee on the Rights of the Child] and the Human Rights Committee."[51]

In addition to considering reports, the Committee has developed twenty-five general recommendations. These recommendations have contributed "to a conceptual expansion of the understanding of human rights violations suffered primarily or even solely by women, such as domestic violence, including female genital mutilation; discrimination against women in the family with consequent discrimination in civil and political life; and discrimination against women in the area of maternal as well as general health."[52]

International debate: CEDAW and Muslim-majority countries

A total of 189 countries had ratified CEDAW as of September 2016. To date, all Muslim-majority countries (referring here to members of the Organization

47 As of 1 November 2013.

48 CEDAW, article 20.

49 Andrew Byrnes, "The Convention on the Elimination of All Forms of Discrimination against Women" in *Human Rights of Women, International Instruments and African Experiences*, ed. Wolfgang Benedek, Esther M. Kisaakye and Gerd Kisaakye (London and New York: Zed Books, 2002), 129.

50 Hanna Beate Schöpp-Schilling, "Treaty Body Reform: The Case of the Committee on the Elimination of Discrimination against Women," *Human Rights Law Review* 7, no. 1 (2007), 218.

51 Ibid.

52 Ibid., 217. Some of these recommendations are; Committee on the Elimination of Discrimination against Women, General Recommendation No. 12: Violence Against Women,

of Islamic Cooperation [OIC]) apart from Iran, Sudan and Somalia, have ratified CEDAW. It is striking to see the sheer number and similarity of reservations these countries have made to CEDAW.

A reservation to international human rights treaties is a unilateral statement declared by a state when signing, ratifying, accepting or acceding to a treaty. In other words, a reservation "purports to exclude or to modify the legal effect of certain provisions of the treaty in their application to the state".[53] The question of reservations has been one of the more controversial subjects of contemporary international law. In general, reservations to universal treaties bring the "universalism" of rights into question. This is especially true when discussing the reservations made to CEDAW. According to Schöpp-Schilling, CEDAW lacks a number of provisions when it comes to dealing with state party reservations. There is no provision in CEDAW stating that a reservation must be explicitly accepted by other states parties, as formulated in 20(1) of the Vienna Convention on the Law of Treaties.[54] Nor is there a provision determining the meaning of incompatibility, as provided for in Article 20 of the International Convention on the Elimination of All Forms of Racial Discriminations (ICERD).[55] According to a report by the Commission on Human Rights, reservations "have been one of the most contentious matters arising in relation to the Convention".[56] The same report declares that CEDAW has been subject to more substantive reservations than any other major human rights treaty.

(Eighth session, 1989), U.N. Doc. A/44/38 at 75 (1990). General Recommendation No. 14, Female Circumcision (Ninth session, 1990), U.N. Doc. A/45/38 at 80 (1990). General Recommendation No. 15, Avoidance of Discrimination against Women in National Strategies for the Prevention and Control of Acquired Immunodeficiency Syndrome (AIDS), (Ninth Session, 1990), U.N. Doc. A.45/38 at 81 (1990). General Recommendation No. 18, Disabled women (Tenth session, 1991), U.N. Doc. A/46/38 at 3 (1993). General Recommendation No. 19, Violence against women (Eleventh session, 1992), U.N. Doc. A/47/38 at 1 (1993). General Recommendation 24, Women and Health (Twentieth session, 1999), U.N. Doc. A/54/38 at 5 (1999). For a full list of recommendations refer to Compilation of General Comments and General Recommendations Adopted by Human Rights Treaty Bodies, U.N. Doc. HRI/GEN/1/Rev.6 (2003).

53 William A. Schabas, "Reservations to the Convention on the Elimination of All Forms of Discrimination against Women and the Convention on the Right of the Child," *William and Mary Journal of Women and Law, the College of William and Mary* 3, no. 1 (1997), 79–80. For more on the definition of reservations see "Treaty Handbook," Prepared by the Treaty Section of the Office of Legal Affairs United Nations, New York, 2006, 11–15.

54 "Treaty Handbook," Prepared by the Treaty Section of the Office of Legal Affairs United Nations, New York, 2006, 12.

55 Hanna Beate Schöpp-Schilling, "Reservations to the Convention on the Elimination of All Forms of Discrimination against Women: An Unresolved Issue or (No) New Development?" in *Reservations to Human Rights Treaties and the Vienna Convention Regime, Conflict, Harmony or Reconciliation*, ed. Ineta Ziemele (Leiden: Martinus Nijhoff Publishers, 2004), 3–41.

56 "The Implementation of the Human Rights of Women: Note by the Secretary General," U.N. Doc. E/ CN.4 /Sub.2/1996/ 20, Geneva: UN, 11 June 1996.

While some of these reservations are narrow in scope, others are wide-ranging and have the potential to limit the obligations undertaken by the reserving states significantly. They undermine the pursuit of the objectives of the treaty[57] and are "crippling to the Convention's integrity."[58] Comparing the numerous reservations made to CEDAW with "the four substantive reservations made to the Convention on the Elimination of All Forms of Racial Discriminations" you can see how one might be inclined to "suggest that discrimination against women is somehow regarded as more 'natural' and acceptable than racial discrimination".[59] Many of the reservations to CEDAW are based on supposed conflicts with religious laws. This is especially true in the case of the Muslim-majority countries discussed in the following section.

These reservations have encouraged a sense that Islam and human rights are incompatible.[60] Yet many of the gender discriminatory laws that are legitimated in the name of Islam are products of the male hegemony governing the interpretation of Islamic law and politics in so-called Islamic states. In general, attempts to justify discrimination based on Islamic law are feeble; nonetheless, "they have been labeled as necessary for the survival of the Islamic state."[61]

Reservations to CEDAW by Muslim-majority countries

Articles 2, 9, 15, 16 and 29 of CEDAW have been subject to the largest number of reservations by Muslim-majority countries. Algeria, Bahrain, Bangladesh, Egypt, Libya, Morocco, Niger and the Syrian Arab Republic[62] all entered reservations or declarations to the following text:

> **Article 2**
>
> State Parties condemn discrimination against women in all its forms, agree to pursue by all appropriate means and without delay a

57 Ibid.

58 Michele Brandt and Jeffrey A. Kaplan, "The Tension between Women's Rights and Religious Rights: Reservations to CEDAW by Egypt, Bangladesh and Tunisia," *Journal of Law & Religion* 12, no. 1 (1995–1996), 107. See also Sara Hossain, "Women's Rights and Personal Laws in South Asia" in *Human Rights of Women*, ed. Rebecca J. Cook (Philadelphia: Pennsylvania University Press, 1994), 470.

59 Hilary Charlesworth, Christine Chinkin and Shelly Wright, "Feminist Approaches to International Law," *American Journal of International Law* 85, no. 4 (October 1991), 633–634.

60 Ann Elizabeth Mayer, "The Islam and Human Rights Nexus: Shifting Dimensions," *Muslim World Journal of Human Rights* 4, no. 1 (2007), 5.

61 Shadi Mokhtari, "The Search for Human Rights within an Islamic Framework in Iran," *The Muslim World* 94, no. 4 (October 2004), 469.

62 In June 2007 the Syrian Arab Republic made a decision to remove reservations to articles 2, 15 9(4), 16 (1) (g) and 16 (2). See "Concluding Comments of the Committee on the Elimination of Discrimination against Women: Syrian Arab Republic," U.N. Doc. CEDAW/C/SYR/CO/1, 11 June 2007, at paragraph 6.

policy of eliminating discrimination against women and, to this end, undertake:

(a) To embody the principle of the equality of men and women in their national constitutions or other appropriate legislation if not yet incorporated therein and to ensure, through law and other appropriate means, the practical realization of this principle;
(b) To adopt appropriate legislative and other measures, including sanctions where appropriate, prohibiting all discrimination against women;
(c) To establish legal protection of the rights of women on an equal basis with men and to ensure through competent national tribunals and other public institutions the effective protection of women against any act of discrimination;
(d) To refrain from engaging in any act or practice of discrimination against women and to ensure that public authorities and institutions shall act in conformity with this obligation;
(e) To take all appropriate measures to eliminate discrimination against women by any person, organization or enterprize;
(f) To take all appropriate measures, including legislation, to modify or abolish existing laws, regulations, customs and practices which constitute discrimination against women;
(g) To repeal all national penal provisions which constitute discrimination against women.[63]

Most reservations are entered in the name of Islamic Shari'a. Bahrain, for example, explains its reservations to Article 2 as being "in order to ensure its implementation within the bounds of the provisions of the Islamic Shariah."[64] Apart from Bangladesh, which mentions that Shari'a law is based on the Qur'an and Sunna, others use the term "Islamic Shari'a" loosely without providing any definition. If states claim that their reservations are made on the basis of Shari'a, then it should be obligatory for them to provide an accompanying definition of Shari'a. Many reservations are abstract even apart from definitional question. Iraq, for example, does not even provide a reason for its reservation to Article 2 paragraphs (f) and (g). The language of Article 2 and CEDAW in general, is often critiqued as being imprecise. Adam Lars Rehof explains the usage of imprecise language with reference to

63 CEDAW, article 2.
64 A list of states parties' reservations and declarations are available at the website of the High Commissioner for Human Rights, online www.ohchr.org/EN/ProfessionalInterest/Pages/CoreInstruments.aspx, (accessed 6 March 2016).

the "anxiety" of the drafters who believed that states would be less likely to accept a more precisely worded, and therefore more forceful, treaty.[65] This imprecision has been met with reservations that are vaguely worded, making it difficult to determine what is being reserved and what impact the reservation has on the obligations assumed by the reserving countries.[66]

For example, Iraq[67] and the United Arab Emirates made reservations to the whole of Article 9, and Turkey has made a declaration to Article 9(1).[68] Bahrain, Jordan, Kuwait, Lebanon, Malaysia, Morocco,[69] Oman, Saudi Arabia, Syrian Arab Republic and Tunisia[70] all entered reservations to Article 9(2).[71] Apart from Malaysia, which mentions Shari'a as one of the conflicting factors for its reservation, the other states do not mention incompatibility with Shari'a. Rather, they regard Article 9(2) to be in conflict with state nationality acts. Although Shari'a is not mentioned by most of these countries as the

65 Lars Adam Rehof, *Guide to the traveaux préparatoires of the United Nations Convention on the Elimination of All Forms of Discrimination against Women, International Studies in Human Rights* (Dordrecht, Boston and London: Martinus Nijhoff Publishers Dordrecht, 1993), 2–3.

66 See Hanna Beate Schöpp-Schilling, "Reservations to the Convention on the Elimination of All Forms of Discrimination against Women: An Unresolved Issue or (No) New Development?" in *Reservations to Human Rights Treaties and the Vienna Convention Regime, Conflict, Harmony or Reconciliation*, ed. Ineta Ziemele (Leiden: Martinus Nijhoff Publishers, 2004), 3–41.

67 The Government of the Republic of Iraq withdrew its reservation to article 9 on 18 February 2014. Refer to the United Nations Treaty Collection, Chapter IV, HUMAN RIGHTS, online https://treaties.un.org/Pages/ViewDetails.aspx?src=TREATY&mtdsg_no=IV-8&chapter=4&clang=_en#EndDec, (accessed 24 September 2016).

68 Article 9(1) asks state parties to grant women and men equal rights in acquiring nationality. It states, "They shall ensure in particular that neither marriage to an alien nor change of nationality by the husband during marriage shall automatically change the nationality of the wife, render her stateless or force upon her the nationality of the husband." Paragraph 2 of the same article deals with the nationality of children: "States Parties shall grant women equal rights as men with respect to the nationality of their children."

69 On 8 April 2011, the Secretary-General received notification from the Government of the Kingdom of Morocco that it decided to withdraw the reservations made upon accession in respect of articles 9 (2) and 16 of the Convention. Cited in the United Nations Treaty Collection, Chapter IV, HUMAN RIGHTS, online https://treaties.un.org/Pages/ViewDetails.aspx?src=TREATY&mtdsg_no=IV-8&chapter=4&clang=_en#EndDec, (accessed 24 September 2016).

70 On 17 April 2014, the Government of the Republic of Tunisia notified the Secretary-General of its decision to withdraw the declaration with regard to article 15(4) of the Convention and the reservations to articles 9(2), 16 (c), (d), (f), (g), (h) and 29(1) of the Convention made upon ratification. . . . Cited in the United Nations Treaty Collection, Chapter IV, HUMAN RIGHTS, online https://treaties.un.org/Pages/ViewDetails.aspx?src=TREATY&mtdsg_no=IV-8&chapter=4&clang=_en#EndDec, (accessed 24 September 2016).

71 Note that Egypt has withdrawn its reservation on article 9(2). See "Convention on the Elimination of All Forms of Discrimination against Women, Egypt: Withdrawal of Reservation in Respect of Article 9(2)," U.N. DOC. C.N.24.2008.TREATIES-1 (Depositary Notification).

basis for their reservations, the transmission of nationality to children seems to be interpreted similarly to the transmission of religion.[72] As previously observed, this is one of the reasons why laws are set prohibiting Muslim women from marrying non-Muslim men, whereas Muslim men are allowed to marry non-Muslim women. These reservations reinforce the gendered nature of citizenship in the aforementioned countries. For this reason Lina Abou-Habib concludes that for these states, "only men are real citizens."[73] Although women in the region are entitled to "citizenship", it is men who are the bearers of it and who control its transmission to their spouses and children. While men who marry foreign women can, in most instances, pass on citizenship to them and their children, women are not able to do the same.[74]

Another article of CEDAW often subject to reservations, Article 15, sets forth the following provisions:

1 States Parties shall accord to women equality with men before the law.
2 States Parties shall accord to women, in civil matters, a legal capacity identical to that of men and the same opportunities to exercise that capacity. In particular, they shall give women equal rights to conclude contracts and to administer property and shall treat them equally in all stages of procedure in courts and tribunals.
3 States Parties agree that all contracts and all other private instruments of any kind with a legal effect which is directed at restricting the legal capacity of women shall be deemed null and void.
4 States Parties shall accord to men and women the same rights with regard to the law relating to the movement of persons and the freedom to choose their residence and domicile.

The United Arab Emirates has made a reservation to Article 15(2). Algeria, Bahrain, Jordan,[75] Morocco, Niger, Oman, Syria and Tunisia all made

72 "'Best Practices': Progressive Family Laws in Muslim Countries," *Woodrow Wilson International Centre for Scholars Middle East Program* (August 2005), 39, online www.wilsoncenter.org/sites/default/files/Best%20Practices%20(English).pdf, (accessed 29 July 2016).

73 "Claiming Equal Citizenship: The Campaign for Arab Women's Right to Nationality, Women's Learning Partnership for Rights," *Development, and Peace*, no. 14 (March 2006), online www.learningpartnership.org/lib/claiming-equal-citizenship-campaign-arab-women's-right-nationality, (accessed 29 July 2016).

74 "'Best Practices': Progressive Family Laws in Muslim Countries," *Woodrow Wilson International Centre for Scholars Middle East Program* (August 2005), 40, online www.wilsoncenter.org/sites/default/files/Best%20Practices%20(English).pdf, (accessed 29 July 2016).

75 On 5 May 2009, the Government of Jordan informed the Secretary-General that it had decided to withdraw the reservation made upon ratification with regard to article 15(4) of the Convention. Cited in the United Nations Treaty Collection, Chapter IV, HUMAN

reservations to Article 15(4). Turkey entered reservations to 15(2) and 15(4). However, Tunisia's declaration concerning Article 15(4) has since been withdrawn. It had stated:

> In accordance with the provisions of the Vienna Convention on the Law of Treaties, dated 23 May 1969, the Tunisian Government emphasizes that the requirements of Article 15, paragraph 4, of the Convention on the Elimination of All forms of Discrimination against Women, and particularly that part relating to the right of women to choose their residence and domicile, must not be interpreted in a manner which conflicts with the provisions of the Personal Status Code on this subject, as set forth in chapters 23 and 61 of the Code.[76]

The United Arab Emirates flatly declares the following in its reservation to Article 15(2): "The United Arab Emirates, considering this paragraph in conflict with the precepts of the Shariah regarding legal capacity, testimony and the right to conclude contracts, makes a reservation to the said paragraph of the said article and does not consider itself bound by the provisions thereof."[77]

These reservations restrict women's rights to free movement and choice of residence. In the cases of Algeria and Morocco, Article 15(4) is held to be in conflict with the Algerian Family Code and the Moroccan Code of Personal Status. In most of these countries a woman's freedom of movement is contingent upon the permission of her husband if she is married, or a male family member if she is single. A married woman in many cases needs the written permission of her husband to obtain a passport.[78] Such practices clearly discriminate against women. Such discrimination has far-reaching consequences. It presents an "obstacle to the educational and economic advancement of

---

RIGHTS, online https://treaties.un.org/Pages/ViewDetails.aspx?src=TREATY&mtdsg_no=IV-8&chapter=4&clang=_en#EndDec, (accessed 24 September 2016).

76 Tunisia's declaration to article 15(4), online CEDAW/SP/2010/2, 54, www2.ohchr.org/english/bodies/cedaw/docs/AdvanceVersions/CEDAW-SP-2010–2.pdf, (accessed 6 March 2016).

77 United Arab Emirates' reservation to article 15(2), online CEDAW/SP/2010/2,56, online www2.ohchr.org/english/bodies/cedaw/docs/AdvanceVersions/CEDAW-SP-2010–2.pdf, (accessed 6 March 2016).

78 For example, in Syria a husband can prohibit his wife from traveling abroad. In Jordan a married woman needs the permission of her husband to obtain a passport. See "'Best Practices': Progressive Family Laws in Muslim Countries," *Woodrow Wilson International Centre for Scholars Middle East Program* (August 2005), 39–40, online www.wilsoncenter.org/sites/default/files/Best%20Practices%20(English).pdf, (accessed 29 July 2016). See also Janet Afary, "The Human Rights of Middle Eastern and Muslim Women: A Project for the 21 Century," *Human Rights Quarterly* 26, no. 1 (2004), 106–125.

societies that tolerate such infringements."[79] Jordan's reservation has since been withdrawn. While it was still extant the CEDAW Committee expressed its concern regarding Jordan's reservation to Article 15(4) in the following way:

> It is particularly concerned that the State party is unwilling to withdraw its reservation to Article 15, paragraph 4, despite its assertion that this reservation has become redundant owing to an amendment to the Passport Act removing the requirement of male consent to the issuance of a passport to a Jordanian woman. The Committee is concerned about the State party's assertion that it cannot, for political reasons, amend its nationality law to allow Jordanian women to pass their nationality to their children and foreign spouses and, for religious reasons, amend provisions of its Personal Status Act to give women equal rights with men in matters of marriage, divorce and custody of children.[80]

The committee continued:

> The Committee calls upon the State party to speedily withdraw its reservation to Article 15, paragraph 4, which it acknowledges has become redundant in the light of legal reform. It also urges the State party to recognize the negative impact of its nationality law on Jordanian women married to foreigners and on the children of those women and, accordingly, to revise its nationality law and remove its reservations to Article 9, paragraph 2.[81]

Consequently Jordan withdraw this reservation. Algeria, Bahrain, Egypt, Iraq, Jordan, Kuwait, Lebanon, Malaysia, Maldives, Morocco, Niger, Oman, the Syrian Arab Republic, Tunisia and the United Arab Emirates all filed reservations exempting themselves from implementing all or parts of Article 16 on the basis of it being in conflict, prejudiced or incompatible with the provisions of Islamic Shari'a. Article 16 reads:

1 States Parties shall take all appropriate measures to eliminate discrimination against women in all matters relating to marriage and family relations and in particular shall ensure, on a basis of equality of men and women:

   (a) The same right to enter into marriage;

79 "'Best Practices': Progressive Family Laws in Muslim Countries," *Woodrow Wilson International Centre for Scholars Middle East Program* (August 2000), 39, online www.wilsoncenter.org/sites/default/files/Best%20Practices%20(English).pdf, (accessed 29 July 2016).

80 "Concluding Comments of the Committee on the Elimination of Discrimination against Women: Jordan," U.N. Doc. CEDAW/C/JOR/CO/4, 10 August 2007, at paragraph 11.

81 Ibid.

(b) The same right freely to choose a spouse and to enter into marriage only with their free and full consent;
(c) The same rights and responsibilities during marriage and at its dissolution;
(d) The same rights and responsibilities as parents, irrespective of their marital status, in matters relating to their children; in all cases the interests of the children shall be paramount;
(e) The same rights to decide freely and responsibly on the number and spacing of their children and to have access to the information, education and means to enable them to exercise these rights;
(f) The same rights and responsibilities with regard to guardianship, wardship, trusteeship and adoption of children, or similar institutions where these concepts exist in national legislation; in all cases the interests of the children shall be paramount;
(g) The same personal rights as husband and wife, including the right to choose a family name, a profession and an occupation;
(h) The same rights for both spouses in respect of the ownership, acquisition, management, administration, enjoyment and disposition of property, whether free of charge or for a valuable consideration.

2 The betrothal and the marriage of a child shall have no legal effect, and all necessary action, including legislation, shall be taken to specify a minimum age for marriage and to make the registration of marriages in an official registry compulsory.

The main justification for reservations to Article 16 has been that all or part of the article is incompatible with Islamic Shari'a. Yet no state has taken upon itself to explain the meaning of Islamic Shari'a, or what indeed incompatibility with Shari'a entails. Drawing on equality/complementarity debates, Egypt justifies its reservation to Article 16 as follows:

> Reservation to the text of Article 16 concerning the equality of men and women in all matters relating to marriage and family relations during the marriage and upon its dissolution, without prejudice to the Islamic sharia provision whereby women are accorded rights equivalent to those of their spouses so as to ensure a just balance between them. This is out of respect for the sacrosanct nature of the firm religious beliefs which govern marital relations in Egypt and which may not be called in question and in view of the fact that one of the most important bases of these relations is an equivalency of rights and duties so as to ensure complementarity which guarantees true equality between spouses, not a quasi-equality that renders the marriage a burden on the wife. The provisions of the

sharia lay down that the husband shall pay bridal money to the wife and maintain her fully and shall also make a payment to her upon divorce, whereas the wife retains full rights over her property and is not obliged to spend anything on her keep. The sharia therefore restricts the wife's rights to divorce by making it contingent on a judge's ruling, whereas no such restriction is laid down in the case of the husband.[82]

The word "equivalency" rather than "equality" is used in the foregoing statement as a means of ensuring complementarity and balance between spouses. This, it is claimed, is "true equality" rather than "quasi-equality". This "true" equality in marriage is explained by the husband's obligation to pay *mahr* to maintain the wife during marriage or upon divorce. Because a woman has no obligation to pay household or family maintenance and can hold on to the property she owns (if she owns property), her right to divorce is restricted.[83]

Algeria, Bahrain, Brunei Darussalam, Egypt, Indonesia, Iraq, Kuwait, Lebanon, Morocco, Niger, Oman, Pakistan, Saudi Arabia, Syrian Arab Republic, Tunisia, Turkey, the United Arab Emirates and Yemen have all made reservations to Article 29(1). Article 29(1) states:

> Any dispute between two or more States Parties concerning the interpretation or application of the present Convention which is not settled by negotiation shall, at the request of one of them, be submitted to arbitration. If within six months from the date of the request for arbitration the parties are unable to agree on the organization of the arbitration, any one of those parties may refer the dispute to the International Court of Justice by request in conformity with the Statute of the Court.

Reservations to this article generally follow the line of logic pursued by the United Arab Emirates:

> The United Arab Emirates appreciates and respects the functions of this article . . . This article, however, violates the general principle that matters are submitted to an opening for certain States to bring other States to trial in defence of their nationals; the case might then be referred to the Committee charged with discussing the State reports required by the Convention and a decision might be handed down against the State

82 Egypt's reservation to CEDAW, article 16, available online at CEDAW/SP/2010/2, 15–16, online www2.ohchr.org/english/bodies/cedaw/docs/AdvanceVersions/CEDAW-SP-2010-2.pdf, (accessed 6 March 2016).

83 "Divorced from Justice: Women's Unequal Access to Divorce in Egypt," *Human Rights Watch* 16, no. 8(E) (December 2004), 1–68.

> in question for violating the provisions of the Convention. For these reasons the United Arab Emirates makes a reservation to this article and does not consider itself bound by the provisions thereof.[84]

As can be seen, a considerable number of the Muslim-majority countries have made reservations that are incompatible with the "object and purpose" of the Convention.[85] As early as 1987, the CEDAW Committee adopted a decision regarding Shari'a based reservations. It asked the United Nations and its specialized agencies to:

> [. . .] promote or undertake studies on the status of women under Islamic laws and customs and in particular on the status and equality of women in the family, on issues such as marriage, divorce, custody and property rights and their participation in public life of the society, taking into consideration the principle of El-Ijtihad in Islam.[86]

The foregoing decision was adopted following the consideration of Bangladesh's report on its implementation of CEDAW. Bangladesh's reservation to Article 2 was criticized and concerns were "expressed about the effects of Islamic law on the rights of Muslim women in Bangladesh".[87] The decision to undertake studies on the status of women under Islamic laws was denounced by many Muslim-majority states, which viewed it as an attack on Islam and a threat to freedom of religion. The Bangladeshi representative in The United Nations Economic and Social Council (ECOSOC), for instance, urged "the greatest caution in using the Convention as a pretext for doctrinaire attacks on Islam",[88] and the Committee's recommendation was rejected.[89]

In 1998 the Committee expressed its estimation that such studies were necessary to carry out its duties under the Convention but insisted that no disrespect was intended to Islam. Absent large-scale studies, the Committee has recognized that the Convention allows reservations in order for a

84 United Arab Emirates Reservation to CEDAW, article 29(1), online CEDAW/SP/2010/2, 56–57, online www2.ohchr.org/english/bodies/cedaw/docs/AdvanceVersions/CEDAW-SP-2010–2.pdf, (accessed 6 March 2016).

85 Article 28, paragraph 2.

86 "General Recommedation No. 4, Report of the Committe on the Elimination of Discrimination against Women," Sixth Session, 42 UN GAOR Supp. (No. 38), paragraph 579, U.N. Doc. A/42/38 (1987).

87 Belinda Clark, "The Vienna Convention Reservations Regime and the Convention on Discrimination against Women," *The American Journal of International Law* 85, no. 2 (April 1992), 288.

88 Economic and Social Council, 1 Regular Session of 1987, U.N. Doc. E/1987/SR.11 (1987).

89 Hilary Charlesworth, Christine Chinkin and Shelly Wright, "Feminist Approaches to International Law," *American Journal of International Law* 85, no. 4 (October 1991), 636.

maximum number of states to become parties. Yet this has led to the paradox of CEDAW: in trying to gain universal application it has jeopardized its integrity.[90] According to Article 28 of the Convention, "A reservation incompatible with the object and purpose of the present Convention shall not be permitted."[91] However, the frequency and pattern of reservations to the Convention highlight "the inadequacy of the present normative structure of international law".[92] It may be the case that the international community, while ready to acknowledge the issues of inequality faced by women, has recognized individual states must be allowed to keep patriarchal practices in place to preserve the doctrine of sovereignty. On the other hand, it may be that international human rights law simply lacks the legitimacy necessary for its full implementation. As Charlesworth et al. note, "The Women's Convention, the international legal flagship with respect to women, is an ambiguous offering."[93] Muslim-majority states' reservations to CEDAW are largely the variable outcome of politics.[94] The reservations themselves, although entered in the name of Islam, are not absolute and can be withdrawn at any time. This was done by Bangladesh in 1997, Malaysia in 1998 and by Egypt in 2008.[95] In the practice of entering and withdrawing reservations, "evolving political contingencies, not Islamic beliefs, turn out to be determinative factors."[96] It is therefore important not to confuse reservations entered by Muslim-majority countries with the exercise of religious freedom, as Theodore Meron does when he writes, "(t)he application of religious laws may itself constitute the observance of and practice of religion."[97] Neither state-interpreted Islam, nor so-called Islamic reservations are necessarily directly related to the beliefs of the overall population in any of these Muslim-majority states. Rather, they more accurately reflect decisions taken by a segment of the population that has a hold on political power.

90 Ibid.

91 "The Implementation of the Human Rights of Women: Note by the Secretary General," U.N. Doc. E/ CN.4 /Sub.2/1996/ 20, Geneva: UN, 11 June 1996. U.N. Doc. E/CN.4/ Sub.2/1996/20.

92 Hilary Charlesworth, Christine Chinkin and Shelly Wright, "Feminist Approaches to International Law," *American Journal of International Law* 85, no. 4 (October 1991), 633.

93 Ibid., 634.

94 Ann Elizabeth Mayer, "The Convention on the Elimination of All Forms of Discrimination against Women: The Political Nature of 'Religious' Reservations," (March 2005), 2, online www.univie.ac.at/recht-religion/kultur-religion/isl/a%20e%20mayer%20en.pdf, (accessed 2 August 2016).

95 "Egypt: Withdrawal of Reservation in Respect of Article 9 (2)," U.N. Doc. C.N.24.2008. TREATIES-1 (Depositary Notification) (2008).

96 Ibid.

97 Theodor Meron, *Human Rights Law-Making in the United Nations: A Critique of Instruments and Process* (Oxford: Clarendon Press, 1986), 156.

Iranian debates on CEDAW

Iran is one of the few Muslim-majority countries, alongside Somalia and Sudan, which has neither signed nor ratified CEDAW. However, Iran has witnessed a considerable number of debates for and against CEDAW at the national level. The debates were particularly intense at the end of the 1990s and the beginning of the 2000s. As already mentioned, the authorization to ratify CEDAW was passed by the *majlis* in 2003. However, this decision was later vetoed by the *shoray-e negahban* (Guardian Council), which held that CEDAW violated Iranian and Islamic laws.[98]

It is possible to identify, in the main, three general approaches to CEDAW that are operative in Iran. First, there are the conformists who vehemently oppose Iran's accession to CEDAW and regard it as an imposition of Western cultures and values. Second, there are the religious modern thinkers who, allied with the reformists, believe that Islam and human rights are generally compatible, but that some provisions of CEDAW may be regarded as unIslamic, and are therefore met by reservation with integrity. Third, there are the women's rights activists and feminists who see CEDAW as a powerful advocacy and lobbying tool that Iran should ratify without any reservations.

The conformists

The conformists' stance on CEDAW reflects the West-East and the North-South dichotomies of the colonizer and the colonized. The conformists employ *fiqh-e sonnati* (traditional jurisprudence), as did their forbearers, the traditionalists. This traditional approach, in essence, resists any law reform.[99] The conformists' discourse can be regarded as a response to Western power. I use the word "conformist" to describe a category of scholars who not only have a traditionalist view of gender in Islam, but are also allied closely to, and are dependent upon, conservative government actors. In Iran, the conformists "insist on keeping intact the ideological discourse of the Revolution".[100] Their views are at times reflected in the governments' legislative actions towards women. Examples that follow illustrate a few conformist jurists' reactions to CEDAW as well as the way CEDAW is portrayed in more conservative state-sponsored media. These jurist views seem to reinforce Samuel

98 See, for example, Kambiz Fattahi, "Women's Bill 'Unites' Iran and US," *BBC News*, Washington, 31 July 2007. See also Miranda Eeles, "Iran Women's Bill Rejected," *BBC News*, 12 August 2003.

99 Ziba Mir-Hosseini, "The Conservative-Reformist Conflict Over Women's Rights in Iran," *International Journal of Politics, Culture and Society* 16, no. 1 (Fall 2002), 37–38.

100 Ibid., 38.

Huntington's idea of a "clash of civilisations".[101] In surveying the opinions of conformist jurists and articles written in the same vein, one common theme is that rights and the UN system are inherently Western in nature. If one is inclined to give some credence to this vein of criticism, it is also important to ask why the same level of criticism has not been levied to address Iran's ratification of other multi-lateral human rights treaties. These include: ICESCR (signed 4 April 1968, ratified 24 June 1975); ICCPR (signed 4 April 1968, ratified 24 June 1975); ICERD (signed 8 March 1967, ratified 29 August 1968); Convention Relating to the Status of Refugees and its protocol (acceded 28 July 1976); Supplementary Convention on the Abolition of Slavery, the Slave Trade, and Institutions and Practices Similar to Slavery (acceded 30 December 1959); Convention on the Prevention and Punishment of the Crime of Genocide (signed 8 December 1949, ratified 14 August 1956); International Convention on the Suppression and Punishment of the Crime of Apartheid (acceded 17 April 1985); International Convention against Apartheid in Sports (signed 16 May 1986, ratified 12 Jan 1988); International Convention on the Rights of the Child (signed 5 September 1991, ratified 13 July 1994);[102] and International Convention on the Rights of Persons with Disabilities (acceded 23 October 2009). Iran has also ratified thirteen conventions of the International Labour Organization (ILO).[103] Although the majority of these conventions were ratified or acceded before the 1979 Islamic Revolution, nonetheless, Iran still remains party to them. Mehrangiz Kar, referencing the non-discrimination clauses of a number of the aforementioned-mentioned treaties, states that these existing international commitments should pave the way for reform of gender discriminatory national laws and the consequent ratification of CEDAW.[104]

101 Samuel P. Huntington, "The Clash of Civilisations?" *Foreign Affairs* 72, no. 3 (Summer 1993), 22–49. See also Ann Elizabeth Mayer, "Debating the Universality of Human Rights: A Plea for a Critical Perspective," n.d.

102 It is important to note that Iran entered into reservation upon signing and ratifying CRC. The reservations read as follow:

Upon signature: Reservation: "The Islamic Republic of Iran is making reservation to the articles and provisions which may be contrary to the Islamic Shariah, and preserves the right to make such particular declaration, upon its ratification." Upon ratification: Reservation:

"The Government of the Islamic Republic of Iran reserves the right not to apply any provisions or articles of the Convention that are incompatible with Islamic Laws and the international legislation in effect."

See, online http://treaties.un.org/Pages/ViewDetails.aspx?src=TREATY&mtdsg_no=IV-11&chapter=4&lang=en#20, (accessed 6 March 2016).

103 For a full list of ratification of ILO conventions by Iran see, online www.ilo.org/dyn/normlex/en/f?p=1000:11200:0::NO::P11200_COUNTRY_ID:102800, (accessed 6 March 2016).

104 Mehrangiz Kar, *Raf-e Tabeez Az Zanan, Moghayesey-e Convension-e Raf-e Tabeez Az Zanan ba Qavaneen-e Dakheliy-e Iran (End Discrimination against Women: A Comparison between*

In contrast, Ayatollah Makarem Shirazi, a conformist Shi'a *marja*,[105] regards Iran's potential ratification of CEDAW as a possible imposition of Western culture on Islamic values and culture. He declares, "These strangers insist in every possible way to impose their cultures on all aspects of our lives. This forcefulness does not only concern women but also includes our culture, politics, morals, family and all other social matters."[106] Shirazi explains that "if they succeed in forcing their culture on us, we will not be able to combat them as an independent nation. The force that they exert on our women's affairs is only a subset of their master plan."[107] It is difficult to read such words and not recall Iran's past struggles for independence from the influence of colonial powers. Indeed, Shirazi continues:

> . . . some of the contents of this convention are against the laws of *Shari'a*. Thus it is better for us not to become a party to such conventions . . . It is apparent that this forcefulness would not only take our religion away but also our independence. This is true because the colonizers do not negotiate with a country, unless it is colonized. We have then to protect our pride in standing by our Islamic and national culture.[108]

Ayatollah Javadi Amoli,[109] another conformist jurist, warns, "Be sure that the West is heading in the direction of demolishing the family unit and objectifying its women, it is changing men into women and women into men."[110]

---

the Convention on Elimination of All Forms of Discrimination against Women and Iranian Laws) (Tehran: Nashre-e Qatr-e Publications, 2000), 31.

105 Ayatollah Makarem Shirazi is one of the *Shi'a marja taqleed*'s (source of emulation) residing in Qom. His views on women's rights in particular are controversially conservative. He has also been active in politics after the Iranian Revolution, allied to the right-wing conservatives. After the revolution he was appointed to the *Majlis-e Khobregan* or assembly of experts, and took part in writing the first Constitution. Ayatollah Shirazi's books in Farsi, Arabic and English may be accessed on his official website, online www.makaremshirazi.org/, (accessed 6 March 2016).

106 Ayatollah al-Uzma Makarem Shirazi, "Bayanat-e Ayatollah Makarem Shirazi (Ayatollah Makarem Shirazi's Statements)" in *Majmoe Maghalate Dafe Az Hughugh-e Zanan Ma va Hughugh-e Beynolmelal (A Gathering of Articles on Women's Rights: Us and the International Laws),* ed. Women's Centre for Studies and Research, Tehran (Qom: Mosassesye Farhagye The, 2001), 9.

107 Ibid.

108 Ibid.

109 Ziba Mir-Hosseini, "The Conservative-Reformist Conflict Over Women's Rights in Iran," *International Journal of Politics, Culture and Society* 16, no. 1 (Fall 2002), 37–53.

110 Abdullah Ayatollah Javai Amoli, "Chekide Sokhannane Hazrate Ayatollah Javadi Amoli (Summary of Ayatollah Javadi Amoli's Speeches)" in *Majmoe Maghalate Dafe Az Hughugh-e Zanan Ma va Hughugh-e Beynolmelal (A Gathering of Articles on Women's Rights: Us and the International Laws),* ed. Women's Centre for Studies and Research, Tehran (Qom: Mosassesye Farhagye The, 2001), 16.

Ayatollah Hussein Noori Hamedani[111] also has a similar view of CEDAW: "This is just like other stereotypical Western slogans that seem to support human rights, democracy, political prisoners and, very recently, the war on terrorism. All these plots are meant to undermine Islam."[112]

A survey of articles on CEDAW from conformist and conservative statist magazines, including *Shamim Yaas*,[113] *Kothar*,[114] *Ravagh Andishe*,[115] *Houra*,[116] *Faslnameh Ravagh Andishe*,[117] *Baztab Andishe*,[118] *Payam-e Zan*,[119] *Sabaah*,[120] *Banovan Shi'a*,[121] *Shoraye Farhangi Ejtemai Zanan*[122] and

111 For more information on Ayatollah Noori Hamedani, refer to his official website at, online www.noorihamedani.com, (accessed 6 March 2016).

112 Abdullah Ayatollah Javai Amoli, "Chekide Sokhannane Hazrate Ayatollah Javadi Amoli (Summary of Ayatollah Javadi Amoli's Speeches)" in *Majmoe Maghalate Dafe Az Hughugh-e Zanan Ma va Hughugh-e Beynolmelal (A Gathering of Articles on Women's Rights: Us and the International Laws)*, ed. Women's Centre for Studies and Research, Tehran (Qom: Mosassesye Farhagye The, 2001).

113 Kobra Hakim Zadeh Abiyneh, "Konvansion Raf-e Tabiz alyeh Zanan (1) (the Convention on Elimination of Discrimination against Women (1))," *Shamim Yaas*, no. 13, July 2002, 8–13. Kobra Hakim Zadeh Abiyneh, "Konvansion Raf-e Tabiz alyeh Zanan (2) (the Convention on Elimination of Discrimination against Women (2))," *Shamim Yaas*, no. 14, August–September 2002, 13–18.

114 Ibrahim Kameli, "Konvansion Raf-e Tabiz ra Behtar Beshnasim (To Know Better the Convention on Elimination)," *Kothar*, no. 42 (22 August 2000), 1–8.

115 Masoud Rai, "Zanan, Asnad Hughugh-e Bashar va Mavazin Fiqhi," *Ravagh Andisheh*, no. 36 (26 June 2008), 1–16, online www.hawzah.net/fa/article/view/65733, (accessed 2 August 2016).

116 Esaam Ahmad al-Bashir, "Dar Tarazoye Eslam va Ghanoon (The Balance between Islam and Law)," *Houra*, no. 11 (February–March 2005), 32–40, online www.hawzah.net/fa/Magazine/View/6432/6520/75278/کنوانسیون-د-رترازوی-اسلام-و-قانون, (accessed 2 August 2016).

117 Editorial, "Konvansion Raf-e Tabiz alyeh Zanan (1) (the Convention on Elimination of Discrimination against Women (1))," *Faslnameh Ravagh Andishe*, no. 22 (26 October 2009), 1–4, online www.hawzah.net/fa/Article/View/82276/سخن-سردبیر-کنوانسیون-رفع-تبعیض-علیه-زنان-(1)-, (accessed 2 August 2016).

118 Daftar Motaleat va Tahghighaat Zanan (the Office of Women Studies and Research), "Sayeh Roshanhaye yek Konvansion (the Shadows and Lights of a Convention)," *Baztab Andishe*, no. 41 (10 February 2010), 1–10, online www.hawzah.net/fa/Article/View/86349/سایه-روشن-های-یک-کنوانسیون-دفتر-مطالعات-و-تحقیقات-زنان, (accessed 2 August 2016).

119 Ahmad Heydari, "Konvansion Kolyie Ashkal Tabiz alyeh Zanan (the Convention on Elimination of All Forms of Discrimination against Women)," *Payam-e Zan*, no. 173 (August 2006), 38–49, online www.hawzah.net/fa/Magazine/View/3992/5188/47823/کنوانسیون-منع-کلیه-؟؟شکال-تبعیض-علیه-زنان, (accessed 2 August 2016).

120 "Konvansion Raf-e Koliyehi Eshkal Tabiz Zanan (the Convention on the Elimination of All Forms of Discriminations against Women)," *Sabaah*, no. 9 and 10 (Fall and Winter 2003), 1–15.

121 "Konvansion Raf-e Tabiz az Zanan va Payamadhaye Ejtemai On (The Convention on Elimination of Discrimination against Women and Its Social Outcomes)," *Banovan Shi'a*, no. 3 (26 June 2008), 1–18, online www.hawzah.net/fa/Article/View/65732, (accessed 2 August 2016).

122 "Esarathaye Kohne dar Tarhaye Nou/ Tarikhcheye Konvansion (Ghesmant Aval) (Old Enslavements in New Plans/ A History of the Convention)," *Shoraye Farhangi Ejtemai*

Faslnameh Marefat,[123] reveals the common arguments that authors employ to denounce Iran's ratification of the Convention. Some of these arguments include:

1 The Convention is Western in its values and therefore promotes Western individualism and secularism.
2 The Convention's notion of "equality" is that of "total equality" ("*tasavi kamel/koli/motlaq*"), which treats men and women as the "same", denies their duties towards each other, and undermines the Islamic concept of complementarity of genders.
3 The values set forth in CEDAW are designed to destroy the family unit.
4 The Convention is incompatible with Islamic law where the rights of women are concerned and is consequently incompatible with the Iranian Civil Code, Penal Code and Constitution.

In addition to these types of articles, there are, of course, many similar books. A good example is Farbia Alasvand's[124] *Naghd Konvension raf-e koliyeh Ashkal Tabiz alyeh Zanan* (*A Critique of the Convention on Elimination of All forms of Discriminations against Women*), (Qom: Entesharat Markaz Modiriyat Qom, 2003).[125] Alasvand is lecturer in one of the largest female Shi'a *hawzas* in Iran, Jami'at al-Zahra, and her book is particularly interesting for having been written by a female religious scholar with a *hawza* education. Although Alasvand has not reached the level of *ijtihad*, her book is nonetheless important because it conveys a conformist woman's position on CEDAW.

Alasvand starts the book with a critique of "feminism". She describes feminism as a uniform Western movement comprised of white women which is void of any sensitivity towards cultural difference and race. She adds that feminists are in favour of individual rights, while ignoring the womanly duties of a mother and a wife within the family unit.[126] Alasvand's criticisms of CEDAW

Zanan, no. 9 (10 February 2010), 1–8, online www.hawzah.net/fa/Article/View/86347/%20یربارابان=SearchText?/(لوا-تمسق)-نویسناونک-هچخیرات-ون-یاهحرط-رد-هنهک-یاهتراسا%20یاه%20نز%20درمو&LPhrase=, (accessed 2 August 2016).

123 "Nim Negahi be Hughugh-e Zanan dar Islam/ Naghdi bar Konvension raf-e koliyeh Tabiz alyeh Zanan (A Brief Look at Women's Rights in Islam/ A Critic of the Convention on Elimination of All Forms of Discrimination against Women)," *Faslnameh Marefat*, no. 7 (10 February 2010), 1–40, online www.hawzah.net/fa/article/view/86346, (accessed 2 August 2016).

124 For more on Jami'at al Zahra, see Roja Fazaeli and Mirjam Künkler, "Training Female ʿulamāʾ in Jamiʿat al-Zahra – New Opportunities for Old Role Models?," in *Knowledge and Authority within the Hawza*, ed. Robert Gleave, forthcoming.

125 Fariba Alasvand, *Naghd Konvension raf-e koliyeh Ashkal Tabiz alyeh Zanan (A Critic of the Convention on Elimination of All Forms of Discriminations against Women)* (Qom: Hawza Elmiyeh Qom, 2003).

126 Ibid., 10–11.

are closely linked to her critique of feminism. According to Alasvand, CEDAW, which she identifies as a feminist document, is incompatible with certain Islamic norms and laws. Alasvand criticizes the concept of the "equality of men and women" enshrined in the Convention, which she terms "absolute" equality with reference to Ayatollah Morteza Motahhari's work "Women' Rights in Islam".[127] She declares that this level of equality means "sameness" rather than equality. According to her this "sameness" or "absolute equality" is against "Islamic Shari'a". To prove this, Alasvand details physical and emotional differences between men and women. She states that women are not suited for certain roles and duties because of their emotional makeup. She adds that women should be barred from these roles and duties, but clarifies that being barred does violate their rights, as the roles and duties she has in mind, that is, judgeship, *jihad* and *shahadat* (testimony in a court of law), ought to be classified as duties, and not rights. In her words, "If one looks at this correctly, it should be said that religion has taken the burden of certain duties off the shoulder of women, and not that it has violated their rights."[128] Her other arguments against CEDAW are identical to those of the conformists previously listed.

These conformist views on women's roles and duties and the Western nature of the rights regime have also made it into the international arena. Fatimah Ajorloo, a member of the ninth *majlis*, in her address to the 55th Session of the UN Commission on the Status of Women (CSW) in February 2011, spoke of the failure of "global decisions and policies adopted in the area of women's issues". She explained that they "have failed to consider diversity of cultures and characteristics of various civilizations, and as a result of being one-dimensional, prescribing a single remedy for all societies. Hence, they have failed to remove the obstacles and challenges women [are] facing at global level."[129] Eshagh al-Habib, ambassador and deputy permanent representative of the Islamic Republic of Iran to the UN, similarly used his address to the 56th session of CSW to make the following declaration on behalf of Maryam Mojtahedzadeh, advisor to President Mahmood Ahmadinejad, and the head of the Center for Women and Family Affairs of the Islamic Republic of Iran:

127 Morteza Mutahari, *Nezam-e Hughugh-e Zan dar Islam (The Rights of Women in Islam)*, 45th ed. (Tehran: Sadra Publication, 2007).

128 Fariba Alasvand, *Naghd Konvension raf-e koliyeh Ashkal Tabiz alyeh Zanan (A Critic of the Convention on Elimination of All Forms of Discriminations against Women)* (Qom: Hawza Elmiyeh Qom, 2003), 19.

129 Statement by H.E. Mrs Fatimah Ajorloo, member of the Parliament of the Islamic Republic of Iran, 55th Session of the UN Commission on Status of Women, On agenda Item 3: "Follow-up to the Fourth World Conference on Women and the 23rd Special Session of the UN General Assembly," (New York, 24 February 2011).

> We, in the Islamic Republic of Iran believe that men and women are equal in respect to dignity and human rights. This right is not to be confused with equaling men and women's role in family, society and in the development process. Hence, we believe, equality, complementarity and justice as well as taking complementary role is part of the basic concepts of the role of men and women in the family and society.

Ajorloo's and al-Habib's CSW remarks confirm the black and white views of the conformists in regard to women's rights. They seek to institutionalize the complementarity of gender roles while criticizing the equality paradigm, and they see the international human rights system as a failure, lacking in cultural diversity.

Islamic modern thinkers and dynamic ijtihad

If the aforementioned conformists who resist changes in law are proponents of *fiqh-sonnati*, then the religious modern thinkers (*rohsanfekran-e dini*) associated with the reform movement must be understood as champions of *fiqh-e pouya*.[130] This has led to new perspectives on Islam and its relationship to modern life, and has generated calls for democratic and legal reforms. One striking difference between the conformists and reformists has been the contrast in their use of the language of *Hughugh* (rights) and *takalif* (duties). While the language of duties has been the preferred discourse of the Islamic Republic, the Iranian reformist discourse has contributed greatly to the expansion of rights language in Iran. The reform movement has been accompanied "by a lively debate on women's rights in the seminaries and in various government and independent publications".[131] This has occurred concurrently with ayatollahs and *mujtahids* in Iran pronouncing favourable decrees regarding the rights of women. It is possible to explain this correlation in causal terms by way of *ijtihad*. *Ijtihad* may be translated as "exertion of oneself", or understood more colloquially as the effort of the jurist to use independent reasoning to form an opinion or to deduce a rule.[132] It is a principle established in Article 2(6)

130 Ziba Mir-Hosseini, "The Conservative-Reformist Conflict Over Women's Rights in Iran," *International Journal of Politics, Culture and Society* 16, no. 1 (Fall 2002), 38.

131 Ibid., 37–38.

132 According to the orthodox schools, *ijtihad* has been classically classified into three categories: independent *ijtihad*, semi-independent *ijtihad* (*al-ijtahid al-mutlaq al-muntasib*) and *ijtihad* within the framework of the juristic and legal position of a school (*al-ijtahid al-fatwa*). In the modern reform debates, a fourth category, or dynamic *ijtihad*, is regarded as a tool for reformists to change legislations based on Islamic law. See Murteza Mutahari, "The Role of Ijtihad in Legislation in Alse-e ijtihad dar Islam," trans. Qara'i, Ali Quli, *al-Thani* 1407 (December 1986 – February 1987), 26.

(1) of the Iranian Constitution, which promotes the use of *ijtihad* by *fuqaha* (jurists). Shi'a *fiqh* (jurisprudence) is deemed to be adaptable to changes of time and place, and Shi'a jurisprudence is kept vibrant by the use of *ijtihad-i pouya* (dynamic *ijtihad*). Ayatollah Mohammad Ibrahim Jennaati writes:

> One of the blessings of *ijtihad-e pouya* is that Islamic *fiqh* will not halt or stagnate in the face of any new modern events and life manifestations. *Ijtihad-i pouya* moves the same direction as life. This is why *fiqh* qualifies as *pouya* . . . therefore *ijtihad* is a necessary rule for the Islamic *fiqh*. Without it, *fiqh* will never be dynamic or able to adapt to the changes of human life.[133]

However, the principle of *ijtihad* itself has been affected by the sclerosis of patriarchy, and on many occasions this is reflected in its practice and outcomes. Because of constraints on the voices of female *mujtahids*, *ijtihad* has become the preserve of male scholars.[134] Women's rights activists in Muslim-majority countries must lobby male *mujtahids* to lend support to their demands to reform gender-discriminatory laws. This in turn creates gendered hierarchies and dependencies, and these dependencies ultimately institutionalize the power of the male clergy. Still, in the near absence of female *mujtahids*, women's rights activists only have recourse to male *mujtahids* for support. One clear example of this can be seen in the composition of the *shoray-e negahban* (Guardian Council). According to Article 91 of the Iranian Constitution the *Shoray-e Negahban* (Guardian Council) is to comprise six *faqih-e adil* (just clerics), who are conscious of the present needs and issues of the day, and six jurists specializing in different areas of law. The six *faqih-e adil* (just clerics) are to be selected by the supreme leader. The six jurists are to be elected by the *majlis* from the Muslim jurists nominated by the head of the judiciary. Although there have been a number of female *faqihs* and jurists in the history of the Islamic Republic of Iran, there have never been female members of the Guardian Council.

Male reformists must assume some responsibility for this. Women religious scholars seem to be veiled conveniently from the reform process. To

133 Ayatollah Ibrahim Mohammad Jennaati, *Advar-e Ijtihad Az Didgahe Mazhab-e Islami (Time of Ijtihad in the view of Islamic School of Thought)* 1st ed. (Moasseseye Keyhan, Summer 1372), 33–34 cited in Mehrangiz Kar, *Raf-e Tabeez Az Zanan, Moghayesey-e Convension-e Raf-e Tabeez Az Zanan ba Qavaneen-e Dakheliy-e Iran (End Discrimination against Women: A Comparison between the Convention on Elimination of All Forms of Discrimination against Women and Iranian Laws)* (Tehran: Nashre-e Qatr-e Publications, 2000), 38.

134 Azizah Al-Hibri, "Islam, Law and Custom: Redefining Muslim Women's Rights," *American University International Law Review* 12, no. 1 (1997), 5.

understand the new Iranian reform movement and the place of religious intellectuals within it, one must recognize the following:

> Initially, Iranian religious intellectuals were supporters and promoters, but are now reformers, of an Islamic regime that has relied on brute force to impose standards of how a "proper Muslim woman" should look and behave in public. As such, in comparison with their secular male counterparts, they have been increasingly pressured to explain their position, in light of their emphasis on a modern and more democratic "reading" of Islam.[135]

It is important to remember that many who are now called religious modern thinkers also played "an important role in turning Islamic law into a powerful ideological tool to suppress other voices", particularly the voices of women.[136] Abdulkarim Soroush is an example of one such intellectual. Soroush has been claimed as one of the most influential Islamic modern thinkers, but he has yet to address women's issues comprehensively.[137] Such failures undermine the reform movement and its influence on the rights discourse in Iran.

Women's activists and CEDAW

The Iranian feminist movement is regarded as one of the strongest social movements in any Muslim-majority country. Women parliamentarians in Iran, in particular those in *majlis-e sheshom* (sixth parliament), have been able to make some headway concerning women's rights in the country. Yet, Fatemeh Haghighatjoo, a member of the sixth *majlis* and a proponent of Iran's ratification of CEDAW, points out that despite the support given by reformists and activists to keep the debate on CEDAW alive in the early 2000s, there were also loud oppositional female voices.[138] In response to whether there is hope for renewed work on CEDAW, she replies:

> Unfortunately, as defined by the Constitution, the Expediency Council does not have any time limitations for approving or reviewing laws and therefore it (CEDAW) has been dormant in the Council since 2003 and it has nothing to do with the *majlis* anymore. This Convention is neither

135 Ibid.

136 Ziba Mir-Hosseini, "The Conservative-Reformist Conflict Over Women's Rights in Iran," *International Journal of Politics, Culture and Society* 16, no. 1 (Fall 2002), 38.

137 In a 2007 interview with Soroush, he expressed his intention to write a volume on women's rights and Islam. See Roja Fazaeli and Margaret Scott, "An Interview with Abdulkarim Soroush," Columbia University, (December 2007).

138 I categorize these women as conformist. Haghighatjoo describes them as Islamist.

> the concern of the *majlis*, nor is it the concern of the Guardian Council. I do not think that they would put (CEDAW) on their agenda and if they do, it will be vetoed. Therefore, it is better if it stays quiet until the political atmosphere is favourable. It is not even good for women activists to work on this right now and demand the Council to follow up on the Convention.[139]

Women's rights activists firmly believe that Iran should ratify CEDAW without entering any reservations. However, they are also aware that by ratifying CEDAW, without reforming discriminatory laws at the national level, Iran will only be paying lip service to the international community in the same way as is done by countries such as Saudi Arabia. Additionally, it is recognized that reformation of laws alone does not necessarily better women's position in society. To this end, Kar underscores that the Convention's ultimate goal is to institutionalize equality and non-discrimination in the states' social and legal structures.[140]

The national debate on Iran's ratification of CEDAW lost momentum to a large extent following the 2009 Iranian presidential elections. However, before the elections a coalition was formed: the Coalition of the Iranian Women's Movement for Voicing Their Demands in the Election (*hamgari-e Jonbesh Zanan baraye Tarh Motalebat dar Entekhabat*). The coalition was composed of 700 individual Iranian women's rights activists (both men and women) as well as forty campaigns and organizations. It urged the presidential candidates to "actively pursue the re-joining of the Convention of Elimination of all Forms of Discrimination against Women (CEDAW)" and explained:[141]

> We are aware that this proposal was submitted to the Sixth parliament in the Seventh government (the first cabinet of Mohammad Khatami) and ratified by the members but was rejected by the Council of Guardians. This proposal was later presented to the Expediency Discernment Council, [of] which the president was a member. We urge the presidential candidates to put this proposal at the top of their priorities with respect to the principles of equality and non-discrimination of citizens.[142]

139 Interview with Fatimeh Haghighatjoo, September 2010 (with Maryam Hosseinkhah).

140 Mehrangiz Kar, *Raf-e Tabeez Az Zanan, Moghayesey-e Convension-e Raf-e Tabeez Az Zanan ba Ghavanin-e Dakheliy-e Iran (End Discrimination against Women: A Comparison between the Convention on Elimination of All Forms of Discrimination against Women and Iranian Laws)* (Tehran: Nashre-e Qatr-e Publications, 2000), 53.

141 "Statement on the Occasion of the Presidential Elections in June 2009 in Iran," *The Feminist School*, Thursday 30 April 2009, online www.feministschool.net/english/spip.php?article281, (accessed 23 August 2012).

142 Ibid.

The coalition also made the following statement:

> We endeavour to eliminate discriminatory laws against women, specifically Articles 19, 20, 21 and 115 of the Constitution with respect to the principle of unconditional gender equality. We are aware that the president has no power to change laws but we are also aware that if the government is committed to the principle of equality and views it as its responsibility, it is able to utilize its capabilities and to encourage the parliament to include the principle of equality in the Constitution.[143]

The two requests, which go hand in hand, are crucial to women's rights, equality and non-discrimination in Iran. Unfortunately, the demands of the coalition were not met. Instead women's rights activists, along with civil and political activists, faced prosecution, threats and widespread arrests following the contested election of Mahmoud Ahmadinejad. Despite this, the very process of forming the coalition provided a benefit to the women's movement: different categories of feminists were together. Secular feminists, such as Mehrangiz Kar and the poet Simin Behbahani, came together with Islamic state and non-state feminists, such as Elahe Kolai and Azam Taleghani; this proved to be one of the movement's strengths.

According to Jelveh Javaheri, one of the coalition's weaknesses was the fact that it paid so little attention to the historical experience of the women's movement In Iran. She explains:

> It seems women reformers who support the coalition's demands and who were previous members of the *majlis*, no longer remember that in the sixth *majlis* they spent most of their time and energy in trying to have Iran ratify CEDAW, and at last they were convinced that it was better to concentrate on reforming national gender discriminatory laws, which according to them comprised 70 per cent of all Iranian laws. Or the activists from the independent spectrum of the Iranian women's movement forgot that in the gathering of 2006 in relation to reforming laws in commemoration of the anniversary of the solidarity of the women's movement, they came to the conclusion that they needed to propose more tangible demands than the reform of the constitution. So that their demands were not too big for the candidates (presidential) to solely nod a yes and the next day when they come to power to say that this too risky . . .[144]

143 Ibid.
144 Jelveh Javaher, "Koneshgaran bi Tarikh Nabashim (Naghdi az Daroon), We should Not be Ahistorical Activists (A Critic from Within)," *Change for Equality*, 15 March 2012, online http://news.gooya.com/politics/archives/2010/03/101909.php, (accessed 24 August 2012).

A comparable coalition that formed as an opposition movement to the Family Protection Bill seems to have had a slightly better historical memory.[145] According to Elahe Amini, it was "one of the largest coalitions formed to protest a bill in recent years".[146] This coalition too was made up of a "strikingly diverse group of women activists, feminists, human rights defenders, as well as secular and religious groups (including some conservative women's groups)".[147] And in contrast to *hamgari-e Jonbesh Zanan baraye Tarh Motalebat dar Entekhabat*, and as detailed previously, this coalition was able to successfully lobby the *majlis to* remove and reframe some of the Family Protection Bill provisions. Such victories have been few and far between for the women's movement. However, despite the arrests and repression around the 2009 presidential elections, Azadeh Kian notes, "Some vocal Islamic (and secular) women continue to struggle against conservative bills, laws and perceptions that are to the detriment of women and their rights."[148]

145 The "Family Protection Bill" was passed by the *majlis* in July 2008.

146 Elahe Amani, "From Bad to Worse and Beyond . . .," *Iran Women Solidarity*, Friday 15 August 2008, online www.iran-women-solidarity.net/spip.php?article430, (accessed 28 August 2012).

147 Ibid.

148 Azadeh Kian, "Gendering Shi'ism in post-revolutionary Iran," in *Gender in Contemporary Iran, Pushing the Boundaries*, ed. Rokasana Bahramitash and Eric Hooglund (Oxon, UK: Routledge, 2011), 31.

Conclusion

A personal account

Charlotte Bunch writes that "[women] are one of the groups that are transforming the concept of human rights to address the degradations and violations that are fundamental threats to our human dignity and rights to life, liberty, and security of person."[1] However, the human rights of women have too often been assigned a secondary status in the human rights arena. Because of the public/private divide and existing power hierarchies, men have dominated the rights milieu as they have other public spheres. There has also been a lack of intentional and explicit female cooperation in shaping the international human regime. I'm particularly aware of this because of the manner in which I found myself pulled into the Iranian women's movement. Looking back, it seems to have happened almost by accident. At the time I wasn't particularly aware of the importance of vocalizing a feminist identity. I wasn't explicit in my demands for justice. I was simply a woman who somewhat unintentionally wandered into some rooms where the women's movement was taking place and thereby also stepped across one of the Iranian state's bright lines. I quickly discovered that what I had thought of as my private life was in fact a public statement. Ironically, though not exceptionally, it was my personal experience with the authoritarian intervention of the Iranian state that ensured I became a public advocate for women's rights in Iran. It is a story that bears telling in full in conclusion.

The last time I visited Iran was in 2004. After visiting family, and holidays with my sister and her husband, I made plans to work for three months in Tehran. At that point I was preoccupied primarily by questions of children's rights. Thanks to some connections made on a prior visit in 2003, as previously mentioned, I started working for an NGO, the House of Culture and Sustainable Development (HCSD). While I was working for HCSD a call was sent out by the United Nations Development Program (UNDP) to

1 Charlotte Bunch, "Transforming Human Rights Form a Feminist Perspective" in *Women's Rights, Human Rights, International Feminist Perspectives*, ed. Julie Peters and Andrea Wolper (London: Routledge, 1995), pp. 11–17.

different NGOs asking them to nominate two young professionals to represent Iran at a United Nations Pan Asian Youth Leadership Summit in Hiroshima, Japan.[2] HCSD nominated me and I was selected. Along with another participant who was active in *Jebhey-e Mosharekat* (Islamic Iran Participation Front, a reformist political party) I set out for Hiroshima on 18 September 2004. A farewell party took us to the Mehrabad airport where we checked our luggage and had a goodbye tea. Following goodbyes we headed straight for passport control. As we waited in line we were approached by a man who asked for our passports. The man asked if I was a European resident. He then took my passport from my hand and asked me to follow him. I was taken to a room on the same floor and asked to sit in one of the chairs facing an empty desk. Once I sat down the door opened and another man came in. He wore green khaki trousers and a safari vest with large pockets in the front. When he started to speak, his northern Iranian accent was unmistakable. Later he introduced himself as Mr Jafari from Lahijan, a city not too far from where I grew up. While Mr Jafari spoke to me, another man came in and began searching through my handbag. At this point I became nervous, more so when Mr Jaafari began asking about people I had met and worked with over the past few months, including two Americans I lived with. My level of anxiety rose when they asked me what my relationship with the Americans was. I had met one of the Americans, Liz, on her first day in Iran when she was a guest of the HCSD. We were good company for each other. I helped her set up interviews for her Ph.D. dissertation and accompanied her as an interpreter. She shared thoughts and advice I might want to consider heading in to my Ph.D. programme. We decided to share a place and joined another student from the U.S. to rent a flat. Mr Jaafari and Co. knew all of this and I was alarmed at the extent of the knowledge they had about my activities and whereabouts over the past few months. The questions shifted from my American housemates to the trip to Japan. After a couple of questions the interrogation suddenly ended. Jafaari declared that the questioning was just a misunderstanding and then stated that I was the pride of Iran and had better make the country proud in Japan. I took the questions as a mild threat to keep quiet and behave while in Hiroshima.

Our arrival back to Tehran after five days in Hiroshima was uneventful, very much to my relief. I returned to an empty flat in Meydun Mohseni; Liz had left to go to Turkey before returning to the U.S. The next two days were filled with meeting friends, doing interviews about the Summit with SYNA (Society of Iranian Youth News Agency) and ILNA (Iranian Labour News

2 Read more about the Summit, online www.shumei-international.org/youth/hiroshima.html, (accessed 6 March 2016).

Agency), visiting family and attending a meeting about underage execution in Iran. I spent the second night back at my cousin's house and the next morning I went back to the apartment. I showered and was dressing when I heard our landlord knock on the door. He was shouting something about our bin being left out too early. I yelled to the landlord that I would take care of the bin and that he shouldn't worry. But he persisted in his knocking and shouted again that he wanted to talk to me. Once more I told him that I would take care of the bin and that I was not dressed to open the door. But the knocking continued and at this point another voice interjected, "Ms Roja can you please open the door? We need to talk to you." Alarmed by an unknown voice addressing me by my first name in a country and context where formality dictated that the surname should be used, I quickly put on my scarf, closed the buttons of my *manteaux* and opened the door. Outside there were two men in plain clothing and a woman in a black *chador*. The landlord was running towards the stairs and did not look back. My heart sank and I felt very nervous. One of the men, who later introduced himself as Ahmadi, said that they were from the Office of Immigrant Affairs, which I later learned was a branch of the Interior Ministry (*Vezarat Keshvar*) known as BAFIA.[3] They wanted to speak to the Americans I lived with. I asked to see their identity cards and asked if they had any warrants to enter the house. The two men showed me their identity cards while disguising their affiliations and names with their hand. They also let me glance at what they said was a search warrant. Reluctantly I let them in, telling them that Liz had already left Iran and my other housemate was asleep. I asked them to stay in the sitting room while I went to wake my housemate up so that she would not be startled. But the woman in the *chador* followed me to my housemate's room. Once up, they asked my housemate for her passport. They also turned to me and asked me for my passport. I brought them my Iranian passport, but immediately they asked for my Irish passport also. After speaking to my housemate, Mr Ahmadi turned to me and said that they were going to ask me some questions and they needed my full cooperation and the whole truth. The younger man introduced himself as *Sarvan* (Capitan) Moghamdam. Before asking any questions they began to search the house.

Having just returned from Hiroshima my room was a colossal mess. Clothes were everywhere and everything I owned was either on the ground or on the bed. My notes and tapes from my interviews and the laptop I had borrowed to take to Japan were all piled together in a corner. Before they entered the room, I made a half-hearted attempt to protest their invasion. I asked why the immigration police were doing a house search. I asked why they wanted to search my room if they had come to talk to my housemates.

3 Bureau for Aliens and Foreign Immigrants Affairs (Edareh Kol-e Atba va Mohajerin Khareji).

I also warned them about my messy room. They smiled and entered the room. Moghadam said, "We have known you for a while and from your appearance we never thought that you would be so messy." The declaration made me shake inside. It confirmed that the search was not about my housemates, but about me. They went through my photos, some from my stay in Iran and some from Europe. They asked about everyone in the pictures, from family to friends to random tourists who happened to have posed for photos at the same time I had. They knew some of the people in the photos, people I worked for or with. They came across photos of my uncles drinking beer, but pretended not to see. They paused on a photo where I was smoking a hooka and Ahamdi said I reminded him of his wife, who also loved to smoke hooka. They held on to about a dozen of the photos, mostly ones I had taken during workshops we ran at the HCSD, and a few of my friends and me walking in parks. They listened to all the tapes and confiscated all my interviews for the civil society book. They also took all my interview notes, the borrowed laptop and a box of empty floppy disks. They searched, they asked, they took and eventually they left. But before they did, they informed me that they had an arrest warrant for me, that I was not to leave the house and that they would call me with further instructions.

Once they were gone I went into my room and lay on top of the pile of clothes, relieved that they only took my stuff and not me, but also worried as to what this all meant. Soon I began to call a number of people I knew, including the UN officer who had coordinated our travel to Japan, and told them about what happened. The UN officer told me to get into a taxi but not to call one and he told me not to use the house phone again. I walked out of the building and out the gate of the apartment complex. There were three cars parked outside. One was a police car (*niroye entezami*). As I walked it drove alongside me at my walking pace. I found a phone booth and called my Hiroshima travel companion to let him know what had happened. At this point a white Peykan pulled up beside the booth and a man, who I assumed to be a government agent, got out and stood nearly attached to the phone booth, too close for comfort. I hastily finished my conversation, crossed the road, hailed a taxi and asked the driver to take me to the UN building on Sharzad Boulevard. At the UN office the security guard asked to see my ID. All of a sudden I was hit with the reality that I had no papers. Ahmadi and Moghadam had taken my passports. I lost my cool and burst into tears, which alarmed the security guard, who gave me tissues, a glass of ice water and a cup of tea all at the same time. I then met with two people from the UN office. When I stepped out of the gate of the UN building, I was greeted by a welcoming party of two police cars and a police motor bike. There was no hiding the fact that I was being followed. I walked down towards Passdaran Street and the motor bike manouvered behind me, back and forth.

A woman in a *chador* and a man in a check shirt also followed me. At first I thought I must be imagining the surveillance of the two in plainclothes and so decided to test them. I went into a shop and stayed for a while. When I came out the woman in the *chador*, whose face I could not see, was waiting on the other side of the street. Once I started walking so did she. I went to the next shop I came across and came out after a while. This time the man was waiting outside and started to walk almost in step with me. More aware of my surroundings than ever, I called one of my uncles from the next phone booth I came across. He was the only family member I decided to confide in. The conversation with him was short, but also made me realize that I was in a real mess. My uncle also told me not to use the phone in the house and not to call him again. Instead, he would contact me himself. I went home. My housemate was not home. Paranoid about what might happen at night, I slept on the ground between two beds. I was woken up at 7.00 a.m. by a phone call. It was Sarvan Moghadam: "Ms Roja, good morning. How are you today? We would like you to please write down the following address: Amaken (Morality Police Station), Motahari Street, The Junction of Mirdamaad. Please be here by 9.30 and come alone."

I rang my UN contact from the house phone and told him about the phone call. To my surprise I was advised to go to the Amaken and to go alone. In my naiveté I thought that once I had gone everything would be over. When they had confiscated my belongings, they had said everything would be given back to me in 24 hours. I was at the Amaken by 9.00. I entered a little room. A soldier sat behind a desk, and there were a few chairs pushed against the wall at each side of the room. I went to the desk and declared that I was there to see Sarvan Moghadam. The soldier did not recognize the name. He asked for my ID. Since my last ID incident I had searched and found my student ID from Trinity College, Dublin, which had a photo of me with uncovered hair. As I took out the ID to hand to the soldier it dawned on me that I was at a morality police station. Women were brought here for having bad *hejab*. Panicking, I withdrew the ID card and searching for anything else offered the soldier a ring I was wearing instead. He was floored by this random gesture, and so was I. He asked to see what I was trying to hide, at this point comically, behind my back. I then handed him the ID. "What is this?" the soldier asked. I explained that it was my college ID. "But you are not wearing a scarf." I explained that I lived and studied in Ireland. "Oh, I see, you are foreign," he remarked. He then took my ID and told me to stay outside the room. Soon he came back and told me to go to a room on the left. Eventually, after visiting five rooms, I was placed in a room with a "Mr Moghadam", but it was not the same "Mr Moghadam" who had questioned me earlier. "Sister, why do you want to see me?" he asked. When I answered that his colleague had demanded I show up at 9.30, I was promptly sent out back to the soldier. At this stage another man came into the small room and shouted at me to stand outside. Five minutes later, the Mr Moghadam that I knew signalled from behind the glass window for me to come in again. He guided me downstairs to one of the basement rooms I had already been to. The room, which resembled a doctor's waiting room, was full of people. Chairs were placed all around the wall and were filled with men and women who were each sitting clutching a slip of paper that stated they had permission to be in the room. The irony that a permission slip was necessary to get into a place no one would wish to enter was not lost on me. I hoped there were exit slips as well. I was taken to an adjacent room where there was a short thin, man with small teeth and stubble; he was wearing a grey suit. Moghadam introduced him as *Hajagha*[4] and said that *Hajagha* wanted to have a chat to clarify some matters. *Hajagha* asked me to sit while he opened a folder on the desk. I looked eagerly at the file. My housemates' names were both on little cards stapled to the inside of the folder. My name appeared beside Liz's on the back of the folder. *Hajagha*'s questions marked the first of many interrogations over the next three months.

After each interrogation I felt my naiveté slip away a little more. During one of the tougher sessions, the notion of feminist dependency explored in Chapter 2 hit me full force. It was October 2004 during *Ramadan*.[5] The *hajagha* started his interrogation:

> So I hear that you are a martyr's daughter. They say that you research human rights? Did you not know that what you (Westerners, he meant) call human rights is against our religion? That woman who won the Nobel Peace Prize (referring to Shirin Ebadi), do you work with her? Did you know that she is a dirty bitch? Did you know that she is a sinner? She goes abroad and takes off her scarf and shakes hands with men. You bitches are all the same! You say that you work for women's rights? But this is only a pretext for all of you feminists to do dirty deeds, to sin and be immoral, and then call it rights. We expect more from a martyr's daughter!

He continued to denigrate Shirin Ebadi, whom I had met for a brief moment at one of her talks in Tehran. "Do you not think that she is a sinner? What has she done for her country after receiving so much money?" My responses

4 *Hajagha* (meaning a man who has gone to *haj*, who has paid his dues in Mecca) is an alias used by many interrogators, I had two different interrogators during my detainment in Iran, both of whom were referred to *hajagha*. See also Habibola Doran, *Dar Mehmaniy-e Hajagha (In the Party of Hajagha)* (Tehran: Entesharate Omide Farda, 2003).

5 The holy month of fasting in the Islamic calendar, *Hejri Ghamari*.

were cut short amidst the *hajagha's* shouts and the sounds of his hammering fists on the table. As if his accusation that all feminists were immoral bitches was not enough, the *hajagha* had to prove that I was a certified "Western immoral bitch", even though, as he stated, also a martyr's daughter and therefore entitled to more respect than others. While shouting at me to cover my neck, he asked me to describe in detail my relationships with all the men I had met with during my stay in Iran. He accused me of *zina*[6] and demanded a written confession. He also wanted me to tell him what one of my American roommates did when she was alone with her boyfriend. He indicated a few times that he wanted every detail, as if expecting I looked through a peephole each time the couple was alone. As Kar points out, in Article 8 of the Iranian Constitution the idea of "*Amre be maroof va nahy az monker*" (the promotion of virtue and the prevention of vice) has become a tool in the hands of extremists to undermine individual rights and terrorize the population.[7]

What I have related in this personal account is but a pale shadow of what many women's rights activists regularly go through in Iran. During the same three months that I was interrogated under house arrest, a number of women's rights activists were jailed. In a subsequent interview with another branch of the Iranian intelligence, I debated the unIslamic actions of the *hajagha* who had wanted to know personal details of my relationships with others and who wanted me to tell him in detail what went on behind the closed doors of someone else's intimate affairs. I asked: How could a self-professed Muslim man, an "officer of Islam" (*pasdar-e Islam*) as he put it, pursue such work with a clear heart? I asked: What is righteous in two men badgering a woman half their age in an interrogation room, especially during *Ramadan* when everyone else in the station has gone to *eftar* to break the fast? I asked: Is this their interpretation of Islam? I wondered: Why should Iranian feminists be dependent, either financially or ideologically, on a system where *hajaghas* abuse their power to humiliate women and women's rights defenders?

Gender is often isolated as the social category used by fundamentalist leaders to mobilize their supporters and discredit their opposition.[8] For the

6 *Zina* has almost the same meaning as adultery, defined by Article 63 as the act of intercourse, including anal intercourse, between a man and a woman who are forbidden to each other, unless the act is committed unwittingly. The punishment for *zina* extends from 100 lashes to death by stoning.

7 Mehrangiz Kar, "Shari'a Law in Iran" in *Radical Islam's Rule, the Worldwide Spread of Shari'a Law*, ed. Paul Marshal (Lanham, Maryland: Rowman and Littlefield, 2005), 41.

8 Sucheta Mazumdar, "Moving Away from a Secular Vision? Women, Nation, and the Cultural Construction of Hindu India" in *Identity Politics and Women: Cultural Reassertions and Feminism in International Perspective*, ed. Valentine Moghaddam (Boulder, CO: Westview, 1994), 243–273. See also Khawar Mumtaz, "Identity Politics and Women: 'Fundamentalism' and Women in Pakistan" in *Identity Politics and Women: Cultural Reassertions and Feminism in International Perspective*, ed. Valentine Moghaddam (Boulder, CO: Westview, 1994), 228–242.

hajagha I was part of the women's rights movement; I was the opposition. I had not seen myself in that light but, as is often the case, state repression did not deter my enthusiasm for women's rights. Rather, the opposite occurred: The state's attempts to negate my feminism only confirmed it. My story began on the periphery of one side of the women's rights movement that has undergone significant repression. Some women remain untouched and unthreatened; they work with government support from large offices in the luxury of north Tehran. At the same time other women receive knocks on their doors, summons to be interrogated, arrest warrants, and worse. In such a context some feminists have decided to write their own warrants for solidarity. My hope in writing is that all Iranian women and women's advocates will be caught up together in the movement towards the realization of women's rights and freedoms. Efforts such as the One Million Signatures Campaign demonstrate that contemporary women's rights work in Iran is innovative and unflagging. Across the generations Iranian women have worked to advance the cause of women's rights in different ways; this book has attempted to chronicle the outlines of that movement, unfinished as it is.

Index